HAHNEMANN HOMEOPATHY

(Recommended for PG Students)

Includes
- High Potency
- Miasm Theory & Remedies
- Small Doses
- Potency Selection
- Psychiatry

Dr. PETER MORRELL

B. JAIN PUBLISHERS (P) LTD.
An ISO 9001 : 2000 Certified Company

First Edition: 2003
Reprint Edition: 2006

No part of this book may be reproduced, stored in a retrieval system or transmitted, in any form or by any means, mechanical, photocopying, recording or otherwise, without any prior written permission of the publisher.

© Copyright with the publisher.

B. JAIN'S SPECIAL PRICE BHMS BOOKS Rs.175.00

Published by Kuldeep Jain for
B. Jain Publishers (P) Ltd.
An ISO 9001 : 2000 Certified Company
1921, Street No. 10, Chuna Mandi,
Paharganj, New Delhi 110 055 (INDIA)
Phones: 91-11-2358 0800, 2358 1100, 2358 1300, 2358 3100
Fax: 91-11-2358 0471; *Email:* bjain@vsnl.com
Website: **www.bjainbooks.com**

Printed in India by
J.J. Offset Printers
522, FIE, Patpar Ganj, Delhi - 110 092
Phones: 91-11-2216 9633, 2215 6128

ISBN: 81-8056-298-0
BOOKCODE: BM-5679

PREFACE

*T*his volume brings together most of my essays about Hahnemann that have been published in various journals in the last ten years or so. It is my sincere hope that the reader will gain from these essays a deeper appreciation of the phenomenal energy and staggering achievements of this multi-talented medical rebel and pioneer, and especially, perhaps, some insights into his personality, mode of thinking and how homoeopathy came to be brought into being.

By the year 2005, it will be 250 years since Hahnemann's birth in 1755. In that quarter of a millennium medicine has changed a great deal, yet the same problems exist today as existed in his day. Though great progress has been made in juggling symptoms, and suppressing illness, to alleviate human sickness [palliation], yet very little real progress has been made towards the type of radically curative medicine that Hahnemann envisaged, and which he described in his *Organon*: "*to restore the sick to health*...[1; Aph. 1]...*rapid, gentle and permanent restoration of health...in the shortest, most reliable, and most harmless way,* [1; Aph. 2]...*it is only this spiritual, self acting (automatic) vital force, everywhere present in his organism, that is primarily deranged by the dynamic influence upon it of a morbific agent inimical to life*...[1; Aph. 11] *for it is the morbidly affected vital force alone that produces disease,* [1; Aph. 12] [and cure must remove] *all such morbid derangements (diseases)...by the spirit-like (dynamic, virtual) alterative powers of the serviceable medicines acting upon our spirit-*

like vital force, [1; Aph. 15]...[for] *it is only by their dynamic action on the vital force that remedies are able to re-establish and do actually re-establish health and vital harmony."* [1; Aph. 16]

By these remarks, and their frequent and emphatic repetition, Hahnemann makes it unambiguously clear that he regards homoeopathy as a vitalist system of medicine in a direct line with previous similar systems such as those of Stahl [1660-1734], van Helmont [1577-1644] and Paracelsus [1493-1541]. Hahnemann's vision of a radically curative medicine will hopefully become established in the next quarter millennium and then natural, healing therapies will at last begin to dominate medicine and take up their long-deserved position of greater prestige. Hahnemann had a very clear understanding of the position of homoeopathy in the grand scheme of things. He harboured few illusions that it would meet easy acceptance in the medical schools, but rather, that opposition and hostility would greet its arrival at every turn.

Though it is naturally disappointing that it has not achieved greater dominance already, yet we should be grateful that it has survived at all and that it is once again expanding steadily through winning over patients rather than professors. The future of homoeopathy looks very bright indeed. The writings and medical preoccupations of Hahnemann are therefore just as vivid and relevant today as when they were written. It seems certain that they will serve as a source of deep inspiration for medical thinkers and practitioners for centuries. It is unlikely that homoeopathy will ever convert medical professors of the Old School, and therefore its future lies in the hands of patients and the unrelenting increase in numbers of enlightened practitioners.

Certainly, *"the resurgence of non-traditional medicine is being spearheaded by the lay public and non-traditional thinkers in medi-*

cine," [2; 7] rather than by hidebound professors and drug companies with vested interests quite distinct from whole-person wellness or patient totality. The medicine of today has indeed *"reduced the patient's autonomy to a therapeutic choice of drugs or surgery,"* [2; 11] which stands as a chilling indictment of its claim to cure disease, which is nothing other than a sorry state of medical dependency masquerading as true cure. This woeful situation obviously flies in the face of Kent's insistence that cure should: *"leave the patient in freedom always."* [3; 160-1]

Some explanation might be deemed appropriate of a view of history I find myself very sympathetic towards. Giambattista Vico [1668-1744] was a thinker and convinced that *"what men have made, other men can understand."* [4; 60] How we understand people in times past became the puzzle of his life, which he eventually solved to his own satisfaction. He concerned himself very much with considering not just the 'external' knowledge we have about times and places but also that special knowledge *"we acquire as agents, from [being] inside,"* [5; xxix] the core of human affairs. This form of knowledge requires that *"we enter into the mental universes of other ages and peoples by recreative imagination."* [5; xxix] Vico realised that *"there existed a field...which men could know from within human history,"* [6; 342] and so he sought a key to *"enter into their worlds, to see through their eyes,"* [4; 60] so as to begin to interpret their actions and utterances *"as intelligible responses to the natural conditions in which they find themselves,"* [4; 60] rather than to write them off as unintelligible aliens, lying mostly beyond our own understanding.

Vico rejected the dead knowledge of an outsider's view, that of a spectator, the gloss or external features of events, people, times and places, which dismally fails to deliver the intimate details of the inner world of human thoughts and the feelings of people at a specific time. Such an 'outsider's account' lacks the deeper, living world of human narrative and motives, which can only be obtained by mysteriously entering *"into the minds and hearts of [history's] major figures with greater empathy."* [5; xxxi] Without such ability, the past remains dead knowledge: *"opaque and impenetrable to human understanding."* [6; 342] Empathy is Vico's secret key to deepening one's understanding of the nature of a people or place in time. Such is a subtle means of *"entering into minds and situations,"* [6; 353] of the past and thereby obtaining, through an act of creative imagination, completely new knowledge, just as if we can *"hear men's voices...[and surmise] their values, outlook, aims, ways of living,"* [4; 64-5].

That elusive something which historians forever yearn to distil out of the raw historical facts and data, primarily revolves about *"what men did and thought and suffered, of what they strove for, aimed at, accepted, rejected, conceived, imagined...their motives, purposes, hopes, fears, loves and hatreds...outlooks and visions of reality...ways of seeing, and ways of acting and creating..."* [6; 342] How can the historian *"grasp the acts, the thoughts, the attitudes, the beliefs, explicit and implicit, the worlds of thought and feeling of societies dead and gone?"* [6; 343] From such an endeavour it becomes clear that *"to understand history is to understand what men made of the world in which they found themselves, what they demanded of it, what their felt needs, aims and ideals were."* [6; 352]

An artist can easily undertake an *"interrogation of the visible,"* [7; 562] but as the past is dead and gone, no such interrogation is possible. At best this leaves the hope of revivifying the corpse, but as with the artist empathising with his subject, close study *"brings you closer to the object, until finally you are, as it were, inside it: the contours you have drawn no longer marking the edge of what you have seen, but the edge of what you have be-*

come." [7; 10] Or, as Auden says, *"one must be passive to conceive the truth."* [8]

Such knowledge is radically different; it is *"not knowledge of facts or of logical truths, provided by observation or the sciences or deductive reasoning; nor is it knowledge of how to do things; nor the knowledge provided by faith...it is more like the knowledge we claim of a friend, or his character, of his ways of thought or action, the intuitive sense of the nuances of personality or feeling or ideas."* [6; 352-3] Such is the *"God-like 'insider's view,"* [6; 343] obtained solely through empathic attunement with the human thoughts, feelings and aspirations that distinguish a certain person or epoch in time.

I therefore offer these vistas into the life of Hahnemann in a similar spirit - accounts of a person I have come to know intimately like a close friend. I hope that this approach proves insightful and that, as Berlin says, even if *"the historical details may be wrong, even absurd, the knowledge may be defective, the critical methods insufficient - but the approach is bold, original and fruitful."* [4; 61-2] In that sense, I hope any errors will be forgiven, if the overall picture is indeed fruitful and that Hahnemann himself comes alive for the reader, rises up and speaks once again, through the mouthpiece these pages provide.

I do not hold any of the sources I have used responsible for any interpretations I place upon them: errors of fact or interpretation are solely mine. I dedicate this work to my wife Dawn and our four children, each of whom has been conceived and raised under continuous homeopathic care. Very rarely have they been sick and even more rarely have they needed an allopath. It is in this manner that homeopathy wins and keeps its staunchest converts, not through so-called clinical trials that prove only the ignorance of scientists: *"those who say they have tested homeopathy and it is a failure have only exposed their own ignorance."* [9]

My sincere thanks are due to those enlightened editors who saw some value in my work: Paul Herscu, George Guess, Misha Norland, Michael Tomlinson, Karen Oakley, Melanie Grimes, Rudi Verspoor, Karen Wehrstein, Charles Wansbrough, Diana Kopatsy, Patty Smith, Ardavan Shahrdar, Gregory Vlamis, Robin Logan, Toni Godden, Eileen Nauman, Julian Winston, Sylvain Cazalet.

PETER MORRELL

Stafford, England,
Winter Solstice, 2002

Sources

1. Samuel Hahnemann, *Organon of Medicine*, combined 5th/6th edition, translated and edited by Boericke and Dudgeon, 1841 and 1923
2. W John Diamond MD, *The Clinical Practice of Complementary, Alternative and Western Medicine*, Washington: CRC Press, 2001
3. James T Kent, *Lectures on Homeopathic Philosophy*, California: N Atlantic Books, 1900, 1980
4. Isaiah Berlin, *Giambattista Vico and Cultural History*, in *The Crooked Timber of Humanity - Chapters in the History of Ideas*, Princeton: Princeton Univ Press, 1991, 49-69
5. Isaiah Berlin, *The Proper Study of Mankind - An Anthology of Essays*, London: Pimlico, 1998, 667 pages; *Introduction*, xxiii-xxxvi
6. Isaiah Berlin, *The Divorce Between the Sciences and the Humanities*, in [5], 326-358
7. John Berger, *Selected Essays*, Edited by Geoff Dwyer, London: Pimlico, 2001
8. W H Auden, *Collected Poems*, London: Faber, 1994, from Kairos and Logos, 1941, 308
9. Kent, *New Remedies, Lesser Writings, Aphorisms & Precepts*, 1925

CONTENTS

A Fragment of Autobiography 1

Hahnemann's Discovery of Homoeopathy 5

Some Reflections on the Origins of Hahnemann's Ideas 17

Coming out of the Darkness like a Meteor 31

Hahnemann as a Scientist 63

Some Notes about Hahnemann's Horoscope 79

Samuel and Melanie in Paris 89

On Hahnemann's Workloads and Consultation Times
   in His Paris Practice 101

Hahnemann: The Adventurous Career of a Medical Rebel 117

On Hahnemann's Coffee Theory 131

Hahnemann and High Potency 137

Hahnemann's Miasm Theory and Miasm Remedies 155

Hahnemann and Paracelsus: a Heavenly Dialogue 171

Hahnemann and Homoeopathy 183

Confusion over Hahnemann's Small Doses 215

Hunter, Hahnemann and The Origin of Homoeopathy 225

Hahnemann's Debt to Alchemy 247

Hahnemann & Others on The Succussion of
    Medicinal Fluids, etc. 275
Hahnemann & Homoeopathy from Romanticism
    to Post-Modernism 283
The Secretive Hahnemann and the Esoteric Roots of
    Homoeopathy 293
Hahnemann's Use of Potency Over Time 323
A Guide to Hahnemann's Translations 341
Hahnemann - the Real Pioneer of Psychiatry 377
Fate Versus Wish 393
Details of Hahnemann's Family Members 399
    Bibliography 403

A FRAGMENT OF AUTOBIOGRAPHY

I was born in 1950 and lived all my childhood in Farndon (which means Fern Hill), a small and pretty village southwest of Newark on the river Trent in Nottinghamshire. The whole area is very flat, like the Fens of East Anglia, and the vast sky dominates the scenery. The dominance by the sky also brought about a love of clouds and light to which I tend to ascribe my love of art and painting and which I share with greats like Constable and Turner, who also came from the east of England. I was fascinated by clouds and skies as a child and recall just gazing up at them slowly moving across the sky with such imperial majesty.

Peter Morell

My mother, Olive Gwendoline Grand-Scrutton (1917-84), was the youngest of 15 children and thus we had many relatives around. There were also 30-odd cousins: sons and daughters of the first 15, which included myself. My mother's family originated from the east, in Norfolk. Her father, George Grand-Scrutton (1865-1945) hailed from Norwich and my grandmother, Susannah Elizabeth Baines (1871-1957) came from Blakeney, then a thriving little port on the north Norfolk coast.

The Morrell's today tend to be found mainly in north Nottinghamshire, the most numerous now being in the Mansfield area. Though I was born in Newark, only 15 miles to the east, my father, Reginald (1912-65), was born in Northampton, 80 miles south, his father, Raymond Morrell (1884-1970) was born in Derby and his father, Samuel Morrell (1850-1920) in Scalford, north Leicestershire, near the pork-pie town of Melton Mowbray.

The first 20 years of my life were hugely dominated by science, especially chemistry and biology. This derives from my having chemistry sets and microscopes as a child. I also liked telescopes and cameras and delighted in all these optical devices from an early age. What I liked about science was the experimental side, that you can discover anything for yourself. You do not need anyone or any book to tell you the way things are. It is there for the taking, all you have to do is look and play around. You can discover anything in that way. This appealed to me very deeply. I never read many books as a child.

Apart from school work I just went outdoors all the time and never sat around reading books or anything like that. Yet in a curious sort of way I was intellectual, in the sense that I thought deeply about things and was a very good observer. So I developed a natural yen for experimentation and observation of all types. I thus became ideal science material.

I also liked about science the fact that it was certain and repeatable. That seemed to make it 'real knowledge' which could be put on the shelf for 30 years and then taken down by someone else and would be just the same as the day it was put up there. This made it enormously powerful and fascinating. That was what the Encyclopedists liked about it and I can still see its big attraction. Yet I was never gifted mathematically and had no interest in the subject. I regret this now as I would love to have been trained in data analysis and statistics. That would have greatly benefited my later interests.

In biology itself I excelled in microscopy and dissection work, which I loved enormously and still enjoy. At college we had an amazing and unconventional teacher who was so brilliant in so many ways. She constantly brought specimens into class and exuded great inspiration on all of us. She greatly encouraged me to have confidence in the self-discovery approach and her approach has remained a very big influence upon me. We were so lucky to have her. I despise book knowledge and people who know much but understand little. She was a great exemplar of the superiority of a person with profound and extensive practical knowledge and who could work anything out from first principles and just straight thinking.

I read Zoology at Leeds University and since 1975 have been involved in teaching, mostly as a College lecturer in sciences. My main other interests have been in art, poetry, astrology, Buddhism and homoeopathy.

My involvement with homoeopathy began in 1978 when I was taught the basics by a student of George MacLeod. I practised on a part-time basis throughout the 1980s but since 1989 have been mostly engaged with researching aspects of the history of homoeopathy. After submitting my thesis in April 1998 and having a viva voce I was elected by the Dean of Social Sciences and the Academic Board as Honorary Research Associate in the History of Medicine at Staffordshire University for a period of 3 years. I have presented research papers on this theme in Stuttgart, Linkoping, Sweden, London and Keele.

■

HAHNEMANN'S DISCOVERY OF HOMOEOPATHY

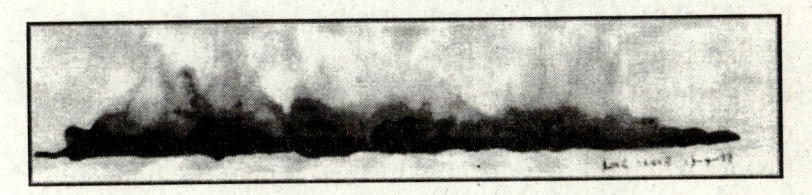

long cloud, April 1999 - Peter Morrell

Firstly there is the problem of where Hahnemann got his ideas from. He mentions no-one from the medical past except Albrecht von Haller (1708-77), and strangest of all he never even mentions Paracelsus (1493-1541), who is most widely regarded as the originator of a form of homoeopathy i.e. a system of medicine based almost exclusively upon the law of similars and small doses.

Secondly, there is the problem of how he developed the processes of provings and potentisation. Again, he seems to credit no-one but himself with these ideas. The solution of these problems is probably only of marginal interest to practising homoeopaths: we have this wonderful system of medicine and that is sufficient. It is, however, of great interest both to philosophers and historians of homoeopathy.

One could take the view that Hahnemann had his own personal, maybe eccentric reasons for writing in the way he did. One might assume, for example, that he was too proud to credit anyone else with the ideas that form the basis of his unique system of medicine. It is also possible that he felt Paracelsus to be too dangerous a figure to associate in any way with his new system. There is some mileage in both these points of view.

He could also have felt that it would cause confusion to link his system with Paracelsus. It might also be argued that he did not know of his medical predecessors. There is no evidence for this and it is extremely unlikely. Indeed his translation work alone makes it almost impossible for him not to have known about all the major trends in medical history. Then there is also the historical material he would have surely covered in his training for a medical degree. Yet none of the above points taken singly or together fully account for the development of homoeopathy.

One can understand how he would have wanted his new system to be seen as just that: entirely new. Yet he could have mentioned with impunity the sources of ideas that led him in the direction of his new system. This would, however, have left his new system with a link-by-association both with metaphysics and alchemy (of which he was not fond) and with the greatest medical rebel of all time: that chaotic, irrational and tempestuous genius Paracelsus.

I think it is highly likely that Hahnemann pursued this line of reasoning and decided at a very early stage that it was better to deliberately leave out all reference to possible sources of his ideas. He probably felt that historically informed physicians would realise anyway who his main influences were and for the rest it was not worth rekindling their ingrained aversion to 'medieval irrationality' by even mentioning the 'beast of Hohenheim' in the same breath as homoeopathy. Finally, he may also have been averse, like most of us, to accusations of plagiarism. Both these arguments carry some credibility.

However, I also feel that there is a new theory that accounts for much of the problem we have discussed above. This involves trying to piece together a clear idea of the situation Hahnemann occupied in relation to medical practice. In order to provide an outline of this, it will be necessary to briefly describe the problems Hahnemann himself faced and how he solved them.

It will be recalled that Hahnemann in the 1780's was becoming disenchanted with his chosen profession and gave up the practice of medicine at an early stage in his career, both out of severe disappointment with its results and to make sufficient cash from translating to support his large and growing family. In the 1780s in Dresden he published many chemical works.. (then)...retired disgusted with the uncertainty of medical practice and devoted himself to chemistry and literature." (5)

"Hahnemann was so disillusioned with the state of medical practice and knowledge that, soon after his marriage in 1782, he totally refrained from practising medicine...so deep was his belief that the tools he had been given would do more harm than good".

Meanwhile, in his translation work he was undoubtedly accumulating a vast knowledge of medical history, the cultural traditions of many different countries and the rich clinical experiences of physicians in those various times, places and cultural environments.

Without doubt, his translation work opened up for him a rich treasure-trove of medical data, therapeutic hints, clinical observations and notes about drug actions, which must have greatly enriched his medical thinking and which no-one else was party to. This was in many ways a gradual, unconscious or intuitive imbibing process. Just as the carpenter develops great skill from the practice of carving wood, or the painter from making pictures, so Hahnemann must have been imbibing a wealth of clinical and therapeutic ideas from his many translations and researches.

"The truly prodigious output of Hahnemann is demonstrated by the fact that these translations totalled no less than 1780 pages."

He also had an unsurpassed knowledge of chemistry, pharmacy and materia medica as evident in his translation of Cullen's Materia Medica in 1790, von Haller's Materia Medica in 1806, his own Pharmaceutical Lexicon of 1799, his Essay on a New Principle of 1796 and finally his Materia Medica Pura of 1811.

Bear in mind also, that throughout all of this there was a doctor trained in a system of medicine he had come to despise for its irrationality and total ineffectiveness. In Desau in 1781 he

"...takes rather a desponding view of medical practice in general, and of his own in particular, as he candidly admits that most of his cases would have done better had he let them alone."

"He had followed the orthodox training of the day, with its insistence on powerful drugs, bleeding, blistering, but he soon grew first disillusioned, then appalled by the failure of these methods."

Here then, was a doctor who was in a state of despair, searching for a rational, safe and effective system of medicine. Combine this with his unshakeable conviction that a rational system could be developed, and that such a system could not possibly bear any of the characteristics of the medicine of his day, I think we can begin to see the essence of his actual situation. Here was that potent mixture of qualities and accidents of fate that so often gives birth to genius.

This sets the scene for us. We can now summarise the problem Hahnemann faced:

1. His clinical experience had firmly convinced him of the total ineffectiveness, destructiveness and danger of the system of medicine in which he had been trained.

    "He had now confirmed his earlier suspicions that the medical profession as a whole was bigoted, corrupt and reactionary and that medical practice was crude, barbaric, unhygienic and ineffective."

2. He conceived therefore that a safe and effective system of medicine could not possibly contain any of these qualities and that it probably contained all or most of the opposite qualities, viz. *similars, small doses, one remedy, gentleness and a new rational materia medica.* It is my contention that he obtained this revolutionary schema from contemplating the main features of the allopathic system he so detested.

3. He was avidly in search of just such a system. Yet how could he produce a new map to replace the one he had rejected?

4. All of these factors led Hahnemann to dwell upon the statements by Hippocrates and Paracelsus (amongst others) about the law of similars and the use of small doses. On reading these great physicians of the past, he was, as it were, haunted by their suggestions, yet without any means of actually using them therapeutically. They were good ideas, but how could he put them into practice? Throughout the 1780s, therefore, he was poised in this frustrating no-man's land, detesting what he could not (dare not) use, haunted by what he wished to use (similars), but unable to utilise the advice of his medical forebears for want of a homoeopathic 'modus operandi'. This was the essence of his situation and his search.

5. What clues he had, pointed strongly towards the law of similars, the minimum safe dose, the use of a single remedy and a gentle system. Yet still homoeopathy as such had not emerged at this point, either in his mind or in fact. This gave him two new problems: how to assess what is meant by the term 'similar' and how to rationally produce a new materia medica.

There was also the problem of how to attenuate the dose, but that was of secondary importance. His biggest and most complex problems undoubtedly revolved around the question of drugs, their properties and therapeutic uses. Without an accurate knowledge of drugs the whole concept of similars was meaningless.

7. In 1790, while translating Cullen, there came the great breakthrough he yearned for.

"...which was to him what the falling apple was to Newton, and the swinging lamp in the Baptistery at Pisa was to Galileo."

The fact that a larger dose of Cinchona would increase the fever of malaria, strongly implied that a curative medicine can cause what it will cure. It clearly established a link between the toxic effects of the drug and its therapeutic effects. This surely must have leapt out of the page at the young Hahnemann and burned like a laser into his soul! One can barely imagine the intense excitement and relief he must have felt when he proved Cinchona himself and confirmed every word Cullen had written, and more besides. And here also was the key to producing a safe, effective and rational system of therapy: the fruit of his heart's desire.

"From this single experiment his mind appears to have been impressed with the conviction that the pathogenetic effects of medicines would give the key to their therapeutic powers."

Here was the solution to his two biggest problems. At long last, he now had the means to scientifically investigate the toxic and therapeutic properties of single drugs. Now he was able to prepare and regulate the remedy in the proving (and, by analogy, in clinical practice) and observe minutely its every action on the mind and body. Now he could confidently push aside a materia medica based upon rumour, dubious clinical hints, 'signatures' and old wives tales, and develop a systematic materia medica based on the actual therapeutic properties of drugs tested on the healthy.

"in the last three thousand five hundred years, not one single physician, to my knowledge...has come upon this so natural, so absolutely necessary, so uniquely valid proving of the pure, characteristic action of medicines..."

It was this breakthrough - *the Proving* - that enabled Hahnemann to understand precisely what the term 'similar' means and to create an entirely new and rational materia medica of individual drugs. The idea came from Cullen, but it was entirely Hahnemann's idea. It was an idea that could only have been formed in the mind of a disillusioned doctor who had been fully ripened by years of disappointment, yearning and searching.

Hahnemann now embarked upon the long series of experiments that are described in detail in all the biographies, the fruits of which were the "Essay on a New Principle" (1796), the "Fragmenta de Viribus" (1805) and finally the "Materia Medica Pura" of 1811. But until he had that idea, it was all meaningless and tangled ideas, fragments, hints, therapeutic insights and clinical concepts mixed up with so much garbled nonsense and mumbo-jumbo.

Finally, the last part of the picture that created homoeopathy as a distinct system, was the regulation of the dose, or rather the method of adjusting the concentration of the remedy. This arose largely as a result of Hahnemann's immense chemical knowledge and simply from his great pragmatism. He had to reduce the dose for the patient's sake, to one as small and effective as possible. More than most, Hahnemann was keenly aware of the damage large doses caused to the patient.

Hahnemann's idea at first was simply to reduce the 'strength' or material mass of his drug, but his passion for accuracy led him to adopt a scale, that he might always be sure of the degree of reduction and establish a standard for comparison. He had always been moving away from large crude doses, not for metaphysical reasons (as had Paracelsus amongst others) but for purely practical reasons. His development of Hahnemann's Soluble Mercury preparation in the 1780s for use against syphilis testified to his rejection of crude drugging and his desire to use minute doses. This was mainly due to his aversion for causing harmful side-effects in the patient, not to a devotion to forms of spirituality à la Kent or Swedenbourg.

> "A hint of his growing conviction that remedies should be prescribed in high dilution was given in..(an article)..published in 1788."

We can now summarise what we have discovered in this review of Hahnemann's formation of homoeopathy by outlining what this theory explains. The theory seems to go a long way to satisfactorily explain certain facts that were formerly resistant to complete or credible explanation. These include the folowing:

1. Why Hahnemann was so vehement in his criticisms of allopathy.
2. Why he was so uncompromising in his promotion of a pure form of homoeopathy of the very highest standard, uncontaminated by other people's ideas or speculations and undiluted by allopathic concepts such as rote prescribing, using very low potencies, or failure to prescribe on the totality of the case. Closely linked to this was his fanatical treatment of those he saw as

opponents and 'failed homoeopaths' (i.e. those who had failed to follow his instructions to the letter).

3. Why he asserted most forcefully, that the therapeutic use of a single drug must and can only be based upon its known effects (mental and physical, coarse and subtle) upon the healthy, rather than its use in clinical practice or upon the speculations of individuals, the dictates of tradition or the so-called 'doctrine of signatures'.

4. Why Hahnemann never credits Paracelsus or Hippocrates, amongst others, as sources of his ideas. They may have given clues, but it was he who had created homoeopathy and no-one else. This has been heretofor misinterpreted as pride and arrogance.

5. Why Hahnemann only eulogised von Haller who had recommended the use of provings of drugs on the healthy and who had possessed an encyclopaedic knowledge of European drugs and their actions.

6. Why Hahnemann stopped practising allopathic medicine out of disgust for its ineffectiveness and its danger to the patient.

7. How a combination of historical, clinical, linguistic and therapeutic knowledge was uniquely blended in the person of Samuel Hahnemann such that he would reject allopathy, remain convinced of the existence of a safe and effective medical system, and actively search for one.

8. Why he always adjusted the dose downwards for purely practical reasons of safety for the patient combined with effectiveness rather than from metaphysical inclination. The idea came from Paracelsus (amongst others) but,

again, was uniquely Hahnemannian.

9. Why Hahnemann was reluctant to associate his new system of medicine with the name of Theophrastus Paracelsus for fear of being misunderstood or being accused of plagiarism. He wanted homoeopathy to have the finest chance to get going as a new and independent system of medicine in its own right, untainted by links with outmoded or denigrated medical systems from the past.

10. His translating work, far from being marginal, was in fact, central to his own development, and without it, it is arguable, he would not have gained such a wide and deep knowledge of medical history and ideas let alone the therapeutic and clinical data from other cultures, times and places that all undoubtedly helped him in his search for a system of safe, effective and rational therapy.

11. Also largely explained is why homoeopathy really is a separate, new and independent system of medicine entirely created by one person. Though the ideas and influences are there, and some had been there for years, if not for centuries, it was only when these were combined in one person that they bore such fruit.

12. It also explains why Hahnemann spent such a lot of his time studying and exploring drugs of all kinds, their properties and alleged clinical uses and why he spent so long pouring over the records of past physicians and apothecaries as to what could kill, poison or cure what.

It is difficult not to eulogise Hahnemann, yet I believe Hahnemann simply solved the problems that he confronted. The fact that he confronted problems of such magnitude and solved them with such skill, devolves at least as much from the situation he found himself in as from his inherent genius. By this I mean that he became a receptacle for such a unique blend of experience, expertise and knowledge that only he could have clearly perceived these problems and solved them. Others may have seen parts of the problem or lacked the means of solution. He was unique in that he saw the problem thoroughly and vividly, explored all its aspects and then set about a slow but systematic solution of each part.

What I feel has been entirely lacking from previous attempts to explain the origin of homoeopathy is the clarity of perception of the exact position Hahnemann found himself in as a physician. This took on a three-part structure. First came his disaffection for and abandonment of allopathy, secondly the search for a new system and translation work (the 'ripening') and thirdly the discovery (via Cullen) of provings and its subsequent train of experimentation and clinical confirmation. Prior to Hahnemann there truly is no homoeopathy.

■

SOME REFLECTIONS ON THE ORIGINS OF HAHNEMANN'S IDEAS

Portwrinkle, 26 July 1999

'The publication [in 1797] of Friedrich Schelling's 'First Draft of a System of Natural Philosophy' was contemporary with the records in which Hahnemann neatly and conscientiously assembled and numbered his observations of the symptoms excited in himself and his children by the most varied of medicines.' [Gumpert, p.114]

With regard to the origin of Hahnemann's ideas, there are two themes, which we can briefly explore. One relates to the influence of Kant upon his writing, and indeed of other eighteenth century German idealists. Second, there is the weird philosophical milieu of Germany in the 1780s and 1790s, which could best be described as ambiguous. Both themes seem considerably to pervade Hahnemann's ideas. In relation to the first of our two themes we can say that probably no other single event in the history of philosophy, and in the history of German philosophy, was as important as the publication in 1781 of Kant's *Critique of Pure Reason*, which 'raised him to the foremost position among living philosophers' [Rogers, p.376]. It placed him in the firmament of German Idealists for all time. At that time, Hahnemann was just embarking upon his 'systematic disenchantment' with allopathy and wondering, no doubt, if there would ever be found any clear 'guiding principles' for the practice of medicine It seems that it was probably Kant's work that inspired Hahnemann to formulate his homoeopathic ideas into an aphoristic style. He cannot really have failed to have seen *Critique of Pure Reason* and probably read it.

> '...for Kant, the truths of the intellect are subordinate to the truths of the practical will...scientific reason [has] the right to induce belief.' [Rogers, p.398]

These were ideas that would most certainly have found fertile ground in the thinking of Samuel Hahnemann in the 1780s and 1790s. Indeed, we read in Hobhouse [pp.104-5] that Hahnemann liked Kant's writings and expressed this in a letter to von Villers.

Not a word is mentioned about Goethe or Schiller.' [Haehl, vol. 1, p.250]

'From his schooldays onwards he had followed Descartes, Spinoza and Leibnitz...and then proceeded to vitalism and to the naturalism of Schelling and Hegel...Wunderlich says in his 'History of Medicine' that the naturalist philosophy of Hegel and Schelling movement actually afforded help to the rise of homoeopathy...' [Haehl, vol. 1, pp.251-2]

Yet any influence by Hegel must have been minimal, for he comes just too late to have any big impact. His first major work, *'The Phenomenology of Mind'*, appeared in 1807, by which time homoeopathy was already up and running, and the *Organon* all but written. Kant's influence therefore still seems central [see also Ledermann, 1944, pp.82-6; 1961, pp.274-6; 1957, p.169; and Ledermann, 1970, for in-depth discussion].

Hahnemann clearly intended his *Organon* (first published 1810) to become refined over time such that its principles could be amplified, clarified and updated, to be elevated eventually to the status of 'natural laws'. That he wrote a further five editions over the next thirty years, might well be seen as good evidence of this tendency to revise and elevate. *The Organon* was clearly modelled on some profound philosophical works [e.g. Bacon's *Novum Organum*; see Close, p.15, pp.27-28, pp.248-9] and he seems to have regarded the veracity of its aphorisms as sacrosanct:

> "...the 'Organon of the Art of Healing' - is presented in sections after the manner of a legal code. [its]...sections manifest the notable and intimidating terseness of legal paragraphs, which, despite their unequivocal and final character, can scarcely be understood without prolific commentaries. Many authoritative minds have expounded them, and have read into them profound significance or nonsense, according to their own estimate."
> [Gumpert, p.133]

It is also true that this tendency to formulate natural laws was at that time very common, for example in Optics and Chemistry in particular, but also in natural science generally. Moreover, Hahnemann was keenly aware of all developments taking place in science, especially his beloved chemistry. Post-Enlightenment, it was a time of great systematisation of knowledge in all fields and the building up of grand systems for the first time.

Thus, quite apart from Kant, the *Organon* actually has two origins. First, it was Hahnemann's personal idea to formulate his ideas and system of medicine into a series of aphorisms, to make it into a system of medicine based upon clear principles, which in his view allopathy certainly was not. This stemmed very largely from the dogmatic, fussy, high-principled or pedantic side of his nature. Second, he had around him in the world, hosts of other scientists doing exactly the same thing in various other fields of endeavour.

These include Michael Faraday [1791-1867], Joseph

Some Reflections

Priestley [1733-1804], John Dalton [1766-1844], Antoine Lavoisier [1743-94] and Karl Scheele [1742-86] in Chemistry. Hahnemann is reported to have met Lavoisier in Dresden in 1786, and to have corresponded with him [Hobhouse, 1933, p.59]. In Botany, there was Carolus Linnaeus [1707-78], in Zoology, Georges Cuvier [1769-1832] and Jean-Baptiste Lamarck [1744-1829] and in Geology, Sir Charles Lyall [1797-1875]. This 18th century phase of prolific experimentation was in turn founded upon the pioneering work of earlier figures like Bacon [1561-1626], Galileo [1564-1642], Descartes [1596-1650] and Newton [1642-1727], who first set thinkers down the road towards experimentation, and away from Church dogma, as sources of ideas and their confirmation.

Antoine Lavoisier [1743-94]

> *"Galileo established a new criterion for truth: truth was only that what [in principle] everyone could test for himself and see to be true. The means used for this was the experiment, that magnificent invention of the western world, brought to perfection by Galileo...before Galileo, theoretical definition was the prime criterion for truth...the completely new element brought in by Galileo had to do not so much with method as such, but rather with truth and authority...the leitmotiv of Galileo's work as I see it was his passionate opposition to belief based on authority."* [Pietschmann, pp.156-7]

Michael Faraday (1791-1867)

Therefore, the development of his ideas into a grand system was not only his own idea, but also part of a 'tide of the times' or 'zeitgeist': an impulse pushing many others along. Experimentation led to the establishment of principles and laws and in this manner the fabric of science theory was gradually woven. Hahnemann undoubtedly drew on the atmosphere of his times. In relation to our second theme, the following quote from Berlin supports the view that Hahnemann was not only living through a time of medical uncertainty, but also through a period of general 'intellectual directionlessness', which pervaded the heart and soul of Germany at that time.

> "This faith in the powers of reason and science was by no means universally held, even in the mid-eighteenth century in western Europe...the first formidable attack upon it, uncompromising, violent and fraught with lasting consequences, came from Germany...a backlash against the French cultural domination of the western world...a growing consciousness of their own provincialism...a sense of inferiority...the pietists, profoundly unpolitical in temper, contemptuous of the world and its varieties...suspicious of hierarchy, ritual, learning and rational explanation ...much of this sentiment was probably at the root of the revulsion against the materialism, utilitarianism, ethical naturalism and atheism of the French lumieres, which one finds

in such thinkers as Hamann, Lavater, Herder and, indeed, Kant himself. They and their disciples Jacobi, Fichte, Schelling, Baader, were in fact the philosophical wing ...of pre-romanticism and, indeed, romanticism itself." [Berlin, 1997, pp.164-5]

An ambiguity arose because of strongly anti-rationalist elements emerging at that time in German culture, and a general backlash against firstly, the general eagerness with which so many were embracing the 'new certitudes' of the Enlightenment and secondly against the French intellectual domination which the Enlightenment involved.

Carolus Linnaeus [1707-78]

'[The Organon] gives clear expression of Hahnemann's originality, but is also the product of a mind steeped in the ideas of the eighteenth-century Enlightenment, and informed by the liberal humanitarianism of Jean-Jacques Rousseau...' [Handley, 1990, p.3]

This was a time of the emergence of a great divide between Enlightenment and Romantic philosophers [Tarnas, pp.367-75] and it seems likely to me that in its origins and its general flavour, homoeopathy became imbued with strong elements of both movements, while being neither entirely one nor the other. In this respect, exactly in Berlin's sense as stated above, Hahnemann's system very accurately mirrors the history of his day, its underlying ambivalence and uncertainty, and the 'cultural schizophrenia' of his

Jean-Jacques Rousseau
[1712-78]

fellow countrymen in the latter half of the 18th century. On the one hand, homoeopathy arose as a powerfully rational critique and a genuinely scientific revision of 'Old Physic', and yet on the other it happily retains nebulous heresies like 'spiritualised substance', 'potency energy', 'succussion', 'case totality' and 'vital forces', ideas which are entirely alien to rational science.

"Day after day, he tested medicines on himself and others. He collected histories of cases of poisoning. His purpose was to establish a physiological doctrine of medical remedies, free from all suppositions, and based solely on experiments." [Gumpert, p.92]

In one sense, therefore, homoeopathy tilts strongly towards Enlightenment and Reason - chiefly through using empirical investigations like provings - and in the other it embraces the blurred mysticism and dreamy pastoralism of the Romantics. And even today, it still retains this weird ambivalence which gives it an almost equal appeal both to rationalists and to romantics. Thus, it is no surprise to still find a somewhat divided movement, with rational scientists residing at one pole, and assorted New Age dreamers and Druids at the other. It still seems as ideologically split as a movement as it was in its origin. That combination still makes it a very attractive and very interesting ideology.

THE ESSENCE OF HAHNEMANN'S SPIRIT OF INQUIRY

By way of summary, we can state several important features about Hahnemann and the foundation of homoeopathy. Firstly, he was clearly in possession of a formidable intellect, brilliant linguistic skills and he was very absorbed by science, even in the modern sense. He was scientific in that primary and fundamental sense of boldly rejecting received dogmas from the past about the nature of truth and the world, and strongly favoured the confirmation of ideas through experiment and observation in the outer world. Hahnemann certainly possessed that elevation of sense data and observations as the sole arbiters of truth, which lies at the very heart of natural science. In that sense he was profoundly scientific and probably more scientific than most of his medical contemporaries. In this sense, he was also typical of the Enlightenment. Like Kant, he also felt that profound truths could be laid out in a logical framework of aphorisms.

John Dalton [1766-1844]

That he thoroughly detested medical systems of ideas and speculations is very apparent in all his writings:

> "No learned brains could unravel the skein of hypotheses and theories which entangled the professors and set them all at odds...there were no experiments, there was no painstaking research; there were only odd and eccentric systems which

were exalted into dogmas, without any possibility of testing senseless methods of treatment." [Gumpert, p.15]

Hahnemann's clear understanding of the dismal value of 'medical systems' is yet further illustrated by the following quotes:

> "There was now the influence of the stars, now that of evil spirits and witchcraft; anon came the alchymist with his salt, sulphur and mercury; anon Silvius, with his acids, biles and mucus...our system-builders delighted in these metaphysical heights, where it was so easy to win territory; for in the boundless region of speculation every one becomes a ruler who can most effectually elevate himself beyond the domain of the senses." [Aesculapius in the Balance, 1805, in Lesser Writings, p.421-2]

> "Physiology...looked only through the spectacles of hypothetical conceits, gross mechanical explanations, and pretensions to systems...little has been added...what are we to think of a science, the operations of which are founded upon perhapses and blind chance?' [Aesculapius in the Balance, 1805, in Lesser Writings, pp.423-6]

> "...because they placed the essence of the medical art, and their own chief pride, in explaining much even of the inexplicable...this was the first and great delusion they practised upon themselves and on the world. This was the unhappy conceit which, from Galen's time down to our own, made the medical art a stage for the display of the most fantastic, often most self-contradictory, hypotheses, explanations, demonstrations, conjectures, dogmas, and systems,

whose evil consequences are not to be overlooked...' [*On the Value of the Speculative Systems of Medicine, 1808, in Lesser Writings, pp.489-90*]

Yet, there is no doubt that he did have a distinct 'system-building' tendency of his own. Like many of his contemporaries, he seems to have enjoyed the aesthetics of delineating great principles and building them up into a tower of ideas. His *Organon* is undoubtedly the best testament to that impulse. It is unfortunate that some historians continue, even today, in simplistically interpreting this impulse as the sole basis for Hahnemann's 'invention' of homoeopathy as just another 'medical system':

**Jean-Bantiste Lamarck
1744-1829**

> "The manner in which critical methods undermined the old order is well illustrated by the history of homoeopathy. This system was established in Germany during the last days of the 'naturphilosophie', and was characterized like the others by a monistic pathology and therapeutics. All diseases save two were viewed as forms of psora or 'the itch' and a single scheme of treatment was recommended for all cases..." [Shryock, 1936, p.160]

> "Hahnemann had cast homoeopathy in substantially the same eighteenth century mold that had given shape to the systems of Cullen, Brown

> and Rush; as regular physicians assessed it, homoeopathy offered an unambiguous example of extreme rationalism informing a dogmatic system of practice with dire consequences." *[Warner, 1986, pp.52-3]*

Yet it is fairly clear that, unlike many of his contemporaries, he conceived this impulse not as an end in itself, to create a 'medical system' based upon speculation—an approach he detested—but springing directly from his practical experimentation.

> "Samuel Hahnemann was not only a physician at war with the medical practices of his time, he was also a great experimental scientist. He observed and collected his observations until gradually a pattern showed itself...observation alone is not sufficient, it must be coupled with right relating, relating in right order until we arrive in the Goethean sense at the idea, the underlying principle or pattern of a thing - the 'urphenomenon'." *[Brieger, p.241]*

From Hahnemann's Preface to the 2nd *Organon*:

> "...the splendid juggling of so-called theoretical medicine, in which a priori conceptions and speculative subtleties raised a number of proud schools...the art of medicine was merely a pseudo-scientific fabrication, remodelled from time to time to meet the prevailing fashion." *[ibid., p.xv]*

In Aphorism 6, he bemoans the

> "...futility of transcendental speculations which can receive no confirmation from experience.." *[ibid., p. 32]*

And, as Dr. Krauss candidly states in his Introduction to the 2nd *Organon:*

> *"Hahnemann was, in all essentials, a flawless experimenter." (p. xxiv)*

> *"The era of scientific medical experimentation begins with Hahnemann and nobody else. Scientific to the core, Hahnemann experimented scientifically for scientific observation..." [ibid., p. xxvii]*

Finally, Hahnemann states in the Preface to his 2nd *Organon:*

> *"The true healing art is in its nature a pure science of experience, and can and must rest upon clear facts and on the sensible phenomena pertaining to their sphere of action."* and that it *"...dares not take a single step out of the sphere of pure, well-observed experience and experiment, if it would avoid becoming a nullity, a farce." [ibid., p. xiv]*

These quotes clearly demonstrate that we should regard Hahnemann as a scientist in the most modern sense and in no way did he devise or invent homoeopathy as a speculative "system" in the manner Warner suggests. Yet, the temptation for Hahnemann to have simply "thrown in the towel" and revert to the allopathic mode of practice, must, at times, have been overwhelmingly strong. We can only admire Hahnemann's astonishing determination to get on with the task he had

Joseph Priestley [1733-1804]

set himself and to be wholly undistracted by every force, which tried to oppose him. His will-power and drive must have been exceptional and there are many people who would have broken under the pressure he faced or who would simply have done something else less arduous. He firmly believed that he was creating a revolutionary new system of medicine for humanity. Frustratingly for his followers, he was addicted to experimentation and improvement and never stopped changing his ideas and techniques right up to the last [see Handley, 1997]. The significance of this is that while most speculators freeze their ideas into a dogmatic system they are then most unwilling ever to change, Hahnemann proved his credentials as primarily an experimentalist, by constantly revising his medical system in the light of new experience.

■

COMING OUT OF
THE DARKNESS LIKE A METEOR

"Medicine has nothing in the whole course of her history which in any way approaches the accomplishment of this man... [Hahnemann was]... primarily a champion - and indeed the most brilliant champion - of internal remedies, the imperfections and manifold unfruitfulness of which he undertook to metamorphose..." [Haehl, vol. 1, 274-5]

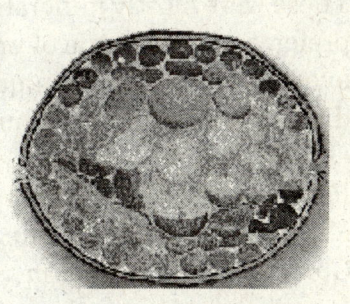

Sorcerer's Amulet, 1977

In his choice of remedies to prove and thus to admit into the new homoeopathic materia medica, Hahnemann reflects certain interesting theoretical and practical medical preconceptions, which may not be apparent to the undiscerning eye. His choice of drugs can be broken down into various categories. It includes two major sources previously unacknowledged. These are firstly those medicines that had already been in long regular use in the old school, such *as Mercury, Aloes, Bismuth, Antimony, Opium, Belladonna, Aconite, China* and *Arsenic*; secondly, those having an ancient alchemical aspect, such as *Copper, Lead, Silver, Tin, Mercury, Gold, Ferrum, Antimony, Sulphur* and *Salt*. Other metals in general might also be subsumed under this category, such as *Cobalt, Platina, Manganum, Nickel*, and *Zincum*. Metallic drugs generally derive mostly from alchemical medicine.

A third group of remedies includes those brand new to homoeopathy, such *as Apis, Calc carb., Arnica, Gelsemium, Graphites, Petroleum, Silica, Causticum, Baryta carb., Sepia, Hepar sulphuris, Terebinthina, Kreosotum, Lycopodium*. These were mostly minerals, which Hahnemann seemed to prefer, and their mode of preparation often employed such overtly alchemical techniques as calcination [roasting] and distillation. A fourth group consists of numerous long-established herbal drugs of ancient origin, such as *Hellebore, Bryonia, Dulcamara, Clematis, Hypericum, Chamomilla, Euphrasia, Hamamelis, Staphysagria, Stramonium, Spigelia, Convallaria, Veratrum, Rheum, Sambucus, Ledum, Symphytum, Hyoscyamus, Digitalis, Papaver*. A fifth group includes those from non-European sources such as *Cimicifuga, Rhus tox., Phytolacca, Lachesis, China, Podophyllum, Colocynthis, Ginger, Licorice*.

What we can conclude from such an appraisal is that homoeopathy did not spring anew overnight, from unknown sources, as a totally original system, "coming out of the darkness like a meteor" [Coulton, regarding Johannes Erigena] and complete unto itself. Yet, Hahnemann does try to give this impression. Although their mode of use, mode of preparation, and mode of study were unique and new, the drugs themselves were very largely drawn from the previous medical systems intimately known to Hahnemann and in regular use. Most of the drugs that were proved and brought into use were already employed in the herbal or mineral medicine of the day. It is therefore quite misleading for any homoeopath to suggest that homoeopathic drugs are unique to it as a system or that their choice and mode of selection were totally new and reflect Hahnemann's pathbreaking originality - they weren't and don't.

Certainly, the proving was new and the methods used in potentisation, but beyond that it is clear that Hahnemann's selection of those drugs that would be allowed admission into his new materia medica strongly reflects herbal, mineral and alchemical considerations which dominated his selection and which must also therefore reflect some theoretical preconceptions of his own. In other words, he did not pick them randomly - they made themselves known to him through their prior uses and long-established associations. Therefore, we can safely conclude that the popular idea that homoeopathy sprang into existence, as a totally new and original system of medicine, "coming out of the darkness like a meteor", is a highly misleading misconception, if not wholly false. While homoeopathy is a carefully honed system, yet it is also highly derivative. It connects in some way with all that preceded it.

TRUE HEALING PROPERTIES

The impact that the homoeopathic provings had upon drug use in general is that their use became greatly clarified and each drug was thrown into much sharper focus, its true healing properties being more clearly identified such that they could be employed thereafter with much greater certainty. Rather than being used on the basis of assumptions and traditions of superstition, astrology, signatures, etc - rule of thumb - they could at last be employed upon the basis of what symptoms they can cause, rather than upon what were previously nebulous uncertainties. Provings "could replace the chaotic amalgam of ignorance, laziness, guesswork, superstition, prejudice, dogma, fantasy..." [Berlin, 1979, 163].

> *"There is, afterall, an important difference between the selection of a medicine on the basis of its ability to reproduce, in a healthy person, the symptom complex manifested in a patient, and the selection of a medicine on the basis of some physical resemblance between it and the organ affected..."* *[Nicholls, 1988, 8].*

Although his first provings of 27 drugs, published in 1805 [*Fragmenta de viribus medicamentorum positivis*], were all Botanics, he soon explored mineral drugs. In *The Chronic Diseases*, for example, of the 48 drugs listed, 35 are minerals, 12 from plants and only one from an animal source [*Sepia*]. Thus, over 70% are of mineral origin. This may show that Hahnemann, like **Paracelsus** before him, had a strong preference for mineral drugs, or that he felt it was an aspect of

Paracelsus

materia medica insufficiently explored at that time compared to the plant world.

> "Undeterred by the magnitude of the task, Hahnemann set about creating a materia medica which should embody the facts of drug action upon the healthy." [Close, 1924, 147]

Prior to Hahnemann, knowledge of the specific and general effects of medicinal compounds on health was very poorly understood, and was often based on the shape, colour, taste and texture of the material, before they were actually used medicinally. This was often referred to as the "doctrine of correspondences" [or "doctrine of signatures"]: a system which assumed that the Almighty had inscribed into the plants of the earth secret signs and features whereby their medicinal virtues could be ascertained by Man. As "healing theologians", it was one of the solemn tasks of physicians to interpret these signs:

> "Although medical theories became increasingly divorced from any specific theological doctrine in the 18th century...physicians still assumed a priestly role because of their divinely given ability to cure." [Gouk, 318]

Examples of signatures include yellow flowering plants for liver complaints, red and peppery herbs for fevers and haemorrhages, etc.

Nicholas Culpeper

> "Lily of the valley...is under the dominion of mercury, and therefore strengthens the brain, recruits a weak memory and makes it strong again." **[Culpeper**, 652, 149]

Yet, *Convallaria* [Lily of the Valley] has very few brain or 'mercurial' symptoms at all, and is mainly used for heart conditions [ruled by Leo?]. Drug use at that time was plainly based on a form of medical speculation and guesswork.

Hypericum Perforatum

Most of the Herbal Materia Medica had, therefore, been compiled by trial and error. Herbs were used based on tradition, a semi-mythical method, stretching back in time before recorded history. This was the case in nearly all cultures on earth.

> "Paracelsus was also a firm believer in the doctrine of signatures, and in illustration of it explained every single part of St. John's Wort **[Hypericum perforatum]** in terms of this belief...the holes in the leaves mean that this herb helps all inner and outer orifices of the skin...the blooms rot in the form of blood, a sign that it is good for wounds and should be used where flesh has to be treated." [Griggs, 1981, 50]

"Hahnemann definitely rejected [the law of signatures]...in his Materia Medica Pura we read under *Chelidonium*... the ancients imagined that the yellow colour of the juice of this plant was an indication (signature) of its utility in bilious diseases...the importance of human health does not admit of any such uncertain directions for the use of medicines. It would be criminal frivolity to rest contented with such guesswork at the bedside of the sick." [Hahnemann quoted in Hobhouse, 1933, 137-8]

Hahnemann was very dissatisfied with this approach and with the whole materia medica of his day, which he regarded as a terrible mess.

"From the earliest beginnings until now, the materia medica has consisted only of false suppositions and fancies, which is as good as no Materia Medica at all. The...virtues of medicines cannot be apprehended by...smell, taste, or appearance...or from chemical analysis, or by treating disease with one or more of them in a mixture... [The Organon, v.110]

"If one has tested a considerable number of simple medicines on healthy people in this way... then one has for the first time a true materia medica: a collection of the authentic, pure, reliable effects of simple medicinal substances in themselves; a natural pharmacopoeia..." [The Organon, v.143]

Conducting the first proving on himself in 1790 [Dudgeon, 1853, 176] with *Cinchona* [Peruvian Bark] Hahnemann followed this in quick succession with many more and increasingly included his co-workers. These co-workers were fellow doctors and members of Hahnemann's and their families. Hahnemann is said to have proved 99 drugs in all [Griggs, 1981, 178], including, for example, *Valerian*, proved by Hahnemann, Stapf and Franz [Blackie, 1976, 203].

The provings started by Hahnemann and his immediate followers, were taken up, and added to by many later homoeopaths. All the greats had a hand in this process and saw it as part of their solemn duty as homoeopaths to add to the materia medica and so 'swell the stream' as best they could. Dr. Constantine Hering [1800-1880], is said to have personally proved 72 drugs [Treuherz, 1984, 139], including *Tellurium* in 1850 [Blackie, 1976, 78], *Hamamelis* in 1848 [Blackie, 1976, 214] and *Glonoine* in 1848 [Tyler, 1942, 391]. Later, many homoeopathic drugs were adopted by allopaths and taken into regular use, e.g. *Belladonna, Chamomilla* & *Arnica*. Many of the American herbs, derived from Amerindian medicine and used in the Eclectic School, were proved and adopted by homoeopaths; e.g. *Ipecacuanha, Caulophyllum* [Blue Cohosh], *Rhus toxicodendron* [Poison Ivy], *Euphorbia* [Spurge]. Many were later to find their allopathic uses; e.g. *Ipecacuanha* and *Lobelia inflata* in cough mixtures. These drugs were originally used in the Eclectic school of US medicine.

Dr. Constantin Hering

PRECISE DRUG PROPERTIES

Much like a modern scientist, Hahnemann demanded a more precise knowledge of the properties of individual drugs than any of his contemporaries. This fact on its own singles him out as an important medical reformer:

> "The task of the great philosophers who break through the orthodoxy is to sweep away the painstaking edifices of their honourable but limited predecessors who...tend to imprison thought within their own tidy but fatally misconceived constructions." [Berlin, 1996, 72]

He wanted drugs to be used singly, not in mixtures, and for medicine to be based on an empirical understanding of individual drug action, based on giving small daily doses of a drug to healthy people, who would record the symptoms they experienced. In this way, a proving produces a 'clean image' of a remedy's symptomatology, called the Drug Picture; i.e. a mild form of poisoning, the precise symptoms of which are unique for any one drug.

> "Provings were carried out according to an exact system and from detailed instructions...the observation of the results, which every individual had to make in himself at definite times, were entered up in a carefully prescribed manner...the power of a medicine was only established after comparisons of different participants..." [Haehl, vol. 1, 101]

> "This inception of the collaborators for the purpose of proving drugs, was of the greatest significance not only for the individual members but also for the whole materia medica and homoeopathic science. All these young people [Leipzig students, 1811] were called upon for accurate observation of medicinal effects and consequently for a detailed examination

of health and of any daily fluctuations...they were trained to an accurate, conscientious and detailed observation..." [Haehl, Vol. 1, 101]

The drug picture is regarded as a 'clean image' because on giving the drug to a healthy volunteer, its action could be observed without the unreliable and misleading variations in symptom information that would inevitably come from giving it to an ill person. This is a very important point, as it shows that Hahnemann by no means trusted the clinical and empirical usefulness of a drug's action as a sole, reliable and consistent source of information. Matching of drug characteristics to the totality of patient symptoms, became the central process of homoeopathy, and not the selection of drugs based upon the false notion of classification, causation and naming of diseases or the rote prescribing of 'specifics':

"The evidence of the homoeopathic provings and of the efficacy of the similimum selected from the specific symptoms totality demonstrates the fact that for every possibility of personality as well as organismic pattern, hence for every possibility of illness pattern there is also a substance pattern out there which minutely duplicates it." [Whitmont, 1980, 9-10]

Hahnemann thus inadvertently became heir to heretical medical knowledge which he used with great effect, never shrinking from what life tasks destiny had laid before him:

"The principal function of philosophy at its best is to break through, liberate, upset." [Berlin, 1996, 66]

He was also aware that the symptoms a person manifests at any given time are partly due to their illness, and partly due to the drugs they are given.

> "Hahnemann in an 1816 essay 'Spirit of the New Doctrine of Healing'...suggested that the living organism is far less affected by the natural diseases than by drugs, so that the latter annul the former by their stronger dynamic effect - provided they have a tendency to produce a change in the state of health similar to that of the disease." [Haehl, vol. 1, 103]

This single paragraph very beautifully illustrates the discourse that was constantly trickling along in Hahnemann's mind - a weighing-up of practical observations and matching them to theoretical assessments of events in the organism. We all do this to some degree, it is a human trait, but it is clearly illustrated because Hahnemann always approached practical matters soaked in theoretical ideas as well and was always keen both to accurately observe and to draw the appropriate conclusions from the observations. He soon became a formidable genius of medical iconoclasm, brilliantly unravelling a new medical system from deep thinking and experiments:

> "Men of authentic genius are necessarily to a large degree destructive of past traditions. Great philosophers always transform, upset and destroy. It is only the small philosophers who defend vested interests, apply rules, squeeze into procrustean beds." [Berlin, 1996, 70]

Every experiment he undertook had a specific purpose. In a certain sense, he adored drawing conclusions, even on the scantest evidence. That was his mental inclination. It was the philosopher in him. Two examples of this trait are first the Coffee theory of chronic disease [1803] and then the later Miasm theory [1827]. Successive generations of homoeopaths have often experienced difficulty in following his line of reasoning in these topics.

> "He instituted 'provings' of drugs upon himself, members of his family, friends, students and fellow practitioners, keeping all under the most rigid scrutiny and control, and carefully recording every fact and the conditions under which it was elicited. This work continued for many years, parts of it being published from time to time, until the mass of material reached enormous proportions." [Close, 1924, 147-8]

Hahnemann clearly regarded the technique of 'the proving' as his most unique, important and valuable contribution to medical science, and as the bedrock of his system:

> "In the last three thousand five hundred years, not one single physician, to my knowledge...has come upon this so natural, so absolutely necessary, so uniquely valid proving of the pure, characteristic action of medicines..." [Hahnemann, 1810, v.108]

> "There is no other possible way of correctly ascertaining the characteristic action of medicines on human health, no single surer, more natural way, than administering individual medicines experimentally to healthy people in moderate doses..." [Hahnemann, 1810, v.108]

By including the effects of the material dose, he felt this gave a more complete picture of a drug's effects upon health. This was a matter of combining in the final drug-picture such gross effects with the more subtle effects deriving from minute doses.

"...I found from the toxicological reports of earlier writers that the effects of large quantities of noxious substances ingested by healthy people...largely coincided with my own findings from experiments with those substances on myself or other healthy people." [Hahnemann, 1810, v.110]

HISTORICAL BACKDROP

Hahnemann was not working in a vacuum, and we need to briefly become cognisant of the time-frame in which he can be located.

The Age of Science [1600s] can in many ways be seen as a product of the religious Reformation of the 1500s which immediately preceded it, and which in many respects set it in motion by clearing ground ready to make it all possible.

"The effect [of philosophy] is necessarily in the direction of wider freedom, of upsetting of existing values and habits, of destroying boundaries, transforming familiar contours, which is at once exhilarating and disturbing." [Berlin, 1996, 70]

Most of the main figures in this age were Protestants and most of the developments took place in the north European lands, especially England, Germany and Holland. This is no coincidence. The Reformation had in effect allowed the sprouting in northern Europe of a new freedom, fresh air and new light.

"A philosopher...is bound to subvert, break through, destroy, liberate, let in air from outside..." [Berlin, 1996, 67]

In essence, it meant that most intelligent people could

henceforth choose to be religious in an independent way, no longer answerable to the centuries-old suffocative domination by Rome or subject to the stifling authoritarian blanket of religious domination, which acted as a severe 'belief dictatorship' holding back progress, which had degenerated into an 'arid and obfuscating scholasticism.' [Berlin, 1996, 62] or 'the elaborate manipulation of hollow symbols.' [Berlin, 1996, 62].

This change undoubtedly assisted the growth of science through encouraging man's innate inquisitiveness about his world - a natural curiosity that had never been allowed such freedom before. This assisted the growth of science in a way unfiltered, uncensored and unrestrained by Church dogma. Arguably, therefore, and stated in its starkest terms, it seems clear, that if there had been no Reformation, then there would have been no age of science.

The next age of medicine can be seen as an age dominated by the machine. Just as the first sciences were concerned with mechanics, the laws governing the movement of physical objects, so too in the 1500s and 1600s the main focus is upon the physical body itself, its dissection, drawings of the organs and the machine-like conception of blood flow, the mechanics of muscle action and the pneumatic principles of breathing. The anatomical work of Harvey [1578-1657] and Vesalius [1514-64], Boyle's work on gases, and the drawings by Leonardo [1452-1519] are therefore very typical advances of this period. We might realistically conceive these advances to be the 'medical analogues' of the machine cosmology of Newton, Copernicus [1473-1543], Galileo and Kepler [1571-1630], and probably reflect an excessive 'admiration for the triumphs of the sciences since Galileo and Newton.' [Berlin, 1996, 28].

This age also sought to displace all those previously dominant magical and religious elements in medical conceptuality, and what had become a 'period of conformity...mechanical, and in the end meaningless, through mere repetition...are the blankest patches in the history of human thought...a great and arid waste.' [Berlin, 1996, 74].

The supernatural fabric of medieval medicine gradually became abandoned and dismantled and so fell into neglect, to be replaced by the new passion for 'mechanism' extolled by figures like Hoffmann [1660-1742] and Boerhaave [1668-1738]. What happened in medicine certainly reflected things happening, and conceptual shifts occurring in the natural sciences and philosophy. Mechanics dominated everything at that time.

The great age of science really covers and wholly dominates the 16th and 17th centuries. It was during this period, that the cosmic and mechanical sciences were brilliantly unravelled, and the main thrust of scientific method established, by figures like Newton, Galileo, Boyle [1627-91], Copernicus, Kepler, Descartes [1596-1650] and Bacon with a specific purpose in mind - to show that the world as we see it is indeed a separate thing in itself, composed of physical identifiable things and forces and working according to predictable principles. That the world is demonstrably not a part of the mind of God, as the Church had maintained, but a vast physical thing in itself that can be dissected and analysed and its principles finally laid bare, just like a machine. Yet, even a figure like Boyle engaged in healing work for the poor:

"The 'reluctant philanthropist' Robert Boyle...collecting and dispensing remedies was a major part of Boyle's charitable activity." [Gouk, 317]

Medicine might be regarded as becoming 'too deeply infatuated with Newton's mechanical model.' [Berlin, 1996, 8]. Inspired by the exciting developments in science, Hoffmann, Boerhaave and **Sydenham** [1624-89] - "the father of clinical observation" [Bloch, 1994] - tried to develop a more rational system of medicine – one wholly devoid of magical tendencies. They were the first physicians to attempt to introduce the "use of reason...a logically connected structure of rules, laws, generalizations, susceptible of demonstration..." [Berlin, 1979, 163] within a medical sphere wholly dominated by the suffocating Medieval dogmas of theology, metaphysics and astrological symbolism, which began to be regarded as a huge "chaotic amalgam of ignorance, laziness, guesswork, superstition, prejudice, dogma, fantasy..." [Berlin, 1979, 163].

Dr. Thomas Sydenham

The results were mixed, but they represent the pioneers of an impulse that was to be picked up again in the 18th century, only to reach its full flowering in the 19th and 20th centuries. It is especially in the work of Sydenham that this mechanical trend really began to penetrate, sufficiently to change, the conceptual fabric of medicine profoundly and irreversibly. And this was an entirely new phenomenon.

> "Sydenham applied his objective investigations to both the treatment and to the description of diseases. Divesting himself of much medieval tradition, he approached therapeutic problems in a relatively empirical manner." [Shryock, 12]

Sydenham is most highly regarded for liberating medicine from the flowery and absurd excesses of speculation in academia and restoring it as a practical concern of viewing the disease and observing the patient. He effectively re-grounded medicine in the observation of patients and diseases, rather than in theoretical notions deriving from previous generations, which had become hardened into dogmas. Such an arid, dead-end approach was derided as "casual impression, half-remembered, unverified recollections, guesswork, mere rules of thumb, unscientific hypotheses." [Berlin, 1996, 41].

Several important aspects of his approach stand out. He based his ideas on what he saw at the bedside, rather than in textbooks, which he condemned as unreliable perverters of medical science [Porter, 229]. Sydenham did indeed regard "the old overthrown philosophy...as a mass of superstition and error." [Berlin, 1996, 62] and its antiquatred corpus of ideas as little more than "...metaphysical and theological explanations unsupported by...evidence, conducted by methods the opposite of rational, the happy hunting ground of bigots and charlatans and their dupes and slaves." [Berlin, 1979, 133].

He minutely observed actual cases of illness at firsthand, formulating a classification of disease based upon multiple cases, thus giving credence to the view that a disease was *a real entity separate from the patient* [Porter, 230] and infecting various individuals as circumstance might dictate. This in turn gave support to the notion that diseases are really *external entities that invade patients*, being 'independent of the sufferer' [Porter, 230; Keele, 1974] and causing broadly similar symptoms in them all. He thus spawned the idea that disease is separate from the patient, rather than an aspect of him, and that it should be viewed as an entity in itself. At the time, this was a revolutionary notion, yet it soon became an integral and unquestioned cornerstone upon which was built the conceptual fabric of modern medicine.

Being a near contemporary of such giants as Thomas Hobbes [1588-1679], Sir Isaac Newton, William Harvey, Rene Descartes, Francis Bacon [1561-1626], John Locke [1632-1704] and Robert Boyle, gives a clue to the powerful secularising attitude pervading all divisions of natural science of his day. To be sure, these were those famous pioneers whose work began to systematically dismantle and displace the magical worldview in the name of Reason! Would it not seem strange if Sydenham were cast from an entirely different mould?

Being a close friend of Locke and corresponding with Boyle, Sydenham especially revered Bacon's inductive method and was in turn admired both by Locke, his single greatest admirer [Porter, 243], and by the Continental medical schools, where he won great influence [CDNB, 2911]. He relied "on Bacon's critique of metaphysics and his call for a return to observation and experience." [Coulter, vol. 2, 180]. Sydenham also "converted Bacon's neo-Platonic 'form' into a wholly new concept - the specific disease.." [Coulter, vol. 2, 180]. It is therefore clear that he approved and applied in medicine the same sort of secularising, anti-magical influence as his illustrious contemporaries mentioned above. It is supremely ironic that Hahnemann also revered Bacon as the founder of the inductive scientific method [see Close, 1924, 15, 27-8, 248-9].

In broad outline terms, Sydenham's approach comprised a revolt against the holism of medieval 'medical theology', and represents the first major impulse towards medical reductionism.

> *"...as late as the 1650s, doctors still spoke largely of the sick man's humors rather than of any particular entity from which he suffered."* [Shryock, 12, my emphasis]

He derided the ancient medicine as having "as much to do with treating sick men as the painting of pictures with the sailing of ships..." [Dewhurst, 40, quoted by Coulter, vol. 2, 182].

Previously embedded in the 'spiritual holism' of medical theology, and already being divorced from formal religion, medicine had therefore begun to cast doubt on any meaningful interpretation of disease with reference to the life of the individual, or of seeing the disease against the karma or sin of the person; arguably a tendency that had already run its course.

Sydenham ruthlessly stripped disease of any deeper philosophical relevance to the life of the patient as a being, made individuality inconsequential, and regarded any disease as merely another example of an *infection* by some *noxious external agent* that has *invaded* the patient for no particular ethical or spiritual reason. No special meaning was to be attached to any disease.

There are two radical elements here – separation of *the disease* from *the patient* as 'clear and distinct entities ripe for taxonomy' [Porter, 307]; separation of the disease from any metaphysical conception as to its purpose or meaning in the life of the patient or the wider universe. Like others of his era, Sydenham asserts the former and denies the latter.

> *"Sydenham...devoted himself enthusiastically to the differentiation of specific disorders." [Shryock, 12-13]*

According to this radical view, treatment and classification of disease must therefore proceed, not by viewing it against the backcloth of the whole person, in its individual variations, minutely observing its uniqueness, or by integrating the illness into the individual psycho-physical continuum of the patient, but of viewing it solely in generalist terms, as the manifestation of an *externally invading entity* [Keele, 1974] that could *affect anyone* in much the same way. This was a revolutionary change in attitude.

> *"Where the ancients had seen an inseparable connection between the patient and his malady, Sydenham saw in the patient certain pathological symptoms which he had observed in others and expected to see again...he distinguished between the sick man and the illness, and objectified the latter as a thing in itself. This was a new outlook, an ontological conception of the nature of disease which was eventually to prove of the utmost significance." [Shryock, 13, my emphases]*

Sydenham's view portrayed any disease as merely a localised affair, a specific malady [Porter, 230, 307] - a result of *some generalised entity* having no personal connection to the sin or karma of the individual sufferer, and thus bereft of theological meaning. This was clearly a momentous turning point [a secularisation] in which, for a further four centuries, the medical gaze would never again fall upon the individual or his metaphysical inheritance, but come to rest solely upon the externally conceived *invading entity* and its possible causes. Again, he irreversibly shifted the focus of disease causation from the internal, nebulous or metaphysical and person-centred arena [preferred by medievalists], to the material forms of the outer world - preferred by his contemporaries. This fundamental division in medicine has persisted. The eventual triumph of this approach came in the 1880s with Pasteur and Koch in finding actual bacilli as being the root causes of many diseases.

"The transition from a theoretical, systematic medicine to an empirically-based 'scientific' pathological anatomy...occurred largely between 1794 and 1830, years of revolutionary turmoil in France..." [Aisenberg, 145]

The other track of medicine that comes down from Paracelsus [1493-1541] to **Stahl** [1660-1734] and Hahnemann [1755-1843], amongst others, betrays a more vitalist impulse, sceptical of the concrete reality of *the disease* as a separate entity from *the patient*; or that its causes must inevitably be material in nature. Respecting the obvious physiological holism and vitalism of the body, and always seeking by all means to strengthen its innate healing power or vital force [Haehl, vol. 1, 64, 284, 289], this approach does not deny, but embraces, the subtle differences between individual cases of *a disease*, and reaffirms that

Georg Ernst Stahl

disease and patient comprise inseparably dual aspects of one united biophysical continuum. A view of disease as a 'dynamic derangement of the life force' [see Close, 1924, 37-8, 74], which Hahnemann, and most homoeopaths since, would heartily endorse. Such is undoubtedly a philosophically finer-grained and more subtle medical conception. Some of them also explore meanings and purpose for illness to the life of the patient. The re-emergence of these modern holistic therapies, and the revival of such a rich cargo of medieval ideas they carry, offers an undoubted challenge to future medical philosophy. To a large extent, these modalities represent the factors that Sydenham helped to hastily eject as irrelevant to the art of medicine. A bad case of throwing the baby out with the bathwater, perhaps!

> "The majority of elite men and the medical establishment no longer valued astrology by the early 18th century and it ceased to occupy a central place in English culture." [Gouk, 317]

Just as Hoffmann, Boerhaave and Sydenham had applied the physical and mechanical scientific advances of their day in an attempt to transform medical theory and practice, and to clear out the 'dead wood' of magic and astrology, so too in the 18th century, thinkers of the Enlightenment tried

Coming out of the Darkness like a Meteor

in their own way to 'improve' medicine through developing and indulging various wild theories. Examples include those of Brown [1735-88], Cullen [1710-90] and the Montpellier vitalists, all of whom had only a transient influence.

> *"This...made the medical art a stage for the display of the most fantastic, often most self-contradictory, hypotheses, explanations, demonstrations, conjectures, dogmas, and systems, whose evil consequences are not to be overlooked..."* [Hahnemann, 1808, 489-90]

> *"The effort to identify and classify specific diseases, which Sydenham had encouraged, went to unexpected lengths during the eighteenth century."* [Shryock, 25]

> *"Medicine seemed to have fallen behind the other sciences...and their science was of little utility...so encouraged, various theorists revived the doctrine that there was one cause and therefore one cure of disease."*a [Shryock, 1966, p.171]

The unfortunately chaotic and un-unified dissemination of conflicting theories, caused great confusion, and merely reflected the warring factions of the day, belief being controversially riven between hard-line Enlightenment fanatics on the one hand, and the equally hard-line Romantics on the other. This deep polarisation of 18th century beliefs impacted upon everything at that time, including medicine.

THEORETICAL ORIGINS OF HOMOEOPATHY

Hahnemann claimed to have found case histories and cures from many ancient cultures based upon the 'law of similars' [*Organon*, v110]. He additionally claimed that from these historical studies the poisonous effects of a drug clearly point to its potential therapeutic properties.

> *"Within the infant rind of this small flower*
>
> *Poison hath residence and medicine power."*
>
> *[William Shakespeare, Romeo and Juliet, act 2, scene 3]*

In other words, toxic and therapeutic effects are frequently dose-dependent. This was the vital clue, which initiated his research into potentisation. It seemed to confirm to him the 'law of similars' as a 'resonance', which exists between the toxic and the therapeutic action of a drug. Toxicity and therapeuticity he regarded as opposite poles of the same phenomenon.

> *"...Hahnemann had to stand on foundations built more or less by himself...the current theories of his time about the causes and phenomena of diseases lost their value for him as soon as he felt certain of his similarity idea, which resulted from careful experimental evidence...the longer he lived, the more strenuously Hahnemann rejected and fought against the theories of disease origin and diagnosis, as known in his time. Whoever desires to criticise him should keep this in mind....he did so because they allowed him no insight into those disease conditions and processes." [Haehl, vol. 1, 290]*

> *"He was indisputably the first to give the new therapy its solid foundations by proving remedies on the healthy subject, by diluting medicines and by experience of the sick-bed repeatedly confirmed...he built up a therapeutic law which has*

resisted unflinchingly the most desperate onslaughts of a whole century." [Haehl, vol. 1, 274]

"...at last he had succeeded in completing one hundred provings...the dependable accuracy accompanying the gigantic task...the conscientious pains he took to check and compile personally the results obtained by students and followers, before they were published..." [Haehl, vol. 1, 274]

Hahnemann also observed primary and secondary actions to a drug; rather like 'action and reaction', they are often opposed to one another. They clearly represent a sequence of 'impact' and 'recovery' on the part of the organism. For example, in the case of *Opium* its first effect is drowsiness and then secondly sleeplessness; *Cannabis indica* gives firstly euphoria followed later by depression of spirits; *Alcohol* stimulates and then depresses the system. He even conceived of the curative influence of a homoeopathic drug and the homoeopathic aggravation along similar lines, ascribing the toxic and aggravatory effects to the primary action of the drug and the therapeutic response being due to the secondary action of the drug combined with the response of the body's vital force.

Hahnemann conducted the first proving on himself in 1790 with *Cinchona* [Peruvian Bark]:

"Hahnemann having, by his simple and rational experiment with Cinchona bark in 1790, conclusively established the great therapeutic law, that to cure diseases medicines must be used which possess the power of exciting similar diseases, at once perceived that the whole edifice of the old Materia Medica must be rebuilt from the very

foundation, as that Materia Medica furnished nothing positive regarding the [true] pathogenetic actions of drugs." [Dudgeon, 1853, 176]

The information Hahnemann gleaned about the first Cinchona bark proving he described in his *Essay On A New Principle* [1796], and the material from his further provings were compiled first into his *Fragmenta de viribus medicamentorum positivis* [1805] and later into his *Materia Medica Pura* [1811] [*Organon*, v.109a]. From studying these drug pictures, Hahnemann was able to indicate the most appropriate drugs for many illnesses.

The drugs proved in the early days included many important herbal drugs [e.g. *Aconite, Belladonna, Digitalis, Hamamelis, Arnica*] and some from other continents that appeared to show peculiar or important therapeutic properties, such as might suit them for certain conditions. Hahnemann also introduced completely new remedies into medicine such as *Silica, Kreosotum, Petroleum, Terebinthinum, Natrum mur.* and *Lycopodium*. Leaning heavily, some might say, upon the pioneering work of Paracelsus [1493-1541], he proved and introduced many minerals, metals and acids into the materia medica such *as Silica, Calcarea carbonica, Sulphur, Acidum nitricum, Aurum, Cuprum* and *Argentum, Kali bichromicum*, etc. These substances were generally regarded as medicinally inert, poisonous or unusable before the provings of Hahnemann. He also greatly refined the medical knowledge and fine-tuned, along new lines, the usefulness of several conventional drugs [through proving them] such as *Carbo vegetabilis, Mercury, Arsenic* and *Sulphur*.

In conclusion, we might point out that Hahnemann was not entirely setting out on uncharted territory, as there had been a few ancient investigations of a similar type.

> "Among the ancients it is only in the school of the Empiricists that we find experiments undertaken for the purpose of ascertaining the pathogenetic effects of drugs and poisons...Attalos Philomenter, King of Pergamos, tested the antidotal powers of Aconite, Hyoscyamus, Veratrum and Hemlock, etc. But it was chiefly the poetical physician Nicander of Colophon...to whom we are indebted for an account of the action of various poisons...it is remarkable, however, that these poetical records...have been pretty closely copied...even to the most absurd errors...and very little else of a positive character is to be met with in the records of ancient medicine." [Dudgeon, 1853, 190-91]

> "Hahnemann was not the first to try drugs on the healthy organism. Anton Stoerck, on June 23 1760, rubbed fresh Stramonium on his hands to see if, as the botanists said, it would inebriate him. It did not, and he then rubbed some in a mortar, and, sleeping in the same room, got a headache. He then made an extract, placing it on his tongue. He wished to know if the drug could be safely used as a remedy. Stoerck says that if Stramonium disturbs the senses and produces mental derangement in persons who are healthy, it might very easily be administered to maniacs for the purpose of restoring the senses by effecting a change in ideas. Crumpe, an Irish physician, tried drugs on the healthy, and published a book in London on the effects of Opium in 1793, three years after the first experiments of Hahnemann. Hahnemann refers in The Organon

to the Danish surgeon, Stahl, who says: I am convinced that diseases are subdued by agents which produce similar affections." [Organon, 4th edition, New York, 91]. [Bradford, 42, 1st edition]

As Dudgeon then goes on to point out, a few attempts are more recent. He mentions Dr William Alexander of Edinburgh, who undertook some near-fatal experiments of self-poisoning with *Camphor*:

"...but this excited very little attention, and had it not been for Hahnemann, who raised them up from oblivion, they would probably have remained altogether unknown." [Dudgeon, 191].

This makes Hahnemann's experiments even more remarkable and original. Yet, all through this brilliant experimentation, we must never forget that 'Hahnemann the theorist' was keeping a watchful eye on the significance, the deeper meanings and implications of his work. Though forsure a brilliant experimental scientist in his own right, like many of his day, he was no less a brilliant theoretician, always keen to weigh-up the evidence and constantly formulate new ideas. In this regard, let us finish by examining the precise way in which Hahnemann had formulated homoeopathy as a distinct system on the theoretical level, by comparison to the other systems well-known to Hahnemann himself. One problem is that homoeopathy arose [1796-1800] at the very time when French medicine was also going through a system-building tendency which lost the trust of doctors.

"Paris medicine developed suddenly in 1794 in opposition to an unsatisfying reliance on theorizing and was replaced in turn, in 1848, with the more *rigorous practices of laboratory science."* [Aisenberg, 145]

Unfortunately therefore, Hahnemann was castigated and written-off as yet another vitalist and yet another system builder.

Through his minute observation of cases and his deep and subtle thinking, not only on cases but also on the theory and history of medicine, with which he was saturated more than most, what Hahnemann conceived about homoeopathy as a system was essentially that Sydenham had been wrong – that you cannot conceive of any disease as an entity that invades the patient from outside and that elicits broadly similar symptoms in each case. Nor can you, through this bogus act of averaging, then reach for a single, mass-applied technique [e.g. vaccines, or the 'specific drug'] that will 'cure every case'.

Hahnemann saw this as a fundamentally mistaken conceptual step to take. He came to profoundly realise that, by contrast, it is in the individuality of symptoms, unique to each case, that provides the real clue to curing the whole case, NOT in any pre-conceived grand picture or 'global average' superimposed upon each individual case like a smothering conceptual blanket. Thus, to summarise, while Sydenham wished to clump together the similarities in a range of cases to arrive at a 'grand picture', Hahnemann chose to differentiate between each case on the basis of its own individual and unique subtle variability. These are very clearly 'conceptual acts' of extraordinarily opposite quality and impulse.

For example, the homoeopathic view of measles [which Sydenham had been the first to differentiate from Scarlet

Fever] is like its view of any other medical condition – treat the patient NOT the disease and all is well. Usually this means remedies like Pulsatilla and Rhus tox. or maybe Belladonna if there is much fever and redness. Its approach is fundamentally different from allopathy – instead of doing what Sydenham set in motion – grouping similar cases together into a grand class of condition and giving it a name and then devising treatment en masse – homoeopathy looks solely at the idiosyncrasy of each individual case – it looks at differences between cases that make each case unique – the very opposite of allopathy which does the reverse. It differentiates, rather than accumulates; separates rather than places together. Both approaches are of course essential to any true science:

> *"The proper aim of the sciences is to note the number of similarities in the behaviour of objects and to construct propositions..."* [Berlin, 1996, 21]

> *"...to bring out what is specific, unique, in a given character or series of events...respects in which it differs from everything...[and] conveys the unique pattern of experience."* [Berlin, 1996, 22]

Furthermore, and most crucially, Hahnemann and many homoeopaths since, would all chorus that only by treating the patient can true cure be achieved, and that 'treating the disease' never cures, but merely conjures an illusion of cure by suppressing symptoms, leading to the eventual degradation of health in the longer run.

Therefore, although Hahnemann garnered his drugs from every realm of Nature, and did so unashamedly, and that he also compiled a completely new materia medica, it is also clear that his profoundly deep knowledge of medical theory and medical history assisted him at every step. He resisted the strong temptation to treat a disease as an all-encompassing entity, or to try and apply a specific drug for all cases of one so-called 'disease'. In doing so, although his materia medica resembles the old Dispensatories and Prescriptoria of previous centuries, the hard-won and accurate information it detailed on each drug, and their mode of use, was manifestly brand new. In that specific sense, and only in that sense, homoeopathy really was 'coming like a meteor out of the darkness.'

■

HAHNEMANN
AS A SCIENTIST

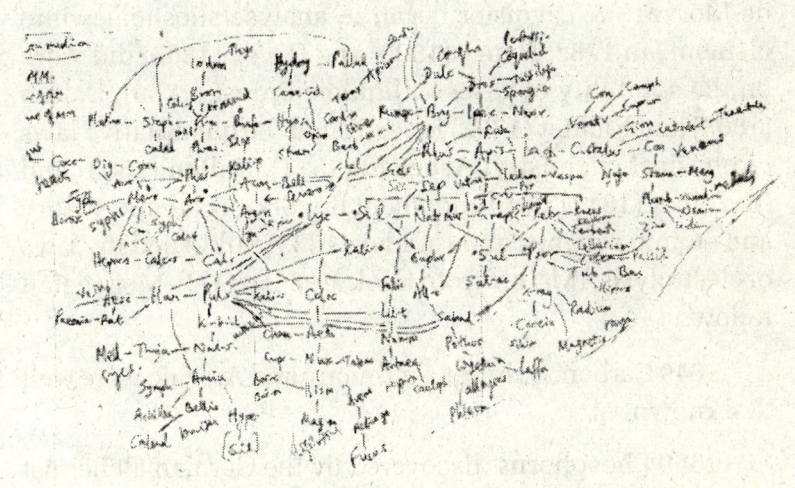

Materia Medica remedy tree 1998

This article concerns itself with to what extent Hahnemann was scientific. If we define science in its broadest sense as the desire to break things down, scrutinise and analyse, then we can easily see that the 18th century was a very scientific century and in no subject more so than in chemistry. But was Hahnemann scientific?

Hahnemann lived during some of the greatest advances in chemistry, during which literally hundreds of natural minerals were successfully analysed and purified into their constituent elements and compounds.

For example, during Hahnemann's lifetime: Black (1755), Cavendish (1766) and Priestley (1770) did fundamental work on gases; Priestley (1774), Lavoisier (1772) and Scheele (1768-73) worked on combustion; Priestley, Cavendish and Lavoisier established the composition of water (1781-5); Priestley did further fundamental work on combustion in 1775; Volta was splitting gases using electric sparks in 1776; de Morveau & Lavoisier began to analyse substances into elements in 1782; Henry (1803) and Davey (1806) did work on the solubility of gases in liquids; Proust (1789), Dalton (1803) and Richter (1792) investigated the quantitative laws of physical chemistry; Avogadro (1811), Dalton (1803) and Berzelius (1811) did fundamental work on atomic theory and atomic weights; and Faraday (1833) published his laws of electrolysis. (Mainly from Cook (1981) p41-2). More detail follows.

> 1649 Carbon, Sulphur, Antimony and Arsenic were well known
>
> 1669 Phosphorus discovered by the German alchemist Brand
>
> 1750 Cobalt and Nickel discovered
>
> 1755 Magnesium shown to be an element by Joseph Black (1728-99)

Hahnemann as a Scientist

1756 CO discovered by Joseph Black

1766 Hydrogen discovered by Henry Cavendish (1731-1810)

1771 Fluorine discovered by Carl Scheele (1742-86)

1772 Nitrogen isolated by the Scot Daniel Rutherford (1749-1819)

1772 Oxygen discovered by Scheele

1774 Manganese discovered by the Swede Gahn (1745-1818)

1774 Chlorine discovered by Scheele

1774 Oxygen discovered by Joseph Priestley (1733-1804)

1777 Sulphur shown to be an element

1781 Cavendish showed water to be a compound

1783 Baryta, Oxygen, Prussic acid and Glycerine isolated by Scheele

1785 Water proved to be made of gases

1803 Dalton discovers atoms have different weights

1807 Sodium and Potassium isolated by Humphrey Davy (1778-1829)

1808 Davy isolates Calcium, Magnesium, Boron, Barium and Strontium

1808 The Atomic Table devised by John Dalton (1766-1844)

1810 Davy coins the term 'element'

1811 Iodine discovered by the Frenchman Courtois (1777-1838)

1813-14 Berzelius published atomic symbols

1818 Table of Atomic weights published by the Swede Berzelius (1779-1848)

1825 Aluminium discovered by Hans Oersted (1777-1851)

1827 Aluminium isolated by Friedrich Wohler (1800-82)

1828 Wohler isolates Beryllium, Calcium carbide and Acetylene

1828 Wohler synthesises Urea from ammonium cyanate

1833 Electrolysis of water by Michael Faraday (1791-1867)

1869 Periodic Table published by Dmitri Mendeleyev (1834-1907)

Christian Friendrich Samuel Hahnemann (1755-1843]

These were obviously developments that Hahnemann could not have failed to know about and indeed, was thoroughly excited about. It is clear from many of his asides, that he regarded chemistry as the most important science. Like Paracelsus before him, he was mad about metals, minerals and acids.

Did all this scientific progress have any effect on Hahnemann's approach to homoeopathic pharmacy and materia medica? I hope to show that it did have profound effects and that

Hahnemann as a Scientist

Hahnemann, like his contemporaries, became swept along with a tide of chemical purification and analysis. However, I also hope to show that Hahnemann had several other reasons for adopting this approach, which were more social and presentational than therapeutic.

Reading some of Hahnemann's greatest works, like Chronic Diseases, the Materia Medica Pura, the Pharmaceutical Lexicon or the Lesser Writings, one is presented repeatedly with very detailed chemical instructions on how to purify the ingredients and remedies and how to rid them of any contaminants.

Examples include, in Chronic Diseases, pp186-7 re Alumina, p231 re Ammon carb, p392 re Baryta carb, p558-9 re Causticum, p762 re Hepar sulph, p783 re Iodium, p805 re Kali carb, p943 re Mag mur, p970-71 re Manganum, p1012 re Mur ac, p1116 re Nitri ac, p1273 re Phos ac, p1301 re Platina, p1397 re Silicea, p1542 re Zincum; in Preface to 'Venereal Diseases' pp1-7 of Lesser Writings, ibid re various mercurial preparations for syphilis, in pp106-116 of Lesser Writings; general instructions in Chronic Diseases pp145-152.

Why did Hahnemann go to such lengths to keep his remedies pure?

When you look at the history of remedies that Hahnemann studied, proved and brought into use, it is clear that he was doing 2 things:

1. he was aware of the natural unrefined minerals and plant mixtures, but by and large, he avoided their use and kept their inclusion in his materia medica to a strict minimum;

2. he strived - like his contemporaries - to use isolated and purified compounds and elements wherever possible.

I am not necessarily suggesting that Hahnemann consciously decided to act in this way, though he may have done. Certainly this is of interest to us today. Judging from the rest of that century, it would be remarkable had he not been excited by chemicals. In any case, he left scant indications as to why he chose the remedies he did or his mode of preparing them. Many require little explanation in any case, as they had been in use for centuries. Examples here include Digitalis, Mercury, Sulphur, Phosphorus, Arsenic, Belladonna and Aconite. What is curious, however, is that he so often opted not to use the natural unrefined minerals, but preferred instead to use mostly purified substances. The care and detail with which he then describes the preparation of his remedies is quite exhaustive. He gives the strong impression that the reader MUST follow these instructions in order to produce an exact copy of the remedy he describes, and that no other impure alternative will do.

For example, in the case of Calc carb he uses oyster shell. This is very curious. Why did he choose oyster shell when you consider that Meissen is over 235 miles (380 km) from the sea? Why did he not use limestone, egg shells, chalk, snail shells or calcite, which would be much more commmon in his own area and basically identical chemically? And why did he call it Calc carb and not Calc ostrea? Further examples include the use of Hepar sulph and Causticum, which must rank as two of the weirdest remedies ever devised. He would have got basically the same product using sulphurous limestone or metamorphosed marble for hepar sulph and slaked woodash for Causticum. Likewise he could have used pure sand instead of flint for Silica, sea salt instead of purified sodium chloride for Natrum mur, burned kelp for Iodum, etc.

For example, is there any major difference in medicinal properties between Ferrum metallicum and Iron oxide as rust? Or between Sea salt and Natrum mur? The list goes on. Were all these possible remedies separately and meticulously proved and Hahnemann chose the best? Extremely unlikely. It would have taken years just to choose one final remedy. He did not have the time or manpower required for this. And probably not the inclination.

We can also go on to ask why he used so many minerals at all, while ignoring so many medicinal plants? Was he biased in his choice? Did he dislike the 'impurity' of plants compared with pure minerals like Kali bich? Or was he by inclination just more of a chemist than a botanist? Where on earth did he get the ideas for using so many of these remedies from? In many cases, these substances had never been used in medicine before, so it was not just a case of refining our knowledge of already existent drugs. In the Chronic Diseases, for example, of the 48 drugs listed, 35 are minerals, 12 from plants and one from an animal source (Sepia). Thus over 70% are of mineral origin.

The same goes for the plants. Why did he use the berries of Hawthorn and not the bark or flowers, the root of Arnica and Aconite instead of the whole plant, the spores of Lycopodium instead of the whole herb? The list is endless. Certainly, some hints and hunches came from herbalism as it was known experientially that certain portions of the plant were more poisonous or medicinally potent. Yet this is not holistic, is it? It is scientific to suppose that the best medicinal power exists only in one part such as the root or the berry and only thinly dispersed (if at all) throughout the rest of the plant. We know today about active ingredients and alkaloids which are more concentrated in one portion of the plant, but they didn't know this in the 1790's. Hahnemann, as a good chemist, probably had a hunch that this was the case. Yet no explanation has ever been offered as to why he chose the remedies he chose and their very precise methods of preparation.

Why did he not use the perfectly natural ('impure') remedies and choose instead weird concoctions, the preparation of which demanded great knowledge of and skill in chemistry?

It is my contention that in part he did this to appeal to the spirit of his times. He wanted, perhaps, to flex his chemistry muscles and reveal to others that in an age of great chemists he was also an expert chemist and that by using these newly purified and isolated drugs he was, like them, eschewing what he and his contemporaries saw as the irrational and unscientific mumbo-jumbo of medieval science - viz, unpurified and unpredictable drugs. It may be the same reason why he so forcefully derided and rejected polypharmacy la herbalism and insisted on the use of separate herbs. Why should herbs be used separately? There is no overriding theoretical reason why they shouldn't be used in combinations. Perhaps it was just part of the puritanism and analysis of the times. Maybe also some of this was macho pride on Hahnmeann's part.

We know that later, through the use of provings, he was to gain a sounder and more rational justification for his preference for individually used drugs, never to be used in combinations. To us today this all seems so logical, but at that time it was a revolutionary concept. One could, of course, find another reason why Hahnemann wanted to deride the errors of his medical forebears. It was very much in his interest to keep his new therapy 'squeaky clean' and to present it to his contemporaries as totally new, modern, scientific and rational, with totally new chemically pure remedies, selected objectively through the use of provings. Were the provings that objective anyway?

He had a strong and justifiable desire to break away from the 'old wives tales' and disorder of herbal lore. He had a yen for scientific accuracy, which comes over very clearly in his writings on pharmacy. He also wanted to present homoeopathy as forward-thrusting and the new medicine of the future. He seems to have devised the accurate system of a potentisation scale - in part - as a way of breaking away from the vagueness and sloppiness of medieval 'bucket chemistry' and recipe pharmacy, which he so detested. His claims for homoeopathy emphasise very clearly that it is new, modern, scientific, rational, futuristic and accurate, based upon the 'new gods' of skill, accuracy, measurement, reason and scholarship. It is difficult not to conclude that all of this was at least in part designed to appeal to his contemporaries, who he fervently wished would take up homoeopathy.

Paracelsus (1493-1541)

Perhaps he also wanted to dissociate himself from his greatest enemy: Paracelsus. The truth is, of course, that Hahnemann was a second Paracelsus, but he felt he had to hide this fact. Both mercilessly derided their contemporaries, rejected the medicine in which they were trained, used small doses and emphasised the law of similars. Both also made extensive use of minerals, acids and metals. Both also obtained brief university teaching posts, but got sacked after abusing their position, 'indoctrinating' their students, castigating the medical

Philippus Theophrastus Bombastus von Hohenheim - Paracelsus
(1493-1541)

system of the day and teaching heretical forms of medicine. How similar to each other can you get? And both were thoroughly castigated by their orthodox brethren. Their biggest difference is that Hahnemann used purified drugs, while Paracelsus tended to use unrefined natural products. Likewise, Paracelsus loved Alchemy, astrology and mysticism, while Hahnemann appears to have loathed all three. Paracelsus was a real problem for Hahnemann about whom he must have thought a great deal: how to shake himself free? Yet he never mentions him in all his writings. One reason is obvious: guilt by association, which had to be avoided at all costs.

Perhaps he decided pretty early on that the only mud that would stick to him was that of plagiarism and that homoeopathy might be seen as just a rehashed form of Paracelsan medicine. And to an informed historian, this is a very valid claim, and almost impossible to refute. One way, however, to rebut the claim was not to use natural minerals, but rather to use refined ones, not to use mixtures of herbs, but to use them separately, and to minimise any fanciful or spiritual overtones, mystical formulae or astrological symbolism, thus keeping to the spirit of his contemporary scientists. In this way he was sure to give homoeopathy a clean start and to successfully dissociate it from medieval medicine in general and Paracelsan medicine in particular.

The point here, of course, is that Hahnemann was far more widely read than any other doctor of his day. He knew medical history intimately. Indeed, some of his works contain references in Greek, Latin and Arabic from authors before the Christian era (eg. On the Helleborism of the Ancients, Lesser Writings, Jain Edition, pp 569-617). He translated works from English, French, Spanish, and Italian, as well as Latin, Greek and Arabic. His linguistic skills were truly astonishing. Of course he knew about Paracelsus, but he kept quiet. It cannot be a coincidence that he put people off the trail leading to Paracelsus by never even mentioning him. The two systems of therapy are unmistakably similar. It is amazing that he is never mentioned. Indeed, many of the metals, acids and minerals in use in 18th century medicine, and later proved by Hahnemann, were actually introduced into medicine originally by Paracelsus, including mercury, arsenic, sulphur, tin, lead, gold, iron, copper and salt.

Hahnemann also needed to break away from the past because he genuinely believed much of it was nonsense, dead-wood that had dogged medicine for too long. He derided the apothecaries for routinely and unquestioningly making up their mixtures from their old formularies without ever really knowing whether they killed or cured. He saw them as colluding with doctors in a form of medicine that was totally irrational, ineffective and corrupt. And he says so repeatedly.

Thus we can conclude that Hahnemann was much like his contemporaries in being very concerned with purifying natural products, plants and minerals, rather than using them in their natural state. Hahnemann clearly believed that great skill in chemistry was essential for the production of a rational materia medica. It is my contention that he went too far in the direction of his contemporaries, being also driven on by his own abiding obsession with chemistry and thus effectively ignored many excellent herbal remedies and natural minerals that he might easily have proved and brought into a rational homoeopathic materia medica.

Some of our Anthroposophical brethren might even feel that he 'threw out the baby with the bathwater', though that may be slightly over stating the position. I also feel he relied too heavily on chemicals and too little on plants. The numerical facts of his materia medica confirm this view. As I have said, the reasons for this were largely the 'tide of the times'. As I said at the beginning, Hahnemann was scientific, in an analytical sense. Some might feel he was too scientific for his own good. On the other hand he was a curious

Hahnemann as a Scientist

mixture of less rational elements, derived mainly from his avid interest in medical history, his translation work and his encyclopaedic knowledge of drugs and chemistry.

Though Hahnemann seems to have 'swam with the tide' of his contemporaries, through his strong interest in chemistry, he then went off at a surprisingly new angle and adopted two completely original ideas, which to an extent, went against that tide. These were the proving and, derived from it, the concept of holism, both of the drug picture or remedy and of the disease - and therefore by implication of the person. Provings were first described in his Essay On a New Principle (1796) (pp249-303 of Lesser Writings). By proving medicines on the healthy - a concept so profound and revolutionary even today that it is still decades ahead of current medical thinking - Hahnemann established that a very complex image of symptoms is produced. He then confirmed - through clinical practice - that a truly curative system of medicine based upon parts, illness names, large doses and polypharmacy was completely unworkable (i.e. uncurative). And this for two reasons:

1. that natural and drug-induced illnesses (and therefore people) are multisymptomatic and
2. that drugs must be tested and clinically used individually rather than in mixtures.

He then built up a materia medica based entirely on these principles. The method of operation was to be similars and small doses. Once he had proved for himself the total ineffectiveness of large doses, many remedies, opposites and using disease-labels, he was left only with the opposites of them all: viz - small doses, single remedy, similars and holism rather than parts (person not disease).

Hahnemann got his critique of allopathy from two primary sources: his own dismal attempts at allopathic practice and translation work, which revealed to him hundreds of cures from the past that had been attained using specific drugs, often through using the law of similars.

The result of this on his part was doubt, confusion and hesitation. Rather than practise, he chose to live on his translation work. This was a sensible choice as it allowed more time for his research and held him back from the chaos and confusion, let alone the emotional drain that bad practice engendered in him. Two out of many possible quotes well illustrate this point:

> "After I had discovered the weakness and errors of my teachers and books, I sank into a state of sorrowful indignation, which had nearly altogether disgusted me with the study of medicine." Opening lines of Aesculapius in the Balance (1805) in Lesser Writings p410, Jain Edition

> "For 18 years I have departed from the beaten track of medicine. It was painful to me to grope in the dark, guided only by our books in the treatment of the sick...In an 8 years' practice, pursued with conscientious attention, I had learned the delusive nature of the ordinary methods of treatment..." From Letter upon the Necessity of a Regeneration of Medicine, (1808) in Lesser Writings pp511-3, Jain Edition.

Yet the demands of his growing family forced him to continue searching for a rational and effective system of therapy.

> "...serious diseases occurred... endangered the lives of my children... caused my conscience to reproach me still more loudly, that I had no means on which I could rely for affording them relief." ibid p512

It is little wonder therefore, that, inspired by his loathing for dismal and ineffective allopathy, Hahnemann took consolation in chemistry, which drew him closer and closer to the rationalising of mainly mineral remedies for use in his materia medica, the isolation and purification of active ingredients, and, somewhat ironically, down the very road that a century later (via the mainly German chemical industry) would lead straight to antibiotics, tranquillisers, analgesics and the other 'magic bullets' of modern allopathy! As we have seen, his development of the proving and the practical and therapeutic necessity of holism - derived from it - proved to be his and homoeopathy's saviour.

∎

SOME NOTES ABOUT HAHNEMANN'S HOROSCOPE

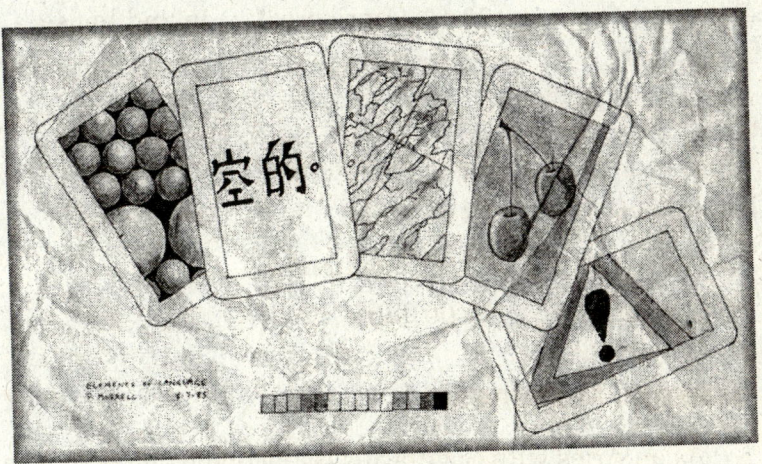

The Elements of Language, 1988

As is well known, Hahnemann was born in Meissen Saxony on 10 April, 1755. I have seen a horoscope published in 1900, for a birth in late evening giving 18 Sagittarius as the rising sign. Hahnemann did have the small and fine features of a Sagittarian. Cook, in his biography of

Hahnemann, says Hahnenann was born close to midnight. I shall use 11.15 pm as the basis for my chart as it just gives Mercury in the 3rd house and Saturn in the 2nd, the importance of which will become apparent below.

The chart details are as follows:

Sun	20 38' Aries	in 4th house
Moon	13 11' Aries	in 4th house
Mercury	1 13' Aries	in 3rd house
Venus	4 54' Pisces	in 3rd house
Mars	7 09' Pisces	in 3rd house
Jupiter	9 31' Virgo	in 9th house
Saturn	28 12' Capricorn	in 2nd house
Uranus	13 27' Pisces	in 3rd house
Neptune	4 39' Leo	in 8th house
Pluto	15 54' Sagittarius	in 1st house
Moon node	29 18' Virgo	in 3rd house
Ascendent	13 00' Sagittarius	
Midheaven	15 00' Libra	

GENERAL FEATURES

As an Aries with Sagittarius rising one would expect a person to have a forceful, daring and passionate nature, easily roused to argument though generally quick to forgive and forget. Sagittarians also make natural students with great curiosity and enthusiasm, a love of systems of thought or philosophy and a natural religious bent. Such people make excellent leaders and administrators and great friends. They also love moving on to new things and to travel of all kinds,

Some Notes about Hahnemann's Horoscope

foreign cultures, etc. They can display strong emotions.

From a technical viewpoint, this chart hinges around Pluto rising in Sagittarius, square (90) to Jupiter in the 9th in Virgo, square a conjunction of 3 planets in Pisces in the 3rd and - perhaps most importantly - exactly sextile (60) the midheaven in 15 Libra.

Pluto rising in Sagittarius square Jupiter in the 9th in Virgo.

Virgo is the traditional sign of healing, service and medicine. Jupiter rules wealth, success, the aristocracy and the Church. There are many elements here. Jupiter - the ruling planet of Sag - is in the 9th house in Virgo. This indicates a love of theories, value-systems and philosophies, possibly a religious tinge and a strong link with medicine and healing (Virgo). But Jupiter is badly aspected both by rising Pluto and by its opposition (180) to Venus and Mars in Pisces. This therefore signifies trouble through theories and philosophies (Sag and 9th) of a medical nature (Virgo) and through writings (3rd house).

There is a strong interest in new systems and grand theories, possibly arrived at hastily or impatiently or on scant evidence. Pluto is the planet of discovery, Sagittarius symbolises systems of thought and ideas, the rising sign signifies the ego and the quest for the new. That these theories and discoveries conflict strongly with the established order is derived from the contact Pluto makes with the Midheaven, dealt with below. Pluto rising in Sagittarius might also be interpreted as 'the creator of a new religion'. This is not so wide of the mark when we consider the sectarianism and philosophical divisiveness of many homoeopaths over the years.

Sun and Moon both in Aries in 4th house.

In the 4th house this signifies a large and nomadic family. In Aries they indicate a person who is a pioneer, even a loner, constantly trying out new things and new ways of looking at (old) things. It signifies someone who sets out alone and wins against all odds. Someone who has a great curiosity and inquisitiveness and who continues to delve into things, push at the boundaries of knowledge and make new discoveries throughout their life. It is this combination that seems to define, for many, the pure essence of 'Sam Hahnemann the Pioneer'. Sun and Moon both in Aries adds the sense of adventure and the pioneer spirit to family life. Moon in Aries also adds strong ties and an emotional and private dimension to Hahnemann's perception of family life.

There is a highly nomadic existence, moving from town to town, constantly moving house, general domestic unhappiness or upheaval. It is the nomadic element that is dominant, not so much the unhappiness.

Saturn in Capricorn in the 2nd house.

This signifies a very slow and difficult rise in life dogged by repeated setbacks in personal fortunes. Especially, it indicates a persistent lack of cash and a person who is poor or destitute for most of their life. Success and wealth only come begrudgingly and towards the end of a long life of hardship and worry. It also signifies thwarted ambitions and a life frustrated by barriers that prevent one being accepted by society. This is due to the reciprocal action between 2nd house taurus and saturn capricorn 10th house symbolisms. Thus the reputation suffers from lack of cash, and the poor reputation deprives one of promotion and progress that would lead to financial improvements. Catch 22?

Some Notes about Hahnemann's Horoscope

Mercury in Aries in 3rd house.

This signifies great curiosity and outstanding linguistic skills. Indeed, it is the linguistic and writing significator par excellence! So we expect to find here a person with an outstanding grasp of several languages and very good writing and reporting skills as well as oratorical ability. What adds even greater force and clarity to this, however, is its position in the sign of Aries. This makes the communicative skills sharper, faster, more robust and pragmatic. It adds the zest of Mars to the sparkle and wit of Mercury in the 3rd. However, Mars adds a coarser element leading to disputes, dictatorial campaign writing and use of harsh language.

Venus, Mars, Uranus conjunction in Pisces in 3rd house.

This also shows remarkable linguistic skills, as an orator and a passionate and eloquent writer and speaker. This can often degenerate however, into abusive, uncontrolled and crude language. Under stress such a person would be expected to have violent outbursts of uncontrollable anger and shouting. There is complete loss of control and an inability to accept another's point of view. Such a person would be extremely sensitive to even the slightest criticism and would probably tend to react violently and abusively. Combined with the 3 planets in Aries and a Sagittarius ascendent, this is a very fiery and bad-tempered feature.

As with all Piscean things, there is here a 'wool-gathering tendency', a tendency to draw in from others, the past and other cultures: a collector of ideas, stories and methods. These are then projected into writings.

Of these aspects the near exact opposition (180) between Mars and Jupiter is the most important. They are also the main ruling planets of the chart, ruling Aries and Sagittarius respectively. This gives great restlessness and energy. It has the aggressiveness, irritation and energy of Mars combined with the great expansiveness of Jupiter. The chief drawback is that such people would tend to exaggerate things. On the plus side it is a fruitful aspect as it generates many ideas and angles on a problem. There is also great impatience and a tendency to excess ideas and a lack of discipline. In the case of this chart this will manifest itself chiefly in writing and communication.

Venus-Mars conjunction in Pisces in direct opposition to Jupiter in Virgo in Midheaven.

This greatly accentuates the above comments about Venus, Mars and Uranus and the communication skills. There is a direct opposition between the new medical creation (Jup Virgo 10th) and the communication skills of the person. Thus Hahnemann can be seen as his own worst enemy, especially in his less moderate writings and rantings. This feature also indicates a student of the past, other cultures and history, a love of detail and precision, and one who creates great conflicts with the established order especially through their writings. Also a love of grand theories. It is in this combination that the linguistic and cultural drawing together of ideas and influences can be traced, and that Hahnmenan appears to have engaged in meticulously over many years. It can be argued that without this linguistic trait there would be no homoeopathy, because he would not have searched through medical history for an answer to his dissatisfaction with allopathy. His linguistic skills allowed him the luxury of a unique window into medical history and diverse medical ideas.

Some Notes about Hahnemann's Horoscope

Uranus in Pisces square the Ascendent.

This shows great intelligence and originality combined with very strange, eccentric methods and a determined, obstinate nature. It also indicates unusual perceptions and procedures and the investigation of the peculiar. The Uranian person is said never to heed advice and to dig in their heels when criticised. Under attack, they become even more convinced that they are right and everyone else is wrong! Sounds familiar!

Uranus square asc.

Wilful, obstinate, determined, strong willed; non-conformist, eccentricity.

Pluto rising exactly sextile the Midheaven.

This alignment basically shows that there is a strong and dramatic link between the discoveries (Pluto) of new systems (Sag), the personal ego (Aries 1st house) and the reputation (Midheaven). There is a rebellious and anarchical streak and there are repeated attacks upon one's reputation and status in society. The ego and the new systems become so tightly welded and in such conflict with the established order, that the attacks are not just directed at the theories themselves but also at the individual.

Pluto tends to destroy everything to ashes only to lift a new system Phoenix-like out of the devastation. As one might expect, Hahnemann's chart shows similar revolutionary and Plutonic features with the charts of Henry VIII, Paracelsus and Martin Luther, all of whom - in their way - challenged and battled with orthodoxy.

Pluto again entered Sagittarius in the autumn of 1995, so presumably bringing with it the start of a new revolution of ideas and new 'voyages of discovery', as it did in 1499 and 1747 - and precipitating the Voyages of Discovery and the Scientific and Industrial Revolutions.

OTHER FEATURES

The chart also contains a few minor details of interest. Jupiter and Neptune both in the ninth, indicate a pure yet traditional religious creed. Saturn is approaching an opposition (180) with Neptune, indicating some scepticism about the more mystical elements of religion and leanings towards the 'sceptical pragmatist' view of religion as taken today by natural science. Sun is semisquare (45) Mars, indicating more impatience and bad temper already covered. Moon is semisquare (45) Saturn indicating losses through all family matters and possibly tragic losses of sons and father (less so of daughters or mother). Mercury is conjunct (0) the Moon's South Node, indicating losses through writings and one's writings being out of tune with public opinion. Also inability to judge the 'mood of the times'.

TRENDS

From the year 1790 major planetary movements begin to strongly influence thisperson, culminating in strong activity in 1802 and again in 1809-11, during which a long series of first family/domestic and then knowledge/theoretical conflicts arise. Basically it is the movement of Pluto into Pisces in the 1790s, eventually passing through the above important degrees of Hahnemann's chart (4-9 Pisces-Virgo) that precipitates first his family upsets and

Some Notes about Hahnemann's Horoscope

then his medical discoveries. This combines with similar movements in his progressed horoscope culminating around 1810. Homoeopathy in general is probably ruled by Hahnemann's Jupiter in 9 Virgo.

Looking ahead it is clear that homoeopathy ruled by Hahnemann's jupiter in virgo will undergo radical developments in the years ahead as pluto enters and moves through sagittarius and especially as it passes through the critical 9-14 degrees. This will be in 1999-2005 approx.

BITS I MISSED

Jupiter square ascendent: Excesses of various kinds; cannot tolerate excess excitement. Depleted energies; takes on too much and can't finish them all; too many irons in the fire; mind restless and full of new ideas and new theories and schemes; bombastic; awkward manner; grandiose ideas; lack of humility; large family, several marriages; tends to exaggerate or overestimate; big schemes, generous to a fault.

Pluto conjunct asc: Revolutionary tendencies, never happy, extremely restless, quarrels and upsets over theories (sag); very wilful and obstinate; argumentative; will not tolerate disagreement; must create new things all the time as well as overthrowing the accepted norms and traditions; great willpower; regeneration; remake & remould things; secretive; a curious mixture of behaviour based partially on egotistic and partly through detached altruism.

Uranus square pluto: Extreme restlessness, like an earthquake, always vibrating at something; wants to destroy everything; strange and eccentric methods; destructive; vehemently opposed to the old, the conventional, the established ways of doing things and theories about life, etc; iconoclastic; turbulent; always at odds with everything; wants to change everything; restlessness and profound dissatisfaction with everything as it is; profound questioning of how things are done, methods and conventions; dissatisfied with conventional explanations, systems, theories or methods of doing things; always at odds with convention, the accepted, the received wisdom, the traditional method; must turn over the old and replace with the new; abundant restless energy and intelligence but very eccentric, wilful and revolutionary; disruptions & upheavals of every kind; revisionist and reforming tendency; insecurity.

∎

SAMUEL
AND MELANIE IN PARIS

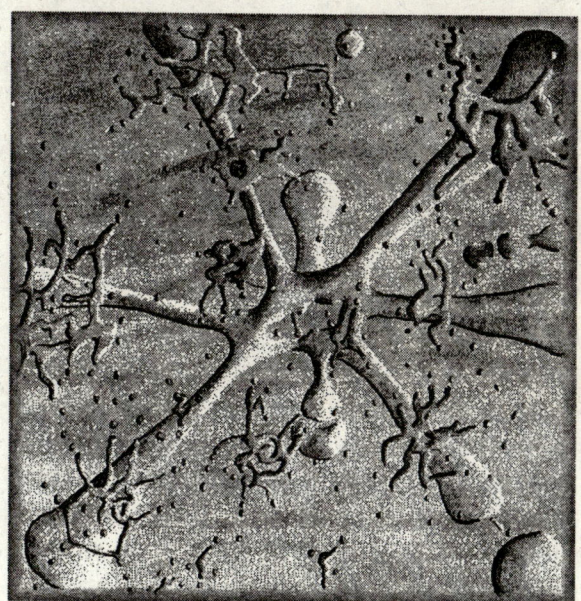

'Study of Water', 1973 - Peter Morrell

This short piece is mainly designed for the visitor to Paris who may wish to lookup some of the places which were central to the lives of Samuel and Melanie when they lived there over 150 years ago.

Samuel Hahnemann and Melanie first met in October 1834, Melanie having travelled from France to Coethen to see him. In the following January - 18th Jan 1835 - they were married. Melanie was not happy in Coethen and wanted them both to move to Paris. Having rewritten his Will on 2 June, they left Coethen (and Germany) for the last time on 7 June 1835, he thereby bidding adieu forever to his beloved Saxony.

**Samuel Hahnemann
(1755-1843)**

Marie Melanie d'Hervilly-Gub

On 21 June they arrived in Paris and took an apartment at 26 Rue des Saints Pères, right in the centre of old Paris, south of the Seine opposite the Ecole des Beaux Arts, near the Hopital de la Charité and the Medical Academy. One of the main bridges, the Pont du Carrousel leads south from the front of The Louvre straight into the Rue des Saints Pères. Some weeks later they moved to a house on the southern outskirts of the city at 7 Rue de Madame, mile further south and on the western side of the Jardin du Luxembourg. In a

Samuel and Melanie in Paris

letter in Jan 1836 to his German friends he describes this house as '...free from noisy streets, our large windows overlook a pretty garden...with backdoor opening into the Park of Luxembourg...a large garden with trees, which is an hour's walk in extent.' (see Haehl, Samuel Hahnemann His Life and Works, 1922, Vol 2, p347 & Vol 1 pp221-237). In 1837 Hahnemann and Melanie moved house again, this time to the north of the city, to **1 Rue de Milan** in 9th District, halfway between the Boulevard Haussman and the Place de Clichy. It is a short east-west street joining the Rue de Clichy with the Rue d'Amsterdam, very close to the railway station Gare St Lazare and to the north west of central Paris. House number 1 is at the eastern or Rue de Clichy end of the street. It was a very noisy and bustling area with fewer trees and less fresh air than they had enjoyed at their former residence. It was at this house that he stayed until his death. It was to this house that the many students, doctors and famous and celebrated visitors came to seek him out for tuition, treatment and advice, such as the virtuoso violinist Nicolai Paganini (1782-1840) and the 2nd Marquess of Anglesey, Henry Paget (1797-1869). It was a house well known to the main founders of English homoeopathy in the 1830s: Dr Quin, Rev Thomas Everest, William Leaf and Dr Paul Curie. Everest, his brother George and Leaf had all been his patients. Despite his great age, Hahnemann clearly had a whale of a time in Paris, being as fluent in French as he was in Italian, English and Spanish. He was feted by the Parisians as a great celebrity in the most fashionable European city of the day. Hahnemann died there at 5 am on 2 July 1843 and Melanie kept his body there before burial until the 11 July. He was buried in the Cimetiere de Montmartre to the north of Paris in what is popularly called the *artists quarter*. He was buried in grave number 8 and in 1878 Melanie was buried in grave number 9. In the early hours, the cortege moved grimly through the streets the short distance to Montmartre in driving rain with only a handful of mourners - Melanie had not informed anyone of his death. On the insistence of wealthy American homoeopaths, in 1898 it was agreed that his grave should be opened, so his remains could be moved to the more prestigious Cimetière du Pere Lachaise. On May 24, 1898 the two graves were opened and the remains identified from a large lock of Melanie's hair around his neck and from his engraved wedding ring. The bodies were moved to a much grander tomb in the Lachaise cemetery which can still be seen. It is a 'celebrity' grave along with many other Paris notables from the last century and also from this.

THE PARIS COLLEGE OF HOMOEOPATHY

The Paris College of Homoeopathy or 'Institut de la Medecine Homoeopathique' was located at 93 Rue de la Harpe. This is a bow-shaped north-south street south of the Ile de la Cité, in the centre of old Paris, just at the top end of the Boulevard Saint Michel. It was opened in Oct 1839 by Dr Croserio with Dr Jahr teaching Materia Medica Pura in German, Dr Mure teaching pharmacology and mnemonics and Dr Croserio running the Homoeopathic Clinic (p400). In July 1840 Dr Croserio says that another College and Clinic had been opened in Rue Git-le-coeur on the south bank of the Seine; both are close to the allopathic 'Ecole de Médecine' and opposite the Palais de Justice. (Bradford, 1895, p401) The expressed objectives of the Paris College of Homoeopathy were outlined by Dr Croserio in a letter to Dr Neidhard of Philadelphia as follows:

1. to teach students the theory and practice of homoeopathy;
2. to spread the benefit of homoeopathy among the lower classes of the capital, by giving consultations gratis to those who will personally apply for them;
3. to give advice in writing to those patients in the country and in the Provinces of France, who, having no homoeopathic physicians near them, apply for it;
4. to prepare Homoeopathic medicines according to the method of Dr Mure;
5. to translate into the French language practical works on homoeopathy;
6. to publish, under the title of 'le propagateur de l'homoeopathie' a monthly periodical, by which all new homoeopathic works and periodicals will be reviewed;
7. to procure for those homoeopathic physicians and other individuals in the Province, or in foreign countries, who would apply for them, homoeopathic books, instruments, medicines and practical advice in particular cases;

8. to open a 'cabinet de lecture' where students, physicians, may read or borrow all homoeopathic books and periodicals published in France or other countries;

9. to consult strangers who come to Paris, either for studying homoeopathy, or for buying homoeopathic medicines, books etc.

10. to serve as a central point for homoeopaths of all nations and to nominate correspondents for that purpose in all foreign countries.

Georges Henri Gottleib JAHR
(1800-1875)

Dr. Benoit MURE

"Dr GHG Jahr will teach Materia Medica Pura, with German as the homoeopathic language; Dr Mure pharmacology and menonics applied to the Materia Medica; and I have accepted the homoeopathic clinic." (Bradford, 1895, p400-1). It is not entirelyclear how long this institution lasted and what number of homoeopaths it trained.

And what a shame it was for British homoeopathy that those noble aims of the Paris Institute were not shared by its founders, Dr Quin & Co, nor imported to the British Isles to create a 'homoeopathy for the masses' rather than a 'homoeopathy for the rich elite', which is what they actually created. And how correspondingly impoverished UK homoeopathy has therefore been ever since. It would be of great interest to determine to what extent the great popularity of homoeopathy in France can be attributed to the above sentiments of Dr Croserio and to Hahnemann's great generosity of spirit. And by contrast, how much its relatively dismal track record in England can be attributed to the absence of the same attributes by the founders of English homoeopathy.

DR. CROSERIO

Dr. Felix Croserio is a little known yet very important figure during Hahnemann's final years in Paris. He was born in 1786 at Condove in Savoy. He studied in Turin, and did military service in 1806 as a French Army Surgeon, following campaigns in Spain, Germany and Russia until 1814. He went back to Turin for his MD in 1812, leaving the Army as a Senior Physician after Napoleon's downfall and settled in Paris as a practitioner. He became acquainted with homoeopathy in 1833 through a Dr Petroz and studied eagerly, learning German at the same time. He edited for some years, along with Dr Leon Simon (1798-1867) and Dr Jahr (1800-1875), the 'Annales de la Medecine Homoeopathique'. He also wrote many essays, his influential 'La Statistique de la Médecine Homoeopathique' and in 1850 'Manuel Homoeopathie d'Obstétrique'. He was Physician for a time to the Embassy of the King of Sardinia in Paris and was attached to several charities. He was trusted completely as an intimate friend of Hahnemann - he and Dr Jahr being the only physicians to attend Hahnemann at his last. He was also Melanie's chief assistant and constant companion after Samuels death, and helped her compile her case for the Lawyers at her trial in 1847. He also corresponded with the American homoeopaths. He died in Paris 69 years old on 13 April 1855, ominously 3 days after the 100th anniversary of Samuel's birth and thus in what must have been a very bleak time for Melanie. (see Haehl, 1922, vol 2, p506)

THE GRAVE OF HAHNEMANN

1993 marked the 150th anniversary of Samuel Hahnemann's death. Rima Handley, in A Homoeopathic Love Story, records his death in Paris in 1843. His grave is at the prestigious Cimetière du Père Lachaise in the north east of the city. "It is easy to get to the cemetery by bus or Metro. At the gate you can buy a plan which shows the whereabouts of the 200 most famous people, out of more than a million who have been buried there over the centuries. You will be glad to know that Samuel figure among these 200. Others include Beethoven, Edith Piaf and Jim Morrison of The Doors! It was a warm Sunday morning in mid-March when we climbed the hill side, bright with crocuses and daffodils, to find Hahnemann's memorial beside a broad path. There is a bust, surmounted by the words, 'Hahnemann Fondateur de l'Homoeopathie' and beneath, the words he asked Melanie to put on his tomb, 'Non Inutilis Vixi, I did not live in vain'. To the left is a list of his major writings and to the right, 'Similia Similibus Curantur. Traitez les Malades par des remèdes produisant des symptômes semblables à leurs maladies'. Let like be cured by like; treat illness with remedies that produce symptoms similar to the illness. A rose and some other flowers had been left on the memorial recently. We took a lot of photos and watched the reaction of others to the impressive memorial." [The above section, written by Richard Palk, has been edited down from an item in 'ONEM, The College of Homoeopathy Student Magazine', which also appeared in the Society of Homoeopaths Newsletter 39, in Sept 1993] The baffling thing about Melanie's destiny is that her grave is also near Hahnemann's, but is in an unmarked plot. Haehl has this to say about it:

"Madame Melanie Hahnemann died on the 27th of May 1878, almost forgotten. She was then 78 years of age, and

Melanie, circa 1875   Pere Lachaise

succumbed to catarrh of the lungs, from which she had suffered for several years. She was laid to rest in Montmartre... she had left her husbands grave without the inscriptions he desired and composed... her own resting place she had chosen to the left of Hahnemann's grave. The assumption that as at first intended, she was to be united with her husband in the grave, led in many cases to a mistaken idea that her grave was also Hahnemanns last resting place. For two decades it was continually described as Hahnemann's Grave, if it was at all remembered as such. Not until 24th May 1898 was the complete and final truth revealed. On this date the grave was opened and found to contain only one coffin with the remains of the widow Hahnemann, Melanie nee d'Hervilly. All the marks coincided with the number of the grave and the entries in the register of the cemetery. In the grave next to it, however, Hahnemann's coffin was discovered containing his remains. These remains of Hahnemann, together with what was left of Madame Melanie now entered upon their very last journey. In the Père Lachaise cemetery the Frenchwoman Melanie lies in a small coffin at the foot of the coffin containing the German founder of Homoeopathy. Stranger shave at last carried out his dying wish: 'bones to bones and ashes to ashes'. (From Haehl, Samuel Hahnemann His Life and Works, 1922, vol 1, p354)

Finally, for the antique collector, try the flea market of Montmartre in the north every Monday for old medicine bottles and pillars. There are some beautiful old pharmacies in Paris, with wood-panelled walls packed with those attractive old medicine jars and bottles that could even be seen in Britain up to the early 70s. These old pharmacies are common around the Ile de la Cite and Ile de St Louis near the Notre Dame. There are also a number of interesting second-hand book stalls along the Seine and a large American Bookstore (second-hand). The latter is bright yellow and close to the banks of the Seine, though I can remember neither the the exact location nor its name as I was travelling on a bus at the time I saw it.

■

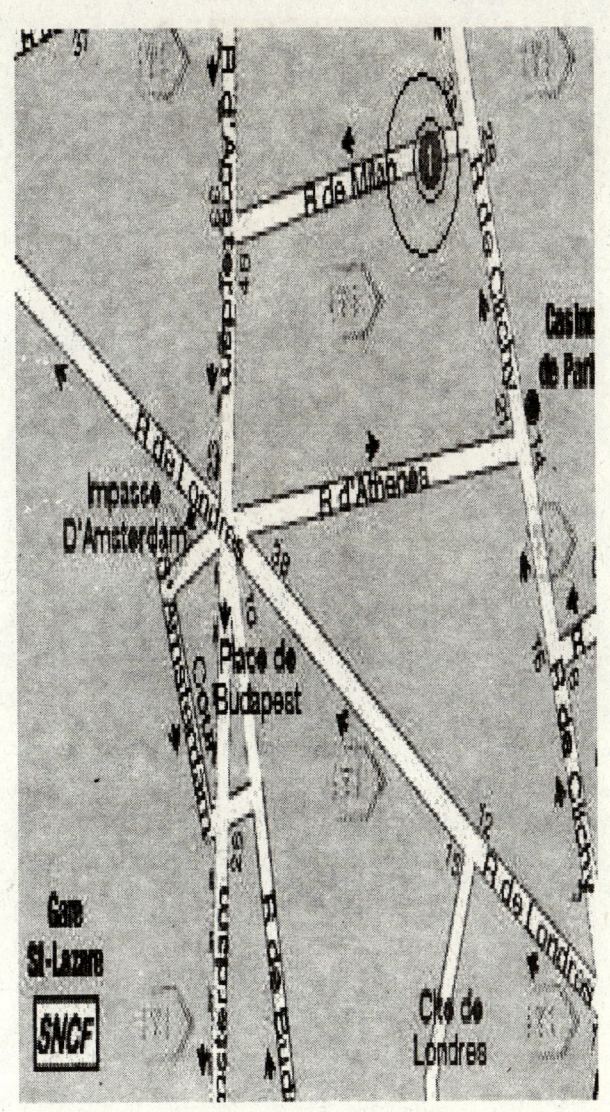

Rue de Saints peres (Paris)

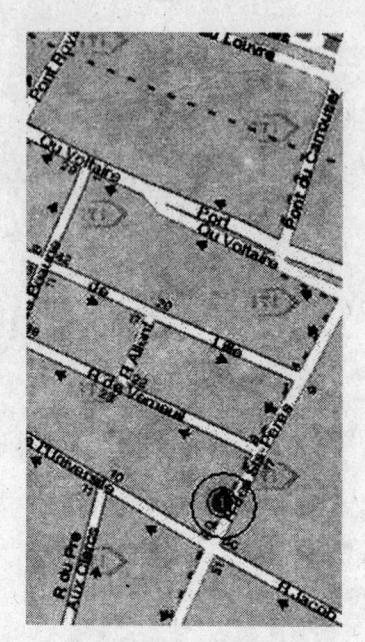

Rue de Milan (Paris)

ON HAHNEMANN'S WORKLOADS AND CONSULTATION TIMES IN HIS PARIS PRACTICE

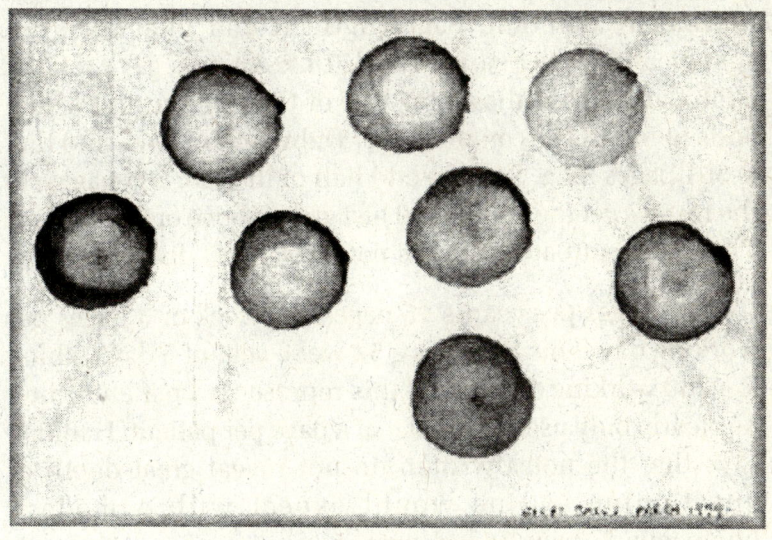

Eight balls, March 1999

"Before long a project was conceived by the newly married pair to visit Paris together. This visit led to a permanent settlement in that city." (Hobhouse, p262)

Two intriguing entries in Rima Handley's new book [Handley, 1997] have led me recently to try and work out the length of Hahnemann's consultation time and to try and estimate how many patients he saw in Paris between 1835 and 1843.

On page 20, Handley says '...*they saw patients for most of the day and then relaxed...*'. On page 24 she says '*it is scarcely likely that the interviews...would have taken as long as one hour and a half...*'. If they did last 1.5 hrs then for a 10 am to 6 pm (8 hour) working day he could only have seen between 5 and 6 patients on this basis. This led me to look at some data in the back of Handley's book.

On page 212 she gives a breakdown of the Kranken journal by date and pagelength. If you total them up specifically for the Paris period, 1836-43, you get a total of 6256 pages. This allows for half of the last journal, which ends in feb 1844, 6 months after Hahnemann died, and that is 591 pages long. So if we add half of that (ie. 295 pages) to the rest we get the grand total just given above of 6256 pages. This works out at 782 pages per year (6256 divided by 8).

782 pages per year is 15 pages per week or 3 pages per working day. This assumes a 52 week year of 5 days which is a 260 working day year. If this represents 5 patients, then he clearly only used about 0.6 of a page per patient. Handley says that the notes written do not reveal great depth of questioning as one would expect with a modern homoeopath (page 24 last para).

Another approach is to say that he had a theoretical maximum of 5 patients per day for 260 days which is 1300 per year and over 8 years that is 10,400 patients. Now we can use that to compare with the pagelengths of the journals.

On Hahnemann's Workloads

6256/10,400 gives 0.6 pages per consultation or 3 pages per day. This also suggests that he was only seeing some 5 patients per day.

Thus from two different angles we can show that it is reasonable to assume that Hahnemann and Melanie were seeing 5-6 patients per day in Paris and that they spent approximately 1-1.5 hrs per consultation.

> "The longest consultations would take about one and a half hours, but were usually much shorter in view of the sixty or more patients waiting outside." (Cook, p173)

It is also interesting that on the pages copied (in facsimile form) in the book several consultations are given per page. On pp42-3 shows 3 feb, 10 feb, 14th and 19th feb, ie 4 on one page. Likewise on pp48-49 we see 12 appointments all on one page: 12 june, 27 may, 18 and 25 june, 6 and 13 july; aug 11th, 13th and 25th as well as sept 1st 15th and 22nd. On pages 56-7 we see march 19th and 26th; 11 march, 6april and 10 april: 5 appointments. On pp 58-9 we see 26may and 13 june. On pp 104-5 we see appts 18 may 27th, 11 june and 26 june: 4 appts. On pp128-9 we 8 appts clearly shown. On pp156-7 we see 5 appts clearly written out. On pp178-9 we see 4 appts clearly written out.

We can summarise this as follows:

1. 4 cons
2. 12
3. 5
4. 4
5. 8
6. 5
7. 4

We can average this as 42 appointments over 7 pages, which is an average of exactly 6 per page. Based upon this we can go back to the size of the journals and see how many appointments in 6256 pages. 6256 multiplied by 6 gives 37,536 appointments over a period of 8 years. That is 37,536 divided by 8 years or 4692 per year. If this is correct then it translates into the following per week and per day: 90.2 per week and 18 per day. This is clearly much higher than our previous estimate of 5 per day and 1300 per year. Even if we assume that 5 consultations per page as a more typical figure, we still get 31,280 in the whole journals and that is 3910 per year which is 75 per week and thus 15 per day.

If Hahnemann was regularly seeing 15-18 patients per day, which seems unlikely for a man of his age, then he would only have been able to spend 20-25 minutes with each of them (based on a 7-hour working day). We must therefore assume that the previous estimate of 5-10 is much more realistic, based upon what we know. Some thus far unpublished surveys of homoeopaths, which I have conducted myself, both of British homoeopaths in 1989-90 and also currently, 1997-8, of world homoeopaths, clearly show that most homoeopaths only see 6-7 patients per day on average and only very few exceed 10 patients per day. This figure ranges up towards 12 and down towards 3. This is by using aids like repertories and computers, which if anything reduces the consultation time taken compared to Hahnemann's time. On the other hand he had much fewer remedies and probably a very intimate knowledge of their use. These would have greatly increased his speed, whereas his lack of modern repertories might have reduced his speed.

Finally, we might highlight a further problem regarding the type of consultation. Homoeopaths may take 1-1.5 hrs for the initial consultation and even 30 mins per follow up, but they get shorter and shorter, so that after the first 5 or 6 appts the visit might only last 15 mins. Thus we are looking at two distinct types of consultation --'initial' for a new patient, which are long, and then 'follow-ups' which are usually a lot shorter. Taking this into account, it is possible for Hahnemann and Melanie to have seen 5 or 5 initial consultations and upto 10 follow-ups all in the same day. That gives a max of 15. Maybe that gives a more accurate picture of his consultation time and workload situation.

And for most homoeopaths, even today, that situation has changed very little indeed. It is hard to imagine how it could change even in the future, as it is in the nature of homoeopathy to discuss in depth with the client the nature and extent of all their health problems, to decide on a remedy and then to discuss the outcome of their treatment. And this necessarily takes more than 15-20 minutes.

HAHNEMANN'S WORKLOADS

> "..it is not clear how long the initial case taking would have lasted. At one point in his career...he saw patients for an hour and a half on their first appointment...in many cases however, the details taken down... were quite few and it is scarcely likely that the interview which produced them would have taken as long as an hour and a half....the intial notes are usually restricted to a few lines and rarely exceed a page....we do have to acknowledge that the case taking was not as detailed as one would expect from the description in the Organon..'"(Handley, 1997, p24)

From DF12, a copy of which I possess, we can see that the notes are usually covering 5-6 lines per appointment (going as low as 1 or 2), but do very occasionally extend to 15-20 lines, or more frequently 8 or 9. An average of 5 or 6 seems acceptable. However, it is clearly very hard to estimate how much discussion time generated those notes and this would also vary from doctor to doctor, from patient to patient and also from time to time. A great many variable factors would influence that and unfortunately it is difficult to gain a certain correlation between the # of lines written and the length of the consultation, even though they will obviously tend to reflect each other to some extent.

We can then consult other data about his practice to find further clues in our search. On p442, Bradford says it is estimated that in the 8 years he spent in Paris, Hahnemann earned 4 million Francs (BJH xxii, 1865, p678); no indication is given as to how this figure was arrived at.

Also that 'he rose at 6 am in summer, 7 am in winter, worked 10-12 am, then had lunch and after lunch a sleep of one hour; then (p445-6) saw patients until 7 pm;

> "*as a physician he was extremely humane and compassionate towards those seeking help*'"(Bradford, p449);

In **Bradford**, p371

> "*he has a select circle of patients and from among the higher ranks; but this much is certain that the ante-room to his office is always filled and that a newcomer has to wait for hours until it is his turn to be admitted*" (from AHZ nov 20 1837);

Also

On Hahnemann's Workloads

"each one takes up more time than is the case in the offices of other physicians." p371; "an examination that lasted about an hour and a half" (Young in ibid, p373);

"..there were generally 60 or more patients at any time in his office when I was there" (J Young, in Bradford, p374)

"In this way, she claimed, he was able to to see more patients before he became tired. Sometimes by four in the afternoon more than one hundred poor patients would be waiting for treatment, and Hahneman would allow her to treat many of them herself." (Cook, p173)

Thomas Lindsley BRADFORD (1847-1918)

"...our consultations [in Paris] begin at 10 am and last until 5 pm or 6 pm" [letter to Gersdorff in Hobhouse, p268]

"during his patients' long wait, often 3 hrs or more, Melanie would circulate...the longest consultations would take about one and a half hours, but were usually much shorter in view of the 60 or more patients waiting outside" [Cook, p172-3]

Hence perhaps why he dished out so much Sulphur to so many patients?

"by 4 in the afternoon more than one hundred poor patients would be waiting for treatment and Hannemann would allow her [Melanie] to treat many of them herself'" [p173] "the fees were calculated on a sliding scale according to the patients means, whereby the very poor would pay nothing at all." [Cook, p173];

"the last of his patients would usually be seen about 6 pm, after which he would have dinner.." [ibid, p173];

"I am writing the 6th edition [during 1840-2], to which I devote several hours a day on sundays and thursdays, all other time being required for the treatment of patients who come to my rooms." [in letter in Bradford, pp176-7]

CALCULATING HIS WORKLOAD

There now follows a series of calculations designed to try and estimate Hahnemann's workloads in Paris 1835-43.

Based upon the above data we can assume he normally worked a 7 hour day from 10-12 and 2-7 pm and only for 5 days a week. If we assume that he worked 90 minutes with a first patient and 40 minutes with a return, then he could see a max of 15 returns per day but only 6 new patients per day. This translates into 5 days per week and 260 days per year. If he saw new patients 2 days a week on average, and returners for 3 days a week, on average, then this gives 2 x 6 + 3x15 = 12 + 45 = 57 max per week; 57 x 52 weeks is 2964 patients per year max.

"Hahnemann's policy on fees for his services had not changed throughout his career...fees were calculated on a sliding scale according to the patient's means, whereby the very poor would pay nothing at all." (Cook, p173)

On Hahnemann's Workloads

If we then accept that he did indeed earn 4 million Francs in 8 years, or 500,000 F per year, then 500,000/2964 = 168.7 F per patient on average. This falls close to the centre of Rima's range of 3-300 F per consultation. This data needs checking for comparison against other fees and prices for Paris of the 1840s.

Alternatively, we might approach the problem purely from the financial angle and assume that if he did receive 500,000 F per year, we can work backwards from that. In this way we can construct a table of data based on consultation fees. If he totalled 500,000 F over each year and charged 100F each, then he saw 5000 per year; alternatively if he charged 200 F each then he saw 2500 per year and so on. Knowing he worked 260 days and 7 hours per day we can then estimate the consultation time for each patient. We can show all of this in handy table form:

charge	50F	75F	100F	125F	150F	168F	200F	300F
# per year	10000	6666	5000	4000	3333	2964	2500	1667
# per wk	192	128	96	77	64	57	48	32
# per day	38.4	25.6	19.2	15.4	12.8	11	9.6	6.4
consult'n time (Minutes)	11	16.7	22	27.3	33	38	44	65.6

I think this gives a fairly good insight into his likely workload. My own feeling is that he saw around 3000 patients per year and thus spent on average 35 minutes with each. That also fits in very well with modern data and allows for a combination of some shorter consultations (10-30 mins) and some longer ones (45-90 mins). It is tempting to up this estimate to 4000 per year but that reduces the average consultation time to only 27 minutes which I feel is too short. But, as Rima says, it is hardly likely that he spent 1.5 hours with each patient. 30-50 mins seems much more likely as an average. On the other hand it is perfectly conceivable that a man of his ability and immense experience could perhaps have worked much faster, and seen 15 or 20 patients a day, employing consultation times of only 20 minutes.

There is one further complicating factor in all this. The Casebooks might not show ALL his patients. He may only have kept records for the rich clientele and not even wrote notes for the numerous poor. Or Maybe only Melanies treated the poor and also without making notes. If this is the case, then clearly our calculations are underestimates of the real picture.

CASEBOOK DATA

In Rima's 1997 book there is a list (p.212) of all the casebooks and their length in pages. The total is 6156 pages, counting the last casebook as 295pp rather than as 591pp and finishing in June rather than in December. This is necessary because Hahnemann died in early July 1843.

Also in Rima's book there are some facsimile pages which give a method of counting the number of lines of writing per page, the number of appointments per page and thus an estimate for the number of lines per appointment. There are 9 such facsimile pages given and the lines are as follows

# lines	# appts
37	11
47	6
42	5
44	8
45	5
44	4
44	4
47	16
43	5
350	64 totals

From this we can show that the average number of lines per page is 43.67 and the average number of appointments per page is 7.111; the corresponding ranges are 37- 47 and 4-16. We can thus calculate the average number of lines per appointment, which is 7.515 and ranging from 2.94 to 11. The number of lines of casenotes per average appointment is 6.14.

I can easily confirm that the appearance of these casebook pages in Rima's book are identical to those in the DF12 casebook, which I possess in microfiche format, and which, by all accounts, are the same dimensions as all those from the same period. Thus we can assume this data to be perfectly reliable.

If we now combine both sets of information we can calculate the total number of lines and appointments contained in the complete casebooks. That would be 6516 X 43.67 and = 268832.52. This assumes of course that all the pages are 43 lines in length and that is not the actual case, as many pages are blank or have only 2 or 3 lines of writing. Some are half filled in.

In order to estimate a good idea of how much space there is in the casebooks we can look at one and count. I looked at DF12 and out of 15 microfiches, covering some 178 pages of the casebooks, a total of only 141.9 pages were filled. Thus we can say that 141.9/178, which is 79.72%, is the total amount of actual writing. Applying this correction to our data now gives a new set of data.

6516 pages now becomes 5194.6 pages of 43 line writing approx.and thus the casebooks actually contain 226848.2 lines of writing. We can now use that figure to make some further calculations. Number of lines per year is 28356. Assuming he worked for 260 days a year then we can see he wrote 109 lines per average working day, or 2.5 pages of casebook [this is also 15.6 lines per hour of a 7-hour working day]. 109 lines is also equivalent to 109/6.14 appointments, ie. 17.8 patients per day. Thus we could say he saw some 18 patients per average day, which is 4628 per 260-day year and thus 108.04 F per average patient, if he earned 500,000F per year. Rima mentions he charged 3-300 francs so this is well within that range. 18 patients per day for a 420 minute [7 hours] working day, gives us 23.3 minutes consultation time spent with each average client. He thus earned 1923F [500000/260] per day or 274F [1923/7] per hour of consultation time. We can expect more of a range. Some days he will have seen fewer patients, say 8 or 10, while on other days he will have seen more, say 26. This would give 10 + 26 = 36 and that is still an average of 18 per day.

I have recalculated this for a 6 day working week (a 312 day year) and for 7.75 years rather than 8 (he did not work

On Hahnemann's Workloads

at all for the June-July of 1835 when first going to Paris, nor the last June of his life in 1843), but the result is still very similar indeed. You still get 15-18 patients per day, 4767 patients per year and 105F as the average fee. He would earn between 1600F and 1900F per day.

On page 29 Rima (1997) gives some examples of fees. She lists 10F (twice), 20F, 50F (twice), 100F (twice), 200F and 300F. A total of 840F/9 = 93.3F as a sort of average, which is surprisingly close to the 108F calculated above.

We can also see from this data that each line of Hahnemann's writing in the casebook represented 3.8 to 4 minutes of consultation time. This is calculated from the above data. It would be interesting to compile some similar data for modern homoeopaths for comparison purposes.

It is also possible, of course, that Melanie saw patients herself on her own and cleared 'the backlog' occasionally by working through many acute cases and poor folks in a shorter time period. If that is the case then we can say he might have seen as many as 20 in one day but that would hardly be sustainable on a regular basis for an 85 year old man.

> "She treats large numbers of poor patients daily, free of charge, under my supervision, which, however, she hardly needs now, because through her own study of homoeopathy she daily progresses more and more..." (from a letter to Dr Hennike in 1837, in Cook, p171)

He also employed other uniformed staff 'footmen in full livery' (Cook, p172) who policed the long queues of his patients and sorted his cases into 'quick acutes' and 'slow chronics', rich and poor, etc. He will probably have received a mixture of each category to treat himself. And with Melanie's help, could have treated between them 40 or 50 a day for at least some of the days in any average week.

CONCLUSIONS

It does seem therefore that Hahnemann was seeing a lot more than 4-9 patients per day in his Paris practice. Indeed, according to some accounts it could have been as many as 20-30 per day. According to our calculations it is more likely to have been 15-18 per day, even though that is still double the workload of most modern homoeopaths and certainly out of line with his own guidelines in the *Organon* about the time required for the proper taking of the case. We are inevitably therefore drawn to formulate some reasons for this accelerated pace of his practice in Paris.

It is also strange for a man who had expressed his desire to retire and to complete his 6th Edition, to have been working at such frenetic speed. Now perhaps we know why he had such little time for writing and that not a single article or new book derived from his Paris years. Apart from eating and sleeping, he was completely absorbed with a very demanding daily work-schedule which many doctors in their 30's would find punishing, let alone an eighty five year old.

How can anyone practise decent homoeopathy when continuously seeing patients in such large numbers for only 20 minutes each? Month in, month out, year in and year out. Surely, such a gruelling schedule is bound to reduce the quality of one's practice? You only have to look at the scrappy and indadequate case-notes, which appear brief, rushed and reflecting very little depth to the discussion which must have preceded them. And then the heavy reliance on *Sulphur* and *Sac lac*. *'he began to prescribe Sulphur to an extraordinary degree.'* [Handley, 1997, p.40]. Why was he prescribing like that? One is tempted to conclude that it was to pack in as many patients per day as possible. The better cases kept coming back, and got well, the rest, in all probability, did neither.

Then the question arises as to why he was behaving in this way, which seems to stand in such marked contrast to his sedate, dignified and methodical mode of practice in Coethen, not to mention his own advice in the Organon about taking the case. And we might then ask who was behind this change? In spite of all the apposite, worthy, high-principled and nice things Rima says about her in 'A Homoeopathic Love Story', we are drawn, again like our forebears, to the almost inevitable and overwhelming conclusion that it was Melanie who was behind it all.

So finally, we seem to have two possible interpretations of these fascinating but somewhat baffling Paris years. One involving the ruthless and calculated exploitation of the unique talents of a great man 'imprisoned' like a caged bird, in the last 8 years of his life, dominated by *'Melanie's flair, personality and ambitious drive'* [Cook, p.171]. Or, a fascinating socio-political experiment in Paris, testing homoeopathy —pushing it to the limits of direct and fierce competition with allopathy —for the first time, in the bustling, fashionable and cosmopolitan urban environment. And in this latter scenario, which we can guess was mostly conceived of and driven by Melanie, Samuel was an equal partner, excited by the whole adventure and enjoying it immensely right up to his dying day. Maybe the truth is that it was a mixture of both and that Samuel was as much in charge as she, and that he was much more a 'willing victim' to her dominant personality than he at first appears. We shall never know for sure. Certainly he had found a great playmate and a great friend in homoeopathy, who also shared his love of hard work, conversation and the French language.

■

HAHNEMANN: THE ADVENTUROUS CAREER OF A MEDICAL REBEL

In Mountains 1, 1983

By Martin Gumpert, L B Fischer Publ Corp, New York, 1945, now out of print, 251 pages, hardback, 8vo; a translation into English of: 'Hahnemann, die Abenteurlichen Schicksale eines Arztlichen Rebellen und seiner Lehre, der Homoöpathie', 256pp, 8vo, S.Fischer, Berlin, 1934; translated from the German by Claud W Sykes.

Reviewed by **Peter Morrell**

I recently purchased this wonderful book from a secondhand bookstore in Vermont, having been recommended it by the Swiss homoeopath Alain Jean-Mairet. It is a most delightful and elegant book. It is a great pity that it cannot be reprinted in paperback (maybe by Jain?) and thus made much more widely available, as it is undoubtedly one of the best and most easily readable biographies about Hahnemann, and also one of the most eloquently written.

According to the dustcover, Dr Gumpert was a 'medical adviser to 'Time' magazine' and managed to 'combine a flourishing New York medical practice with the writing of books'. According to his entry in Who Was Who In America, Dr Gumpert's dates were 1897-1955. He was MD Berlin 1923, moved to US in 1936 and became a US citizen in 1942. Dr Gumpert published several other books, including 'Trailblazers of Science', 'Dunant: The Story of the Red Cross', 'Health Under Hitler' and 'You Are Younger Than You Think'.

On the inner dustcover of the book it says Dr Gumpert 'has brought wisdom and tenderness to the telling of his story', and to have possessed 'shrewd psychological insight and literary intuition to create this portrait'. Never were truer words written! It is a fascinating, indeed enthralling, portrait of the founder of homoeopathy and probably the most profound and insightful. It goes on: 'Hahnemann emerges a half- comic, half-tragic figure, the haunted and somewhat grotesque prophet of a new system of healing, still wandering from town to town and still disappointed at the age of eighty, struggling under the burden of unwanted wisdom'. And also: 'Dr Gumpert's... treatment of the scientific aspect of Hahnemann's life is authoritative and exact.'

I can criticise this book on only two minor grounds: first, that it does not contain an index, and second, that it gives only scant information about his years in Paris. The latter is entirely forgivable because even by the 1940's very little hard factual information was in the public domain about his Paris years.

I cannot emphasise more strongly that Gumpert writes beautifully and lavishes detail upon the reader. He seems to have entered into the world of Hahnemann so completely and blended with it so intimately and so thoroughly, like a truly intuitive historian; he then proceeds to deliver page after page of details about the man that you just cannot find anywhere else. Completely absorbed by his subject, the anecdotes and warm insights about the man simply flow elegantly from his pen. It is easily the best book about Hahnemann I have ever read and so readable that literally anyone could pick it up and read it in a single day. To my mind it easily outshines every other biography. It is meticulously researched.

The rest of this book review will simply be a guided tour of some of the most delightful parts of the book.

Hahnemann utterly despaired at the irrational nature of the medicine of his day, and its learned professors in the university medical schools, who he felt did more harm than good through their quarrelling:

> "No learned brains could unravel the skein of hypotheses and theories which entangled the professors and set them all at odds... the words of

an arrogant and incomprehensible professorial language were in themselves without results, but the applicaion of those same professors' erroneous deductions killed thousands of men and women. There were no experiments, there was no painstaking research; there were only odd and eccentric systems which were exalted into dogmas, without any possibility of testing senseless methods of treatment." [p.15]

Hahnemann's interest in chemistry is legendary, but few know where he studied it on a daily basis when in his twenties. Gumpert tells us:

"But the sole consolation of Hahnemann's existence in Dessau [1779-83] was his daily visit to the apothecary, Haeseler, in whose laboratory he could continue his study of chemistry." [p.26]

No wonder then that he eventually married the daughter of an apothecary.

His ability to upset and shock people was also present from an early age. According to Gumpert he was a pedantic, rude and exacting young upstart and very unpopular with patients and colleagues alike:

"Hardly a day passed without some complaint against him. As a doctor he was intolerant in his attitude to both colleagues and patients. He ruthlessly refused treatment to anyone who did not follow his prescriptions strictly...he spoke harshly, and often unjustly, about other physicians, in violation of the sacred traditions of his calling...'"[p.29]

He was always in trouble with someone. His fiancee and her parents all worried about this serious young man who seemed determined to be rude to people:

> "Whence he departed, he left enmity behind. Whither he went, conflict awaited him." [p.31]

After finally abandoning Old Physic c1784 he embarked on a literary career, launching into a series of translations from French, English and other tongues, with immense eagerness. He did not just translate them, but also impudently added comments and ideas of his own, especially where he disagreed with the writer on a certain point:

> '[in 1784]... he translated Demarchy's 'The Art of Manufacturing Chemical Products' from the French. It was an elaborate work in two volumes, to which he made numerous additions of his own.' [p.34]

It is interesting that his desire to abandon allopathy was not just because it didn't work too well. He was temperamentally quite unsuited to deceive his patients and 'calm their fears' when he knew full-well that most treatments on offer were useless:

> '...he was not more clumsy or stupid than other doctors; he simply lacked that power to shuffle off responsibility which enabled them to face every failure'. [p.43]

Gumpert identifies clearly Hahnemann's attitude towards allopathy, while an assistant to the town's physician in Dresden:

> 'Hahnemann...practised his profession only to obtain definite proofs against it...he was in the

> *fortunate position of being able to examine a very large number of patients and to treat them according to his own discretion, while large experimental stations were at his disposal.' [pp.49-50]*

He yearned to become famous for something and to turn his talents into cash for his growing family.

> *'Hahnemann could invent a number of dazzling diversions in the twinkling of an eye. He translated Demarchy's 'The Art of Distilling Liqour' [in 1785] and 'The Art Of Manufacturing Vinegar' [in 1787] from the French. His name was becoming famous, and his assistance sought by rich and enterprising merchants...' [p.51]*

He especially revered Lavoisier, the famous French chemist, and went to a public gathering for Lavoisier on his visit to Dresden. Unfortunately the two never met, because the room was too overcrowded with people:

> *'Lavoisier came to Dresden. He lodged at the Hotel de Pologne. Hahnemann's heart began to beat wildly at the thought of proximity of the great man. Lavoisier's achievements had set science aflame...he had a view of a handsome, stately man with elaborately dressed hair...the halo of political, financial and social power encircled his head...but not once did their glances meet.' [pp.54-55]*

This failure to meet is an example of those baffling misfortunes of fate, similar to that of Mendel and Darwin, who could theoretically have met up at the Great Exhibition in London in the Spring of 1851. Mendel died a miserable depressive due to the utter failure of the scientific community to appreciate the importance of his work, which remained in obscurity until 1900. In all such cases one is left to wonder how knowledge might have progressed if they had met.

> 'The more definitely Hahnemann passed into oblivion as a doctor, the greater grew his reputation as a writer on medical subjects. Orders for translations poured in on him from Leipzig.' [p.58]

> 'His despair grew with the realisation of his own inability to heal. He could only wait for the moment, as inevitable as the Day of Judgement, which would see him revealed as the apostle of a pure and true doctrine of medicine.' [p.59]

> 'Hahnemann...sat at his desk writing until his fingers were sore. There was no more talk of medical practice. The doctor was a fanatic devotee of the quill-pen, who now drowned his sorrows over his lost medical career in a sea of ink..' [p.61]

It is quite astonishing for us today to behold how truly systematic Hahnemann was:

> 'Day after day, he tested medicines on himself and others. He collected histories of cases of poisoning. His purpose was to establish a physiological doctrine of medical remedies, free from all suppositions, and based solely on experiments.' [p.92]

> 'Hahnemann sent his children into the fields to collect henbane, sumach, and deadly nightshade. They grew up like young priests of the Asclepieion of Cos... they felt the leaves, blossoms and tubers with small but expert hands... everyone was obliged to join in the work...for there was no other way to succeed in his titanic plan of rescuing the wealth of

> *natural remedies from the quagmire of textbooks, and displaying it in the bright light of experience.'* [pp.93-94]

> *'...he fought with redoubled energy for the purity of medicine. He struck deadly blows at three points: first, he believed that the doctor should prepare his own medicines; second, he advocated ever more definitely the administration of small doses; and, third, he was a most passionate opponent of mixed doses that contained a large number of ingredients.'* [p.96]

> *'He sought to discover the specific relations of certain medicines to certain diseases, to certain organs and tissues, he strove to do away with the blind chimney-sweeper's methods of dulling symptoms.'* [p.99]

> *'Even today, his enemies still wave their banners of hatred, and his supporters their banners of blind devotion.'* [p.111]

Once he had started his provings, again he involved the whole family in the venture:

> *'The family huddled together; and every free moment of every one of them, from the oldest to the youngest, was made use of for the testing of medicines and the gathering of the most precise information on their observed effects.'* [p.114]

He was interested in philosophy as well as chemistry, languages and medicine:

> *'The publication [in 1797] of Friedrich Schelling's 'First Draft of a System of Natural Philosophy' was contemporary with the records in which Hahnemann neatly and conscientiously assembled*

and numbered his observations of the symptoms excited in himself and his children by the most varied of medicines.' [p.114]

'Thus in Germany, doctors indulged in the most audacious and obscure philosophical speculations, even with their fingers on their dying patient's pulse.' [p.115]

The accounts of his first provings, the forerunner of his 'Materia Medica Pura', were first published in 1805 as a long essay, the 'Fragmenta de viribus':

'...Hahnemann's 'Fragmenta de viribus medicamentorum positivis... was published in Latin. This two-volume work gives us, for the first time, an insight into the remarkable, and so far unknown, methods of investigation which he employed. It supplies reports on the tests of twenty-seven medicines - the results of years of experiment on himself and his family.' [p.122]

He nursed a growing contempt for hypothetical systems of medical ideas, which did not work in practice, and believed that testing things through direct experiment was the only way to formulate a rational system of medical science:

'Medicine tests [provings] constitute one of the most critical points of Hahnemann's teachings. This grandiose attempt to acquire unhypothetical medical experience was outwardly justified by the complete lack of objective methods of investigation and experimental systems in those days... [Hahnemann had] the courage to break away from hypotheses and systems...' [p.122]

His Organon (first published 1810) was clearly modelled on some profound philosophical works and he seems to have regarded its aphorisms as sacrosanct:

> '...the 'Organon of the Art of Healing' - is presented in sections after the manner of a legal code. [its]... sections manifest the notable and intimidating terseness of legal paragraphs, which, despite their unequivocal and final character, can scarcely be understood without prolific commentaries. Many authoritative minds have expounded them, and have read into them profound significance or nonsense, according to their own estimate.' [p.133]

He was a peculiar, fussy and exacting man:

> 'Hahnemann's pedagogic ideal was discipline. Those who sided with him had no easy life. He was not a martyr but a fighter; not one of the persecuted but a persecutor.' [p.149]

In 1820 Hahnemann faced trial in Leipzig for contravening the apothecaries through 'dispensing his own medicines'. In his defence statement, he clearly indicates the nature of homoeopathy:

> 'My system of medicine has nothing in common with the ordinary medical art, but is in every respect its exact opposite... the new method of treatment, called homoeopathy, being the exact opposite of the ordinary medical art hitherto practised, has no preparations that it could give to the apothecary, has no compound remedies... thus the 'right to dispense' ...can by no means refer to the homoeopathic art of healing' [pp.176-7]

But Hahnemann lost his case:

> 'The old man sat silent, grey, inert, behind his white casebooks, and bowed his heavy head. But before the government could confirm the judgement, a near-miracle occurred. Couriers from Austria arrived in Leipzig, for the purpose of persuading Hahnemann to go to their country to undertake the treatment of Prince Schwarzenberg, who had been ill for some time.... a country where the practice of homoeopathy was forbidden... Hahnemann refused to enter the country which spurned his life-work... he told the couriers that the Prince must come to Leipzig. The Prince came.' [p.178]

> 'Throughout his life, Hahnemann remained a strange mixture of realist and idealist.' [p.185]

The house in Kothen where Hahnemann lived

Gumpert calls him 'the recluse of Coethen', but of Hahnemann's marriage to Melanie, Gumpert tells us:

> 'When this strange marriage had taken place, and had been sufficiently discussed, a storm of slander and vilification broke like a cloudburst...' [p.219]

> Wherever he went, he found trouble: '..scandal trotted behind Hahnemann like a well-trained dog' [p.222]

Gumpert considers the intriguing nature of Melanie in some depth:

> 'Melanie was... for her enemies, an ambitious and self-seeking intellectual... for the man who loved her, a gentle, wide-eyed, enchanted creature.' [p.222]

And his view of Paris:

> 'And the old man from another land came to know this wonderful city of Paris as a vision from the Arabian Nights. He came to know its mysterious magic formula, which combines the maximum of freedom with the strictest observance of tradition.' [p.234]

> 'The old gentleman grew thinner and more dwarflike. His knees bent in slightly; his torso was thrust forward, both when he walked and when he stood still... but the head, which ever more and more dominated the body, remained erect and sovereign.' [p.238]

> 'Hahnemann's fabulous age, and the magnificence which outwardly surrounded him [in Paris], increased the suggestion of his healing powers to a most improbable degree. Numerous tales of his prowess were in circulation.' [p.239]

> '[Melanie] never left his side. She mastered his case-

books, all the symptoms and most obscure notes of the Materia Medica Pura, as none of his pupils had ever done. She became a living compendium of homoeopathy.' [p.241]

Inevitably, I have missed out many other fascinating stories, from every phase of Hahnemann's life, but I hope to have conveyed the essence of this great book and the rare beauty of Dr. Gumpert's writing. Even though it lacks the fine factual detail of Haehl, it is so well-written and so deeply and insistently analytical of Hahnemann as a person, that it stands out as an exceptional work. I could not recommend this book more highly to all homoeopaths. It is an absolute gem and far and away the most engaging biography of the man.

■

ON HAHNEMANN'S COFFEE THEORY

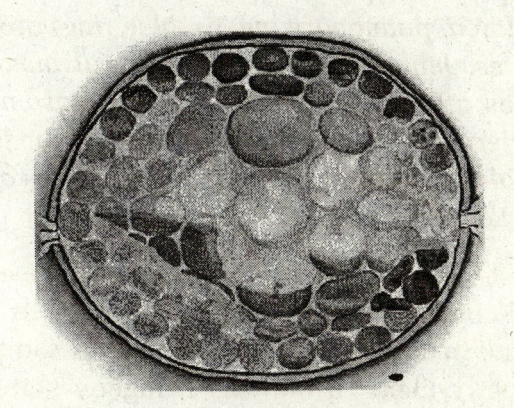

Sorcerer's Amulet, 1977

It is rarely mentioned today the strange theory that Hahnemann created before the Psora theory, that Coffee was the cause of all human illness. Reference is: 'On the Effects of Coffee from Original Observations' (Leipzig, 1803) and listed in his Lesser Writings, pp391-410.

> '...Hahnemann himself alludes to the essay he wrote upon the action of coffee in 1803, where he had ascribed the production of a multitude of chronic

diseases to the action of that all but universal beverage, and he confesses that he thinks he had ascribed an exaggerated importance and gravity to its use; since his discovery of psora as the cause of many chronic diseases, he is inclined to attribute to that agent the production of most of those affections he had imputed to coffee.' (Dudgeon, 1853, Lectures on the Theory & Practice of Homoeopathy, p259)

I will not quote in full length his essay, but in the course of it Hahnemann ascribes the following chronic disorders to the use of coffee:

'constipation, impotence, dental caries, abscesses in children, pulmonary mucus, blue rings around the eyes, leucorrhea, ulcers, general megrim, nervous affections, chronic diseases, insomnia, stammering of speech, lack of appetite for food, ophthalmias, rattling in the chest, etc.' (On coffee, 1803, Lesser Writings, pp401-9)

This list very closely resembles many of the entries in his list of conditions for Psora (given both in Chronic Diseases and in other essays from the 1820's and 30's) and it is perfectly clear to me - as Dudgeon states - that Hahnemann was tempted in 1803 to ascribe to Coffee a grand theory of chronic disease remarkably similar to that which he later, in 1827, ascribed to the Itch Animal of Scabies.

In the Chronic Diseases Hahnemann says this:

'That the drinking of warm coffee and Chinese tea...has further augmented the tendency of this period to a multitude of chronic diseases and thus aided psora, I least of all can doubt, as I have made

> prominent, perhaps too prominent, the part which coffee takes with respect to the bodily and mental sufferings of humanity, in my little work on the 'Effects of Coffee' (Leipzig, 1803). This perhaps undue prominence given was owing to the fact that I had not then as yet discovered the chief source of chronic disease in Psora.' (Chronic Diseases, Jain Edition, 1978, (Tafel translation of 1896), Vol 1, pp13-14)

It therefore follows that he was, through strong mental impulse, trying to develop a theory of chronic disease with a pathological basis in the lives of people - which is fine, I do not object to that per se - it shows great mental powers. He even goes as far as to say (in his essay of 1803) that children and babies accumulate the ill-effects of coffee from their parents and from being in the same rooms as coffee drinkers. Being convinced in his mind of the certainty of the theory apparently impelled him to then find 'evidence' for it, no matter how ridiculous. That was my main point. Further, one might say, he showed a peculiar and recurrent tendency to create 'grand theories' upon what is arguably scant evidence.

It is also of interest to note that he recommends Coffee as the chief antidote (along with Nux vomica) for the excessive action of Psorinum. I can testify personally from clinical experience both to the wide usefulness of Psorinum as a profoundly acting remedy and to Coffee as its chief antidote. I actually believe the Psora theory, but not the one about Coffee. I am not a coffee drinker.

I do not mean to imply that Hahnemann was wrong to look for evidence for grand theories. Quite the reverse, it shows he believed that we live in a meaning-saturated universe, and that through careful observation we can discern patterns and then reveal the meanings that account for those patterns. But the inevitable tendency of such a superior mental tendency is also the occasional and forgiveable (?) lapse of 'jumping to conclusions on scant evidence'. I think the Coffee theory is a good example both of Hahnemann's superior mental powers and of his occasional tendency to make up a grand theory from scant evidence.

I think it is clear from the quote from Dudgeon above, that he was in pursuit of a grand theory and did for a short time hold coffee as such a theory.

Firstly, we have the observation that the deeper-acting psoric remedies help the vital force to bring to the surface and expel the problems of suppressed psora and push them towards outward manifestations. Secondly, we can say that coffee appears to suppress them inwards even further. So here we can see in this a simple dipole action of push in or push out. Maybe it is this which lies at the heart of Hahnemann's observations and the link he made between coffee and Psora, which we have been discussing? Maybe this is also why coffee is the natural antidote for Psorinum?

In other words, the link between coffee and psora is not coincidental and there is a meaningful basis to it. Yet such a suppressive substance can be helpful, for example when the action of Psorinum is excessive and it is throwing too much material to the surface than the patient can cope with. In such a situation coffee can be safely used to dampen and neutralise the activity of the psoric miasm in a positive way. It is also interesting as it illustrates the positive and negative actions of remedies and relates to their primary and secondary effects.

But in general terms, according to Hering's law those things that bring material to the surface and increase expulsion are generally good for the long-term good of the patient, while those things that 'push in' are harmful to the long-term good of the patient. So here we can see that coffee has an opposite (suppressive) effect to what is good for the patient. It suppresses by pushing inwards. This is in the opposite direction to the path of cure.

In nature cure we find a similar situation: that which encourages excretion and expulsion of toxins (eg fruit diet, exercise, fasting, steam baths, etc) is good for the patient, while that which pushes inwards or increases toxins is bad (eg antiperspirants, medicaments applied to the skin and alkaloids like coffee and nicotine). So here we see a direct parallel between nature cure and homoeopathy - based entirely upon separate healing traditions with minimal cross- dialogue - in terms of the effects of a regime of treatment and its value or worth to the longer term benefit of the patient. I suspect this can be duplicated for many other types of natural medicine. Another example: in the case of psychotherapy, in most cases progress is made not through hiding material from the past but through bringing it out and reviewing it.

So I would summarise this by saying that Coffee is very probably a natural suppressant of symptoms and miasms, that pushes inwards the psoric miasm and aspects of it. This is also in accord with Hahnemann's original observations about Psora being both 'hydra- headed' and based upon 'evil suppressions of outer conditions'. And his claim that coffee is a purely medicinal substance. The psoric remedies (and especially Sulphur and Psorinum) and the aims of constitutional homoeopathic treatment, act very largely to bring to the surface and expel that which lies buried. The two work antagonistically and thus coffee in the last analysis - imho - has to be regarded as harmful to the overall and long-term health of the patient (whether it neutralises the action of their remedies or not), while psoric remedies and homoeopathy in general are good for the patient.

The underlying pattern is also that homoeopathy (esp constitutional and miasmic treatment) tends to bring to the surface undigested and unresolved material which needs to be reviewed, resolved and re- experienced (re-integrated) - mental and physical, miasmic or genetic. As Kent said, 'That is the path to cure and there is none other.'

■

HAHNEMANN AND HIGH POTENCY

Welsh Mountains, 1991

Hahnemann's views and practice in relation to potency are very important as they relate both to how homoeopathy has developed since his time and also in relation to how people have viewed and interpreted his teachings in the various editions of the *Organon*. As a result of which many dogmas have arisen. Also there is a link with the high-low split and the purists and pragmatists within homoeopathy. All these problems and issues revolve around the issue of potency use —or strongly reflect it. It is useful to take a brief glance at what some of the early high potency enthusiasts were doing and what Hahnemann thought of them. These include Schréter, Boenninghaussen and Jenichen amongst others.

SCHRÉTER AND HAHNEMANN ON POTENCY

Baron Clemens Maria Franz Von BŒNNINGHAUSEN(1785-1864)

In an article printed in Student Homoeopath 36, (Oct 1995), pp.23-26, by Serena Lambrughi, 'A Question of LM Prescribing', there was a discussion about the use of the higher potencies by Hahnemann.

There are two major points about Hahnemann's use of potency which need stating. First of all, adopting a very flexible approach in general, he experimented continuously with potency and kept an open mind about the whole issue. Secondly, he knew very well that Boenninghausen, Korsakoff, Jenichen and others, for example, had developed and were freely indulging an enthusiasm for using the higher potencies, but he stuck by his assertion that 30 was 'high enough for any homoeopath'.

It is perhaps easy to overstate Hahnemann's actual interest in the higher potencies. Haehl says re a letter to Dr Schréter of Lemberg:

'... there existed a small body of overzealous students, anxious to outstep the Master in potentising... they produced a 60th, 90th, a 200th and finally even a 1500th potency. Amongst these enthusiasts the principal part was played by Dr Gross of Jüterbogk, Dr Schréter of Lemberg and General Korsakoff in Russia. They became the real founders of the theory of high potencies, which later on found an industrious and zealous protagonist in Stapf.' (R Haehl (1922) Samuel Hahnemann His Life and Work (2vols), vol 1, p321)

Hahnemann himself felt, in 1829, the urgent necessity of a limit in potentisation and declared the ultimate degree of dilution to be the 30th centesimal potency. It is true however, that he had already exceeded this limit in 1825, when, as we saw, he recommended Thuja for gonorrhea; in that case he had described the 60th potency as being particularly efficacious.

How anxious he was at that time to set a limit to the over-enthusiasm of his students, is best shown by the following letter to Dr Schréter, of Lemberg, of the 12 Sept 1829:

'I do not approve of your potentising medicines higher than to XII and XXII [my emphasis] - there must be a limit to the matter, it cannot go on indefinitely. But by definitely deciding that homoeopathic medicines should be diluted and potentised up to X (= 30 CH) a homogeneous process arises in the cures of all homoeopaths and if they describe a cure, we are able to work after them in the same degree, since they are operating with the same tools as we are. Then our enemies *cannot reproach us with all having nothing definite, no fixed standard.'*

Thomas Indsley bradford (1847-1918)

A similar reply was sent by Hahnemann to the Russian General Korsakoff, who was desirous of potentising unmedicated globules by mixing them well with one or several granules soaked in the medicine. The General had gone so far as to say that he had succeeded in transmitting all the properties of Sulphur to 13,500 unmedicated granules from one single globule of Sulphur 30.

'In the year 1829, Hahnemann came upon the strange idea of setting up a kind of standard dose for all curative remedies used in homoeopathy. This was to be the 30th centesimal.' (Haehl, Vol 1, pp321-22)

FROM BRADFORD (1895) LIFE AND LETTERS OF HAHNEMANN

He says to Shréter in 1829 *'your want of success in the cases you have recorded is certainly owing to the rapid changes of the remedies, the often unfitting dilution and dynamization, and the too large doses.*

'Once you have spoilt matters with these three faults for about four weeks, it is very difficult to set them right again. My advice is that you bide rigorously

> by the precepts contained in my book on Chronic Diseases; and if possible, go still further than I have done, in allowing a still longer period for the antipsoric remedies to exhaust their action, in administering still smaller doses than I have advised, and in dynamizing all antipsoric medicines up to thirty.' (Bradford, 1895, pp466-7)

Further on, Bradford has this to say about Hahnemann's use of potencies at the close of his life:

> 'In 1853, Dr J Chapman writing to the London Homoeopathic Times says 'My reason for addressing you is to prove what was the actual practice of Hahnemann during his residence in Paris, and to the close of his life. I have before me, while I write, the box of medicines he carried about with him...' (ibid p471)

> 'Since my last letter I have seen two boxes of homoeopathic medicines which Hahnemann selected for a patient in the years 1841-42... among them is Arnica 3 and Euphrasia 6 and other low dilutions. None is higher than thirty...the dilutions are 6, 9, 12, 18, 24 and 30. I have what I consider the best possible authority for stating that Hahnemann used no medicine beyond thirtieth dilution.' (Chapman in Bradford, p473; see also Dudgeon p407).

On balance this is probably a rather rash and misleading claim for Chapman to have made. As Dudgeon candidly states, Hahnemann 'in the last [ie. 5th] edition of the Organon even he speaks approvingly of the 60th, 150th and 300th dilutions.' And 'in the last years of his life he allowed himself...the 60th, 150th and even 300th dilution (Dudgeon, 1853, p407-8).

However, Bradford then lists the entire contents of the medicine box by name and potency. For the sake of brevity, we can summarise the full contents of that medicine box as follows:

Potency	Number	Percentage of Phials of total
6	3	2.1%
9	2	1.41%
12	21	14.8% - 28.2%
18	19	13.4%
24	47	33.1%-68.3%
30	50	35.2%
total	142	100%

As we can see from this data, the 'late Hahnemann' strongly preferred the potencies 24 and 30 above all others (68% = 2/3 of his prescribing). As is also clear, the vast bulk of his prescribing (96%) was done with just 4 potencies - 12, 18, 24 and 30. So it is quite incorrect therefore, to imply that he habitually used the higher potencies. He may have done so very occasionally. But it is clear that these were just occasional excursions into unfamiliar territory and that he had little real interest in the high potencies. In truth, the vast bulk of his practice relied entirely upon the potencies shown above. These are the actual remedies he habitually carried around with him. The authority of the above list rests entirely upon this single fact - he would hardly carry around with him remedies he never used, and he would carry around with him higher potencies if he were in the habit of using those.

The other major point regards the use of the LM potencies. As we know, Hahnemann rejected the use of higher potencies not only because he was opposed to the sort of quasi-mystical ideas some of Kent's predecessors were keen on (see above), but, chiefly, as Serena Lambrughi states (Lambrughi, p23), out of regard for the patient, to protect them from the homoeopathic aggravation and to give them the gentlest yet most curative benefit in infinitesimal doses of the most similar remedy. The LM potencies evolved entirely from this practical consideration as they proved to be very gentle yet also effective, which is why he is quoted at the end of his long life, as praising and recommending them with the highest enthusiasm. Likewise his enthusiasm for the less widely popular olfaction. We must conclude that Hahnemann was an intensely practical man.

This point is also made by Dr Patel in his article in SH 37.

> '...these potencies are a boon to sensitive patients, who react with centesimal scale very badly.' (SH 37 p20).

It is possible to give a brief summary of the main points about Hahnemann's use of potency, based upon an analysis of data drawn from a wide range of major sources about Hahnemann's prescribing habits at different periods in his life, such as Bradford, Haehl, Chronic Diseases, The Lesser Writings, Dudgeon, Cook and Rima Handley.

A definite progression emerges. Firstly, we can see that although he started to use similar medicines around 1790,

Hahnemann did not conduct the first experiments with dose reduction until the year 1798.

> 'We cannot fail to be struck by the sudden transition from the massive doses he prescribed in 1798 to the unheard-of minuteness of his doses only one year later, and we can but guess the causes for this abrupt transition.' (Dudgeon, 1853, pp395-6)

This includes 2x, 4x and 2c. In 1799 he began to reduce the dose further, using 5x, 6x, 3c and 8x, or their crudely 'dilute-and-shake' or 'spoonful-in-a-glass-of-water' equivalents. In 1800 he begins more systematically to use 10x and in 1803 the first of the centesimal potencies, 12c, makes its debut appearance.

In 1805 the 18th centesimal dilution appears, which was to prove one of his most consistently popular potencies, and which he used throughout his long career. Widespread use of this potency appears to have died with him. There is then a long gap in new developments, but in 1814 8c, 15c and 16c all make their first appearance in his writings. In 1816 30c makes its first appearance and this remained his most extensively used and most highly recommended potency of all time. Another one of his favourite potencies, 24c, was one of the last, not appearing in his writings until 1821.

Further developments include the first mention of 6c in 1819 and the first mention of 60c in 1824. In 1830 he first mentions *Olfaction* as a means of drug administration and this remained a very popular method with him until the end of his life. Again, he was motivated entirely by gentleness combined with effectiveness. The method involved:

> '...olfaction (a là last para Organon; see also Dudgeon, 1853, p505 & pp507-9) using small phials of granules, containing 2.5 mls and a cork. Few people knew about olfaction - inhaling deeply the remedy bottle rather than placing it on the tongue. Doctors criticised it as a nonsense. Dr William Boyd hammered that type of criticism saying it was invalid unless you had experience of the technique...' (John Pert, telephone conversation re Scottish homoeopathy, Jan 1991).

Finally, in 1838 the LM potencies make their first appearance. It is also interesting to point out that Hahnemann never specifically mentioned 3x, one of the most popular English potencies of the last century, and still widely used on the Continent and in the Tissue Salts of Schuessler. Nor did he make great use of the now popular 6c before 1820, though he used it extensively in his closing years (1830-43).

We can deduce from all this, that to truly call oneself a Hahnemannian homoeopath one would likewise have to use potencies 12, 18, 24 and 30 for at least three quarters of one's overall prescribing. Those homoeopaths who claim to be Hahnemannian, while mainly using 30, 200 and 10M, are quite clearly exaggerating their similarity to the prescribing habits of Hahnemann himself. And as we have seen, they are in fact much closer to Kent than anyone else.

There is further detailed evidence in an article called: Classical Hahnemannian Homoeopathy Or What Hahnemann really did - Preliminary Observations by Rima Handley (and it comes from The Homoeopath 7:3, Spring 1988 pp106-114). The information it contains is based upon a study of the 17 Krankenjournalen or Casebooks held in Stuttgart which Samuel and Melanie wrote in Paris between 1835 and c1847. Some are just by Melanie after Samuel's death. Each book is handwritten in French and consists of c450 pages. 13 are of the joint practice and four just of Melanie's. It appears from Handley's studies that Hahnemann did all sorts of things in his Paris practise which previously he had in his writings expressly forbidden others to do. These include:

1. Most cases are opened with Sulphur - some 90% of chronic cases. Sulphur was often repeated frequently in the early stages until symptoms of another remedy appeared and then that was given. Sometimes only Sulphur was used throughout.

2. He also prescribed for anything that came up in the course of treatment eg some cough or symptoms of an acute nature.

3. He treated the return of old symptoms in the same way. In every case he regarded the return of old symptoms with delight and saw a new symptom as an indication of the next new remedy.

4. He also commonly used two remedies at the same time.

5. He frequently prescribed one remedy by mouth and another by Olfaction, which he maintained.

6. The LM's he used in many different ways and asserted that they— (a) could be repeated very frequently without aggravation or harm andb. maintained continuous stimulation of the vital healing force. The LM's appear therefore to be mainly a product of his impatience with slow cases!

7. In his early days in Paris he mainly used 3, 6, 9, 12, 18, 24 and 30 potencies He then progressed to using the 200 and the 95. These remedies were often repeated frequently every day sometimes twice a day, or more up to a max of 6 times a day! He often used widely different potencies in the same case, going lower for acute conditions and higher for chronic work. He tended to use LM's for chronic and the centesimals for any acute symptoms that emerged.

8. He often repeated remedies very frequently. He abandoned the centesimal potencies mainly because of their power to produce aggravations. He suspected that the higher dilutions (above 30) would increase aggravations and he was very cautious about them. He used two remedies at once when he felt it necessary. He treated most symptoms as they came up.

The contents of one of Hahnemanns' medicine cases as shown in Bradford:

Potency	Number
6	3
9	2
12	21
18	19
24	47
30	50
sum	142

Gathering data from other sources we can get some ideas of what Hahnemann did in his final years.

As we can see from this data, the 'late Hahnemann' strongly preferred the potencies 24 and 30 above all others (68% = 2/3 of his prescribing). As is also clear, the vast bulk of his prescribing (96%) was done with just 4 potencies - 12, 18, 24 and 30. So it is quite incorrect therefore, to imply that he habitually used the higher potencies. He may have done so very occasionally. But these were just occasional excursions into unfamiliar territory and that he had little real interest in the high potencies. In truth, the vast bulk of his practice relied entirely upon the potencies shown above. This list certainly represents his final view on the potency question. These are the actual remedies he habitually carried around with him. The authority of the above list rests entirely upon this single fact - he would hardly carry around with him remedies he never used, and he would carry around with him higher potencies if he were in the habit of using those.

For Hahnemann data taken from T L Bradford's 'Life and Letters of Hahnemann' (1895, chs 82-85, pp453-75).

Potency	Number	Percent
TINCT	10	4.46
1x	1	0.3
1c	1	0.45
2	4	1.8
3x	1	0.45
5x	1	0.45
3c	3	1.34
6x	2	0.92
4	1	0.45
6	9	4.02
15x	2	0.92

Potency	Number	Percent
9	9	3.02
10 3		1.34
12	32	14.3
15	6	2.7
*16	1	0.45
18	28	12.5
20	1	0.45
21	1	0.45
24	52	23.2
30	59	26.34
TOTAL	224	100

The final phase of his prescribing runs from 1830 to 1843, comprising 27.7% 30c, 25.6% 18c and 25.2% 6c. Also during this phase (from c1840 onwards) he makes increasing use of olfaction and the LM potencies.

OTHER DATA:1. In a photograph of part of the contents of a Hahnemann medicine case from the Robert Bosch collection in Stuttgart, approximately dated c1840, the following remedies and potencies are clearly visible:

Ran b 24; Coccion 24; Aethusa cynap 12; Sabad 18; China 18; Rhus 24; Vinca 24; Natrum carb 24; Capsic 18; Selen 18; Opium 24; Spongia 12; Bryonia 12; Teucrium? mar 18; Calc hydr? 24; Merc sol 24; Cantha 24; Staphy 24 and ? 18 and ? 24. If we process this we get as follows:

Potency	Number	Percent
12	3	15
18	6	30
24	11	55
TOTAL	21	100

We can therefore conclude that he changed his views on potency very frequently and mainly in the light of clinical experience rather than 'neat theories'. It is also clear that he was moving higher and higher and that in his later phase he settled both on Olfaction and the LM or Q potencies as being especially gentle and effective methods of drug administration. He regarded them as superior for practical reasons, not out of any quasi-mystical notions.

If we add up all of the potencies mentioned in Rima Handley's *A Homoeopathic Love Story*, (pp117-143) we get yet another snapshot of his use of potency in the 1835-43 period, as follows:

Potency	Number	Percent
3	2	3.4%
6	3	5.1%
9	1	1.7
12	4	6.8
18	6	10.2
24	9	15.3
30	16	27.1
100	1	1.7
200	12	20.3
M	2	3.4
LM's	3	5.1
Sum	59	100

Another good source of data is that of Michalowski et al (1989) based upon Paris Casebook DF5 dated 1838-42. (Arnold Michalowski, Sabine Sander & Karl-Otto Sauerbeck,

Therapiegeschichte Materialen zu Samuel Hahenamanns Pariser Praxis, (rough translation - therapeutic historical material from Samuel Hahnemann's Paris Practice) Med GG 8, 1989, pp171-196, Stuttgart)

The results for their data is as follows:

Potency	Number	Percent
3	1	0.424
6	2	0.85
9	1	0.424
12	7	2.97
18	22	9.32

Potency	Number	Percent
24	59	25
30	104	44.1
LM's	40	16.95
Sum	2	36

Finally, by combining and re-averaging all the above data we can obtain a final or global average for his last years in Paris. This includes the Stuttgart medicine cases 1 and 2, Bradford 1 and 2, Rima Handley, the 6th phase and the Michalowski data.

This is as follows:

Potency	Number	Percent
3	0.581	0-3.8
6	9.13	0.85-25.2
9	1.36	0.42-3.02
12	13.4	2.97-35

18	17.98	9.32-30
24	22.83	15.3-55
30	27.6	22-44.1
100	2.26	0-1.7
200	3.06	0-20.3
M	0.53	0-3.4
LM's	3.33	0-16.95
Sum	774	Samples

To assess how accurate this final % is we can compare it with the previous data. This is shown in the range column, which gives the max and min for that potency (excluding 0 for some) and thus indicates how widely from the mean the samples vary or are spread. The most compact samples (closest to the mean) are potencies 3, 9, 18, 24 and 30. This means they have a narrow range, cluster tightly about the mean and thus the average shown can be considered to be a very reliable indication of Hahnemann's actual prescribing habits for that potency. It means that most people agree on his actual use of that potency and that there is much less variation in his use of it. I think we can safely assert that an analysis of 774 cases is fairly good and statistically very significant.

Those other potencies with much wider ranges (6, 12, etc) were clearly subject to more variation by the man himself, i.e. he used them a lot at times and little at other times. It also means that those potencies with narrow ranges (mainly 3, 9, 18, 24 and 30) he was generally happy with and made frequent use of compared to those with wide ranges with which we can assume he had problems and his use of them therefore varied more over time.

Finally, we can safely say that Hahnemann at the end of his career mainly used potencies 12, 18, 24 and 30 and that this comprised some 81% of his total prescribing . If we then add potencies 6 and 9, we cover some 94% of his total prescribing. Clearly it is true that he was beginning to experimnt with higher potencies and was making increasing use of the LM's for reasons already stated. Those homoeopaths who can with honesty say they use mainly potencies 12, 18, 24 and 30 can truly call themselves Hahnemannian. The rest cannot.

Most of this flies in the face of what most people think he did and of course, with his directions in the 5th edition of the Organon and also it conflicts with Kent's directions, amongst others. Much more detail will of course be found in Rima Handley's forthcoming book on the same subject.

■

HAHNEMANN'S MIASM THEORY AND MIASM REMEDIES

The theory of miasms originates in Hahnemann's book *The Chronic Diseases* which was published in 1828, around the same time that he decided to fix 30c as the standard potency for all homoeopaths. He declared that the theory was the result of 12 years of the most painstaking work on difficult cases of a chronic character combined with his own historical research into the diseases of man.

Dream of Egypt, 1995

The three miasms given in that work are held to be responsible for all disease of a chronic nature and to form the foundation or basis for all disease in general. This latter aspect was then to receive considerable amplification from Kent. Kent was also able to clearly identify those remedies that relate to each miasm.

Though now generally accepted by most homoeopaths without question, at the time, the theory was generally greeted with disbelief and derision from all but the most devoted followers. This can be explained in part by the primitive nature of medical science at that time, which was not really very willing accommodate any theory for the origin of disease, least of all such a grand and all-embracing one.

The word miasm means a cloud or fog in the being. The theory suggests that if 100% of all disease is miasmatic, then 85% is due to the primary and atavistic miasm Hahnemann called Psora. The remaining 15% of all disease he held to be either syphilitic or sycotic, being derived from suppressed Syphilis or suppressed Gonorrhoea. Hahnemann unlike Kent later attached no moral dimension whatsoever to the sexual nature of the two latter miasms. Kent of course, emphasised this a great deal. Which is hardly surprising in the somewhat Puritanical atmosphere of nineteenth century small town America.

Taking them in reverse order, we can depict the main characteristic features of each miasm.

SYCOSIS

This miasm is held to be responsible for many sexual and urinary disorders, and affections of the joints and the mucous membranes. Also those conditions worsened by damp weather and by contact with the sea. Thus arthritis and rheumatism, asthma, catarrhs, bronchitis, cystitis and warts are all regarded as partly or mainly sycotic in character. The wart came to be seen as the underlying archetype of this miasm as it is also held to be responsible for all warty excrescences and growths. Chief remedies are Thuja, Lycopodium, Natrum sulph, Causticum, Kali sulph, Staphysagria, Calc and Sepia amongst many others.

SYPHILIS

This miasm is held to be responsible for many diseases of the nervous system, the blood and skeleton as well as a range of psychological disorders, including alcoholism, depression, suicidal impulses, insanity, loss of smell and taste, blindness, deafness and ulcerations. It is also associated with many heart conditions, some vesicular skin eruptions and diseases that have a definite nocturnal periodicity. Chief remedies are Arsenicum, Aurum, Mercury, Phosphorus and Lycopodium, Nitric acid, amongst many others.

PSORA

The word Psora is derived from the Hebrew 'Tsorat' and Greek 'Psora' and means a groove or stigma. Hahnemann held that all non venereal chronic diseases are Psoric. That includes most diseases of a chronic nature, all skin diseases, most mental illness other than syphilitic ones, allergies, varicose veins, haemorrhoids, most dysfunctional diseases of organs and systems, etc.

He lists among others, catarrhs, asthma, pleurisy, haemoptysis, hydrocephalus, stomach ulcers, scrotal swelling, jaundice, swollen glands, cataract, diabetes, tuberculosis, epilepsy, fevers and suppressed urine as all being typically psoric manifestations. Plus, of course, the whole gamut of skin problems.

Chief Psoric remedies he suggests include Sulphur, Natrum mur, Calc carb, Arsen alb, Lycopodium, Phosphorus, Mezereum, Graphite, Causticum, Hepar sulph, Petroleum, Silica, Zinc and Psorinum amongst many others.

Hahnemann also claimed that Psora was the most ancient and insidious miasm, and that it was derived from skin eruptions of various types in the past, such as scabies (Itch), leprosy and psoriasis. These had been contracted by ancestors or in one's own early childhood. The suppression of these conditions especially through the use of ointments he held to be the primary cause of Psora.

> 'Psora is that most ancient, most universal, most destructive, and yet most misapprehended chronic miasmatic disease which for many thousands of years has disfigured and tortured mankind... and become the mother of all the thousands of incredibly various chronic diseases...' [Chronic Diseases, p9]

Kent, in his Lectures, then greatly enlarged upon the theory, proposing that Psora was the foundation of all other illness, without which mankind would be pure and healthy both in mind and body, as in the Garden of Eden. He thus regarded Psora as being equated with the 'Fall of Man' and with original sinfulness. He portrayed Psora in this highly moralistic light as also being the foundation of the sexual miasms that came later.

Miasm Theory & Miasm Remedies

'You cannot divorce medicine and theology. Man exists all the way down from his innermost spiritual to his outermost natural.' [Lesser Writings, p.641]

'A man who cannot believe in God cannot become a homoeopath." [p.671]

'The body became corrupt because man's interior will became corrupt.' [ibid, p.681]

'Man...becomes disposed to sickness by doing evil, through thinking wrong...' [ibid, p.664]

'Psora is the evolution of the state of man's will, the ultimates of sin.' [ibid, p.654]

'This outgrowth, which has come upon man from living a life of evil willing, is Psora.' [ibid, p.654]

'Thinking, willing and doing are the 3 things in life from which finally proceed the chronic miasms.' [ibid, p.654]

'...had Psora never been established as a miasm upon the human race... susceptibility to acute diseases would have been impossible... it is the foundation of all sickness.' [Lectures, p.126]

'Psora...is a state of susceptibility to disease from willing evils.' [ibid, p.135]

'The human race today walking the face of the earth, is but little better than a moral leper. Such is the state of the human mind at the present day. To put it another way everyone is Psoric.' [ibid, p.135]

'Psora...would not exist in a perfectly healthy race.' [ibid, p.133]

'As long as man continued to think that which was

true and held that which was good to the neighbour, that which was uprightness and justice, so long man remained free from disease, because that was the state in which he was created.' [ibid, p.134]

'The internal state of man is prior to that which surrounds him; therefore, the environment is not the cause...' [ibid, p.136]

'Diseases correspond to man's affections, and the diseases upon the human race today are but the outward expression of man's interiors... man hates his neighbour, he is willing to violate every commandment; such is the state of man today. This state is represented in man's diseases.' [ibid, p.136]

'The Itch is looked upon as a disgraceful affair; so is everything that has a similar correspondence; because the Itch in itself has a correspondence with adultery...' [ibid, p.137]

'How long can this thing go on before the human race is swept from the earth with the results of the suppression of Psora?' [ibid, pp.137-8]

'Psora is the beginning of all physical sickness... is the underlying cause and is the primitive or primary disorder of the human race.' [ibid, p.126]

'...for it goes to the very primitive wrong of the human race, the very first sickness of the human race that is the spiritual sickness...which in turn laid the foundation for other diseases. [ibid, p.126]

I think it is abundantly clear from these quotes that Kent took a very puritanical and moral line about the origins of disease within the human race and he apparently felt that Psora was equivalent to Original Sin or the Fall of Man.

Miasm Theory & Miasm Remedies

Hahnemann also pointed out the origins of his theory and the remedies that he decided had the power to eradicate the symptoms of a particular miasm.

The lists of miasmic remedies that Kent gives on **page 1406** of his Repertory are as follows:

SYPHILIS : Arg-m., **Ars-i.**, *ars-s-f.*, *ars.*, *asaf.*, **Aur-m-n.**, **Aur-m.**, **Aur.**, bad., benz-ac., *calc-i.*, *calc-s.*, carb-an., carb-v., *cinnb.*, clem., *con.*, cor-r., crot-h., *fl-ac.*, guai., hep., iod., kali-ar., kali-bi., kali-chl., **Kali-i.**, **Kali-s.**, lach., led., **Merc-c.**, **Merc-i-f.**, **Merc-i-r.**, **Merc.**, *mez.*, **Nit-ac.**, petr., *ph-ac.*, phos., **Phyt.**, sars., **Sil.**, staph., **Still.**, *sul-i.*, *sulph.*, **Syph.**, thuj.

SYCOSIS : *Agar.*, alum., alumn., anac., ant-c., ant-t., *apis.*, aran., **Arg-m.**, **Arg-n.**, *aster.*, *aur-m.*, aur., *aar-c.*, bry., *calc.*, carb-an., carb-s., carb-v., *caust.*, cham., cinnb., con., *dulc.*, euphr., *ferr.*, *fl-ac.*, *graph.*, hep., *iod.*, kali-c., **Kali-s.**, lach., Lyc., mang., **Med.**, merc., *mez.*, **Nat-s.**, **Nit-ac.**, petr., *phyt.*, puls., sabin., *sars.*, sec., *sel.*, **Sep.**, *sil.*, **Staph.**, *sulph.*, **Thuj.**

These are exactly the same as the lists given on p86 of Speight's work on the miasms.

Hahnemann lists the following as **Psoric remedies** in the Chronic Diseases: agar, alumina, ammon carb, ammon mur, anacardium, antimon crudum, arsen alb, aurum, aurum mur, bar carb, borax, calc carb, carbo an, carbo veg, caust, clem, colocynth, conium, cuprum, dig, dulc, euphorbium, graph, guaj, hepar, iodium, kali carb, lyc, mag carb, mag mur, manganum, mez, mur ac, nat carb, nat mur, nitric acid, nitrium, petroleum, phos, phos ac, platina, sars, sepia, silica, stannum, sulph, sulp ac, zincum.

To discover the true psoric remedies we must add together the remedies listed in the Repertory for a range of 'psoric' conditions. This means checking carefully all the symptoms and repertorising for all of them, gradually building up a master list of remedies that fit Psoric conditions. This exercise was highly recommended by Kent as a sure way of fixing in the mind the remedies of a particular miasm. It is also an excellent introduction to the miasms generally and is good for revision purposes. With computer programs like Radar and Cara this task become a lot easier than it was in Kent's or Hahnemann's day.

Taking some of Hahnemann's list of psoric conditions given above we can find the corresponding remedies as follows:

Phthisis (Kent p879) : *Acet-ac.*, **Agar.**, ant-t., *ars-i.*, *ars.*, *bar-m.*, *brom.*, *bufo.*, **Calc-p.**, *calc-s.*, **Calc.**, *carb-an.*, *carb-s.*, *carb-v.*, card-m., chlor., *con.*, *dros.*, *dulc.*, *elaps.*, *ferr-i.*, *ferr-p.*, fl-ac., *graph.*, *guai.*, **Hep.**, hippoz., **Iod.**, kali-ar., **Kali-c.**, *kali-n.*, *kali-p.*, **Kali-s.**, *kreos.*, *lac-d.*, *lach.*, led., **Lyc.**, *med.*, *merc.*, mill., *myrt.*, nat-a., *nat-m.*, *nit-ac.*, *ol-j.*, ox-ac., petr., *ph-ac.*, **Phos.**, *plb.*, **Psor.**, **Puls.**, samb., *sang.*, **Senec.**, *seneg.*, *sep.*, **Sil.**, **Spong.**, **Stann.**, still., sul-ac., **Sulph.**, **Ther.**, **Tub.**, **Zinc.**

Hayfever (Kent p326) : Ail., **All-c.**, *ars-i.*, *ars.*, *arum-t.*, **Arund.**, bad., *brom.*, *carb-v.*, cycl., *dulc.*, *euphr.*, *gels.*, iod., kali-bi., *kali-i.*, *kali-p.*, lach., *naja.*, **Nat-m.**, nux-v., **Psor.**, *puls.*, *ran-b.*, **Sabad.**, *sang.*, *sil.*, **Sin-n.**, *stict.*, teucr., *wye.*

Diabetes (Kent p691) : *Acet-ac.*, all-s., alumn., am-c., aml-n., *arg-m.*, *ars.*, *benz-ac.*, **Bov.**, *calc-p.*, *calc.*, camph., *carb-ac.*, *carb-v.*, *chel.*, chin-a., *chin.*, coff., *colch.*, conv., cupr., *cur.*, *elaps.*, *ferr-m.*, **Helon.**, *hep.*, *iris.*, *kali-chl.*, kali-n., *kali-p.*, *kreos.*, *lac-d.*, *lach.*, *lact-ac.*, *lec.*, lith., **Lyc.**, *lycps.*, lyss., mag-s., *med.*, morph., mosch., *nat-s.*, *nit-ac.*, op., petr., **Ph-ac.**, **Phos.**, *pic-ac.*, **Plb.**, *podo.*, rat., sal-ac., sec., *sil.*, *sul-ac.*, sulph., **Tarent.**, **Ter.**, *thuj.*, **Uran.**, zinc.

Varices lower limbs (Kent p1223) : *Ambr.*, arg-n., **Arn.**, *ars.*, calc-f., calc-p., **Calc.**, *carb-s.*, **Carb-v.**, card-m., *caust.*, clem., *crot-h.*, ferr-ar., *ferr.*, **Fl-ac.**, *graph.*, **Ham.**, *hep.*, *kali-ar.*, *kreos.*, lac-c., *lach.*, **Lyc.**, **Lycps.**, *nat-m.*, *plb.*, **Puls.**, sabin., sars., sil., spig., sul-ac., *sulph.*, *thuj.*, vip., **Zinc.**

Eczema (Kent p1312) : Alum., am-c., am-m., anac., ant-c., arg-n., **Ars-i.**, **Ars.**, astac., *aur-m.*, aur., **Bar-m.**, bell., bor., brom., bry., *calad.*, **Calc-s.**, **Calc.**, canth., carb-ac., carb-s., *carb-v.*, *caust.*, **Cic.**, clem., cop., **Crot-t.**, cycl., **Dulc.**, fl-ac., **Graph.**, **Hep.**, hydr., *iris.*, **Jug-c.**, **Jug-r.**, *kali-ar.*, kali-bi., kali-c., *kali-chl.*, *kali-s.*, lach., **Lappa-m.**, led., *lith.*, *lyc.*, merc., **Mez.**, nat-m., nat-p., nat-s., nit-ac., **Olnd.**, **Petr.**, phos., *phyt.*, **Psor.**, *ran-b.*, **Rhus-t.**, rhus-v., sars., sep., sil., staph., **Sul-i.**, **Sulph.**, thuj., viol-t.

Psoriasis (Kent p1316) : Alum., am-c., ambr., **Ars-i.**, *ars.*, aur., bor., bry., bufo., *calc-s.*, *calc.*, canth., carb-ac., chin., clem., cor-r., cupr., dulc., iod., *iris.*, *kali-ar.*, kali-br., *kali-c.*, kali-p., *kali-s.*, led., *lob.*, **Lyc.**, mag-c., *mang.*, merc-c., merc-i-r., *merc.*, *mez.*, *nit-ac.*, nuph., *petr.*, ph-ac., *phos.*, **Phyt.**, *psor.*, puls., ran-b., *rhus-t.*, sarr., sars., **Sep.**, sil., *sulph.*, tell., teucr., thuj.

Herpetic skin eruptions (Kent p1312) : Acet-ac., agar., *alum.*, am-c., ambr., anac., *anan.*, apis., *ars-i.*, **Ars.**, aster., aur., *bar-c.*, *bar-m.*, bell., berb., bor., **Bov.**, *bry.*, bufo., cadm., calad., **Calc-s.**, **Calc.**, caps., *carb-an.*, **Carb-s.**, *carb-v.*, *caust.*, chel., *cic.*, *cist.*, **Clem.**, cocc., com., **Con.**, crot-h., *crot-t.*, cupr., cycl., dol., **Dulc.**, **Graph.**, grat., hell., hep., hyos., iod., iris., *kali-ar.*, *kali-c.*, *kali-chl.*, *kali-i.*, kali-n., kali-p., *kali-s.*, kalm., *kreos.*, *lac-c.*, *lach.*, *led.*, **Lyc.**, mag-c., *mag-m.*, manc., mang., **Merc.**, mez., mosch., mur-ac., *nat-a.*, *nat-c.*, **Nat-m.**, nat-p., *nat-s.*, nit-ac., nux-v., *olnd.*, par., *petr.*, ph-ac., *phos.*, plb., *psor.*, puls., *ran-b.*, ran-s., **Rhus-t.**, rob., rumx., ruta., sabad., *sars.*, **Sep.**, **Sil.**, spig., spong., squil., stann., *staph.*, sul-ac., **Sulph.**, tarax., **Tell.**, teucr., thuj., valer., viol-t., zinc.

The idea is then to compact this data down by deleting all those remedies that only occur once or twice and then totalling up all the scores until we get a master list of 40 or so highest scoring remedies. It is these that are the major Psoric remedies. In essence, this is the method Hahnemann himself used to establish both the miasms and their corresponding remedies.

Since the 1950s it has been claimed that Tuberculosis and Cancer have developed into new miasms in their own right, most probably as offshoots of what Hahnemann termed the 'Hydra headed Psora miasm' (The Chronic Diseases, p14).

59 symptoms and major conditions were selected and repertorised using Kent's Rep. The symptoms were as follows:

TB (p879), TB incipient (p879), TB pituitous (p879), scabies (p1318), pso riasis (p1316), dandruff (p114), hair loss (p120), leprosy (p1314), cancer (p1346), cancer lupus (p1346), leukaemia (p1370), diabetes (p691), cataract (p236), blindness (p281), long sightedness (p280), short sightedness

Miasm Theory & Miasm Remedies

(p283), lack of reaction (p1397), takes cold easily (p1349), swollen neck glands (p474), indurated glands neck (p472), swollen tonsils (p469), swollen axillary glands (p880 1), buboes (p541), goitre (pp471), tooth decay (p431), deafness (p323), insanity (p56), asthma (p763), liver (p563), haemorrhoids (p619), itching anus (p622), offensive stools (p640), varicosities (p1223), numbness (limbs p1035), chilblains (p955), sweaty feet (p1183), offensive foot sweats (p1183), halitosis (p409), nasal crusts (p330), perianal moisture (p623), hayfever (p326), foul flatus (p618), cracking joints (p970), worms (p634), ulcers on legs (p1231), ringworm, Haemoptysis (p813), Hydrocephalus (p128), Stomach ulcers (p531), Scrotal swelling (p712), Jaundice (p1307), Dysuria (p656), Eczema (p1312), Psoriasis (p1316), Herpetic skin eruptions (p1312), Crusty skin eruptions (p1310), pleurisy (p836), epilepsy, swollen inguinal glands (p603),

These symptoms were chosen as they are in the list given by Hahnemann as of 'latent psora' or they are major diseases of modern life, which I have assumed to be predominantly more psoric than syphilitic or sycotic. I have assumed, like Hahnemann, that they are derived from suppressed scabies, leprosy or plague. They are disorders mentioned in Hahnemann's Chronic Diseases as often being the products of suppressed itch, or they are skin disorders in their own right. To an extent one major justification for choosing these symptoms is that they have all increased during for choosing these symptoms is that they have all increased during this century, which many take to be a confirmation of the Psora doctrine. The symptoms come from Chronic Diseases pp52 77 and include the expanded list he gives plus those listed by Juncker. Also included are those symptoms as major past or present diseases. All of these are assumed to be broadly psoric in accordance with Hahnemann's descriptions of the miasm.

If the symptoms used in this analysis are truly psoric; if Kent's Repertory is generally accurate; if the scoring system adopted here is OK; and if Hahnemann's list, expanded list, the assertions of Juncker and my own observations regarding Psorinum and conditions are all correct then the following remedies cannot be seriously considered as being truly Psoric remedies.

These are Am m, anac, ant t, arg m, aur m, borax, bovista, bromium, camphor, cantharis, carb ac, cistus, clematis, occculus, colchicum, colocynthis, crot h, digitalis, euphorbium, ferrum, ferr phos, guaj, kali chlor, kali nit, ledum, mag carb, mag mur, manganum, merc c, mur ac, nat ars, nat phos, platina, podophy, sang, sarsap, secale, selenium, spigelia, spongia, tarantula, veratrum. They are important remedies but they are not truly psoric.

This exercise now reduces Hahnemann's original list of 47 antipsorics to 32. It is possible that Hahnemann based his list of 47 on what he knew about them at that time. He simply fitted maybe? the symptoms of latent psora to those remedies he had proved at that time. The result was his list of 47.

I believe the claims made above are correct and that the remedies listed are not antipsorics. If a remedy is incapable of scoring more than 22 points out of a maximum of 120, then it cannot seriously be considered to cover that range and depth of major human diseases and is thus NOT a very profound remedy. And to be considered psoric a remedy must be profound. It must cover the major diseases of humanity as well as the symptoms of latent psora.

The preliminary results of repertorisation can be given as follows:

agar, alum, anac, ant c, ant t, apis, arg m, ars, ars i, ambr, aur, bar c, bar m, bov, brom, bry, bufo, CALC, calc p, calc s, canth, carb ac, carb an, carb s, carb v, caust, cham, chel, chin, cist, cocc, colch, con, crot h, cupr, dulc, fl ac, graph, hep, iod, kali ar, kali ci, kali carb, kali i, kali p, kali s, kreos, LACH, led, LYC, mag c, mag m, med, merc, merc c, mez, nat ar, nat c, nat m, nat p, nat s, nit ac, nux, petr, ph ac, PHOS, phyt, plat, plmb, podoph, psor, puls, sang, sec, sep, SIL, spig, spong, stann, staph, SULPH, sul ac, tarent, thuja, tub, verat a, zinc.

However, this is not the full results for the entire run. It just indicates the main thrust. There are many remedies here that fail to match up in range or depth to our expectations of a truly psoric remedy.

An alternative method using the page-length entry of the entry of each remedy in Hahnemann gives the following:

agar, alumina, am c, anac, ant c, ARS, aur, aur m, bar c, CALC, carb an, CARB V, caust, con, cupr, dulc, graph, hep, iod, KALI C, LYC, mag c, mag m, mez, nat c, nat m, NIT AC, petr, PHOS, ph ac, plat, SEP, SIL, stann, SUL, sul ac, zinc

Two other problem about miasms relate to (a) where the miasms are stored and what they actually are and (b) to how the miasms can be used in practice. On the first point it may be that the miasms are archetypes in the unconscious mind, or it may be that they are stored in the DNA or some other large molecule within the organism. These are just possibilities. Many would say 'what does it matter?'

On the point about the use of miasms in treatment, many people routinely give the corresponding nosode. For example to a child born with syphilitic skin vesicles, they might give Syphilinum rather than the simillimum say Merc. This would tend to be seen as an inappropriate use of the miasm concept, as the simillimum is what the patient needs, not the nosode. The routine use of Psorinum, Medorrhinum and Syphilinum is in general frowned upon because it is the simillimum that the patient needs and that will cure. Certainly the nosodes can do good work, but it should be used when it becomes the simillimum, not just routinely.

PROBLEMS

The miasm theory presents at least two main problems. The first is whether it is real or not and the second is how it has been variously interpreted in homoeopathy and how it continues to be interpreted in the clinical situation and for guiding and interpreting the unfolding of symptoms in a case receiving treatment. Clearly, if all chronic disease are miasmatic then surely all curative remedies must be miasmatic remedies. Thus Nux vom, Aconite, Belladonna and Rhus tox, etc cannot cure any chronic disorders. So what if they do cure such conditions? Does this prove the theory wrong or are they bigger remedies than people thought?

Another problem is whether all the so called 'miasmatic remedies' are really as important as they appear to be. How many people actually use Manganum, Iris, Am c, Am m, etc. Do such cases ever crop up in regular practice? If so, only very rarely. If they don't correspond to many persons then why are they classed as Psoric? Could it not be that they are more likely 'lesser remedies' that ape some of the features of true psorics?

Maybe modern homoeopaths should more seriously question its validity. Though we do not have space here to discuss this in any great depth, the theory does present these two problems and all I can do here is to outline their nature.

The miasms doctrine has also become unfortunately and perhaps unnecessarily tangled up both with Hering's Law and with Kentian metaphysics. Both of which are suspect on a number of grounds relating directly to actual practice. Hering's Law claims that symptoms get better under treatment in the reverse order of their appearance, from top downwards and from centre to circumference. Is this true? Under the influence of deep constitutional i.e. miasmatic remedies the law should be confirmed in this way. What if it isn't? Does that mean that the case is not cured or that the law is inaccurate? If the cure does not proceed in this way is it a true cure or merely a suppression? Is the remedy the true simillimum? Questions of this kind can lead straight into a wilderness of thorns and brambles where everything seems uncertain and painful!

Finally, on Kentian grounds the miasms and their remedies are regarded as 'high homoeopathy', the ultimate and only true homoeopathy, acting in that hallowed and rarefied realm of disease causation. This somewhat snooty view of homoeopathy has been questioned before. Is it a real claimant of the high ground or a pretender? Again, many years of observant practice are required to answer this question for yourself.

■

HAHNEMANN AND PARACELSUS: A HEAVENLY DIALOGUE

Jean-Baptiste Lamarck [1744-1829]

PARACELSUS: Ah, Dr. Hahnemann, nice to meet you, I have admired from afar your system of homoeopathica, but I at times despair that you perhaps threw away so much that was useful in previous systems.

HAHNEMANN: Yes, that is fair comment, but so each man is to the age he lives in. Your age gave us your complex system; my age of enlightenment and science produced me.

My system is the first true science of therapeutics, based upon clear and rational principles and grounded solely in experiments.

PARACELSUS: I disagree, of course. This so-called science is but make-believe. How can one practice medicine and understand the sick without a knowledge of the Christian universe we live in, God, the Devil and the causes of Sin? This is the problem with the medicine of today, they seem obsessed with evidence, but they only define it in chemical or physical terms; they ignore the inner man, the spirit and the spirit in nature that can be brought to bear upon this complex matter. They talk of causes yet know nothing of the cause of disease. The true causes are internal not external, they are moulded into the mortal souls of individuals. We come to this world with already pre-formed within us the predispositions to certain diseases. They are our specific and individual inheritance. They shadow our life. I despair they ignore so much that would benefit the sick.

HAHNEMANN: Your system, as I said before, was the product of your world and your times. Those times, that world, have been swept away forever since the reformation and the enlightenment. New world and new times came upon us. No-one could understand your system and your copious writings; there was no clear plan or message. You recommended different things on a whim, for no clear reason. The thread was lost and medicine became degenerated. By 1750, there was merely a vast panoply of conflicting systems, all vying with each other and verily none could claim the truth. Most physicians were fools, and very dangerous and incompetent fools at that. Looking for guidance, the intelligent man could find nothing in the past of much service. My system was devised through experiment and thus, as it works along clear principles, I feel justified in claiming it is scientific.

PARACELSUS: Yes, you are probably right and thank goodness, you got rid of those mixed drugs and high doses, which carried many poor souls into a premature meeting with the Reaper. However, I think you misunderstand my methods and ideas. Much of my writing was scribbled in a hurry and when travelling and I did not have time to consolidate, organise and reflect on it in old age, as I would have liked. The time given to me was but brief. This much, at least, the Lord decides. My system of medicine was very like yours, but it was rooted in the philosophy of Christ, Our Saviour, shot through like gold.

I think it was the English poet Milton who spoke of 'man's first disobedience and the fruit of that forbidden tree that first brought death into the world and all its woe'

- such is the basis of true therapeutics. Disease comes from sin and accords in its nature with the nature of the sin and affects the parts in which the sin was committed and forgiveness by Our Lord is the highest art of medicine; we physicians are mere handmaidens, midwives of Christ who dispense things plucked from His Garden. We do well to observe the nature of plants and their parts in order to discern God's secret will. What is more obvious than this? The plants and minerals of this earth are God-given to the physician.

HAHNEMANN: Yes, that is all very well, but does it work?

PARACELSUS - It works after a fashion and according to His design for each mortal soul. Sometimes miracles are performed but most days progress is very slow.

HAHNEMANN: Exactly, physicians are entitled to more accurate knowledge and clear principles. That is what medicine since 1800 has been about. Much clearing of rough ground had to be undertaken, and the removal of encrustations of belief and superstition before establishing clear principles and practical methods that work.

PARACELSUS: systematically removing The metaphysical! Because you could not understand or use it, you arrogantly assumed it was wrong and you were right. Is this sound logic?

HAHNEMANN: Medicine has been subject to the same changes as other disciplines. You seem keen to downsize science for the wrong reasons. Nothing useful has been thrown away; quite the reverse. Everything useful has been retained. What has been thrown away is the centuries-old baggage of claims, superstitions and beliefs that could not be substantiated and which contravened clear principles. For example, venesection. That was abandoned because it was clearly dangerous and it did not conform to any rational principle. It is simply untrue that being drained of a quart of blood does a sick person any good whatsoever. That is how progress has proceeded.

PARACELSUS: But what of the four humours? They are integral to our understanding of the functions of the body. How can you dispense with such a superb and simple idea?

HAHNEMANN: Because it was dangerous in routine use and also untrue. It did more harm than good; well, no good at all!

PARACELSUS: You seem just about as simplistic as these modern clinicians with all their instruments and chemical tests, throwing the baby out with the bathwater.

HAHNEMANN: I am proud to say I am a scientist and you should be more respectful of its achievements.

PARACELSUS: I do not see how you can separate medicine and theology. That is the main problem. You were the first to divorce medicine from theology. I watched you do it!

HAHNEMANN: What has theology got to do with it?

PARACELSUS: It has everything to do with it. What has happened in recent centuries is this severing of the material from the spiritual and a rupturing of the natural order of things. As Plato said, there is always an inner and an outer, invisible 'noumena' lie behind the visible 'phenomena'; thus, any physical medical system is useless if it does not address the inner side of man also. Today, they have so-called psychologia but it seems like a mass of conflicting theories that amount to nothing but baseless and changing opinions, which all deny spirit anyway. What possible use is there for such a thing?

As I understand it, in some respects, your homoeopathica does address both sides of man, because your remedies hit many spots in the organism at the same time - mind, body, emotions, sleep, etc. Thus, some lip-service is paid to the inner, or spiritual, but I am sorely aggrieved that you chucked out all my alchemy and astrology, and the 7 metals and thus the inner has been cast aside, and all you kept is the husk of the great seed. You kept the husk thinking it was the living seed. You threw aside the best part, the nutritious inner kernel. That is the problem with life since my passing. I can see now that the wrong direction has been taken. Human souls need deep remedies for their ailments, not chemicals and not just your potentised plant extracts.

HAHNEMANN: Oh yes, I agree with you that there is no spirit in modern medicine, none whatever. I was the last in the great line of vitalists. Myself and Stahl were the last of a distinguished lineage. Vitalism was finally banished in the 1800s once the idea of germs and vaccines had finally taken hold in the minds of these simple fools who call themselves physicians. Ever since that time, ever since Koch and Pasteur, the only things to interest physicians have been the molecule and the infectious agent. Every other cause of disease, internal or external, has been ridiculed, denied, ignored completely or relegated to the sidelines. It is a woeful business.

A Heavenly Dialogue

PARACELSUS: But this is such folly. This ignores the soul and its conduits in the subtle body. Lately, I have been studying the Chinese and Tibetan systems. They are so close to my own intimations that I am amazed such great minds must have walked this earth so long before us. The flow of this vital fluid, vital energy in the channels of the spirit is truly spectacular. That is verily the source of disorder. What Mesmer called magnetism, is the same as your vital force and the Qi energy of the Confucian scholars. It all goes back to Pythagoras, of course, and the thrice great Hermes.

Swedenborg also made a creditable contribution in his day, reviving my doctrines and inspiring the poet and artist, William Blake, as well as many of your own homoeopathists in the New World, such as the gifted Dr. Kent of Chicago. Drs Dudgeon and Clarke, in England, also gave good accounts of my work. I am also pleased that fragments of my esoteric teachings have flowed down to inspire other great minds like Goethe, Steiner and Emerson. It is all most gratifying.

HAHNEMANN: Yes, I studied such matters after graduating. I spent the best part of two years studying all the esoteric medical systems under the tutelage of von Brukenthal in Transylvania. His extensive library was the finest collection in the whole of Europe on astrology, alchemy and secret arts. Outside of the forbidden texts in the Vatican, his library was unsurpassed. I studied your writings and those of Rhumelius much of the time. I am sorry to say it made little impact upon my thinking. It made little sense to me.

PARACELSUS: I disagree. I think you copied me.

HAHNEMANN: I have been accused of this before by several physicians, but in honesty, I say to you that I did not plagiarise your works. Even Goethe called me *'this new Theophrastus'*. It is merely that I came to similar views through experiment and reading the literature. Mostly I was inspired through the study of poisonings.

PARACELSUS: The whole concept of disease as an imbalance of natural energies, and cure as a re-tuning or re-harmonising of the whole organism, which the Confucian scholars contend, is completely in harmony with my own ancient system. The Ayurvedic system of the Indians and the principles of self-purification in nature cure are also of great interest. There is great merit and wisdom in these ancient healing systems. Why are they completely ignored by modern clinicians?

HAHNEMANN: Regarding the other healing systems, I agree with you that they all possess some features, which modern physicians could usefully adopt or adapt. There is much to be learned from them. The problem is that these modern clinicians are entirely focused on what they call material evidence of efficacy. They have dispensed with holism and want to lead a clinical life dealing solely with specifics - specific drugs and specific diseases. They ramble endlessly about the precise nature of each condition as if each were a real entity separate from the patient, not realising that they speak of constructs that are really phantasms, visible only

> *'through the spectacles of their own hypothetical conceits'.*

We speak a completely different language. It does not matter how many times you tell them that there are no 'conditions', there are only patients, it makes no sense to them.

PARACELSUS: I despair that medicine, the holiest of arts, is now so debased these days. They are such literal-minded simpletons. They should seek to improve healthy functioning not just to palliate symptoms. Their drugs seem merely to juggle symptoms around the body. It is mere window-dressing at best; no fundamental cure occurs. Illness cannot exist in a pure body, in a pure mind. It is impossible. If only they could see. The causes of disease lie within, not in the germs or molecules. Of course, disease is a punishment from God for our sins - we live in a moral universe, a God-given matrix. True cure is a process of purification of the soul and body of man. How could it be otherwise?

I would often say to the weeping and wailing who consulted me - I can only do so much, more lies in God's hands; this is earth - it is by no means Heaven. Even the Muslims agree that this life is by no means Paradise. The Buddhists also assert that life is filled with suffering. Such being the case, there are certain limits upon medicine - theological limits imposed by the Almighty. Some truly are born to suffer. Look to Job and behold this simple fact. Even our individuality is an illusion. We come streaming out from God and stream back in at death. He is the vastness of the heavens and the inner silence of the human heart combined. That is who we are. We are parts of God, parts of a continuum. Thus, illness fulfils part of God's purpose for each one of us.

HAHNEMANN: Yes, that was Berkeley's philosophy too [26]. However, times have changed and we do not believe all that tosh these days!

PARACELSUS: But what of the seven metals, the seven planets, the inner and the outer, the cosmos, that resonance that must exist between all the layers of correspondences? You can cure a Mars person with Mars or Iron drugs or you may occasionally use Venus drugs. This is why your 'similia similibus' is incomplete - Galen was right in certain cases - 'contraria contrariis' - and Hippocrates also knew this. You just took similars as the ONLY principle, when in fact BOTH are of use.

I admit similars is the higher principle, the ideal, but not for every case. Likewise, with doses. Your tiny doses which caused such uproar! Even the physician to an English Queen called your infinitesimal doses 'an outrage to human reason'!

However, small doses are not always applicable. For certain people, and in certain cases, a material dose can do wonders. As with similars, so with doses, you have only half the picture. This vile impulse to concretise and make into fixed dogma that which is merely a guiding principle comes from the flesh, the worldly side of man, not from the spirit. It is to be avoided. It has taken hold of everything in the modern world. It has virtually destroyed medicine. The esoteric concepts are vital - 'as above so below' - surely Brukenthal told you these hermetic doctrines?

HAHNEMANN: Oh yes, but it was lost on me. I could never fathom what he was rambling about. However, your ideas of the three basic drugs and their corresponding maladies did come in useful. In my time, I discovered that your Natrum, Salt, was akin to my Sycosis, the gonorrhoea taint or miasma. Your Mercury became my Syphilis miasma; and your Sulphur corresponds to my Psora, or miasma of the Itch, suppressed inwards through topical salves like Petroleum or crude Sulphur ointment. These inherited predispositions or dyscrasia form the main elements of my Miasm Theory of chronic disease. I feel this discovery greatly improved and extended your work.

PARACELSUS: I must admit to feeling disappointed that only fragments of my teaching have survived into modern times and that the full teaching was very poorly understood at best. I am quite stunned, Hahnemann, I do not mind telling you, that there is no soul in modern medicine. This is its major failing. It is lop-sided and a mere halfling.

HAHNEMANN: Oh no, there is no soul in it any more. It is an outdated concept. No-one ever mentions such an idea. It would be regarded as a medical blasphemy today. There is no soul according to biochemistry. If it cannot be seen or felt or detected, then it does not exist for them. In my system, however, as you know, I retained your 'vis medicatrix naturae' as the 'vital force' or 'élan vital'. It is without doubt a good concept as it explains much that can be observed. Modern physicians find it absurd. I think the path modern medicine treads is wrong. Much that was hastily thrown out centuries ago now needs to be brought back in.

PARACELSUS: I would say they have cut away too much of the important metaphysical element from medicine and thus it has become corrupted by materialism. Like a rudderless ship, it veers this way and that, with no direction and bereft of any true principles. The path home for medicine is the true purpose of the holistic therapies. It seems inevitable that they will become increasingly important. All future roads lead back to the ancient systems and back into greater holism. I feel that reductionism has run its course and is now all but finished.

HAHNEMANN- At least we can agree to end our discussion on such a positive sentiment!

■

HAHNEMANN AND HOMOEOPATHY

ABSTRACT

This article presents an analysis of Hahnemann's personality and then relates the main elements of it to the development of homoeopathy in the world and what I shall call the 'Great Schism'. Based upon his personality and his practice, a critique is then presented, of the claims of modern, self-styled 'classical' homóeopaths.

In brief, Hahnemann is presented as a combination of 'fussy pedant' and 'violent revolutionary'. Most of what he did stems from these two strands. The Organon stems from

Landscape with colour spheres

the first strand, and homoeopathy in toto stems from the second. Classicalism, so-called, rests very largely upon the belief that the Organon represents the most important achievement of Hahnemann and that following it forms the basis for the whole of homoeopathy.

Yet as we shall see, this claim is entirely reliant on only one aspect of Hahnemann. It is a partial and incomplete view both of Hahnemann and of homoeopathy. I therefore recommend a much wider and more balanced approach, both towards Organon scholarship and towards homoeopathic experimentation in general. In so doing, a new balance might be achieved which more truly embraces the full spirit of Samuel Hahnemann, rather than just the lop-sided and rather pedantic view based solely upon the Organon. That would also bring all homoeopaths closer into a unity, rather than as warring and disunited factions.

Once we understand Hahnemann clearly, then it is much easier to see the basis for most of what follows.

No great understanding of homoeopathy and its development can be complete without some account of the life and personality of its founder, Samuel Hahnemann. The reason being the immense impact he had on the system which he created. In order to obtain such an account, we can profitably start by reading the biographies by Hobhouse, Cook, Bradford and Haehl, which give a good account of the man and his life. If we then ignore his many travels and the main aspects of his career, which bear little direct relevance to homoeopathy, we can peer through the details to see the essence of the man. We can focus on three chief aspects as being especially relevant to the study of homoeopathy. These are his personality, the development of his system and his practice. This article considers all three, but mainly focuses upon his personality.

The above sources provide us with more than ample data. But I would also add Rima Handley's 'Homoeopathic Love Story' to see another side both of the man and his later practice. Further detail about his character and practice and the development of homoeopathy is given in Dudgeon (1853), which remains an altogether excellent, though badly neglected source of information, much of it apparently unavailable elsewhere. Unlike most other writers, Dudgeon adopts a surprisingly modern approach and succeeds in placing Hahnemann and homoeopathy within a much wider historical context.

Taken together, if we immerse ourselves in all these sources of information we soon begin to appreciate much more about Hahnemann as a person —who comes alive before us— and of how his system and practice developed. Based upon doing exactly that myself for the past seven years, I present my own assessment of the man, his development and his practice. And I do this in part to delineate the possible origins of the great schism within homoeopathy.

HAHNEMANN THE MAN

After observing him very closely, if we then stand back and observe him from some distance, it is apparent that Hahnemann possessed three main qualities which really stand out as being especially noteworthy, unusual and phenomenal. These are:

1. his astonishing linguistic skills,
2. his revolutionary character,

3. his painstaking, methodical and dictatorial nature.

Of course there were other traits, but as I hope to show, these three stand out as the most significant in relation to homoeopathy.

1. Linguistic Skills

> "A precociously brilliant man, he had mastered eight languages and turned himself into an outstanding chemist by the time he obtained his medical degree in 1779." [Griggs, 1982, p176]

It is true that his linguistic skills really were astonishing and place him in a tiny minority of people throughout history who have fluently mastered 8 languages. For example, many people can master Italian, Spanish and French say, or German, English and Latin, but to have mastered all these languages is very unusual. Even more so when we add Greek and Arabic to the list! It is therefore true to say that he possessed an astonishing gift for languages. And he used this gift in two main ways. Firstly to satisfy his great curiosity about the world and other peoples and cultures; and secondly to give him unique 'windows' into the medical systems and traditions of other cultures. This gave him the opportunity to undertake translations of foreign medical texts into German —a task he threw himself into with great relish in the beginning of his career as a young doctor. All of this gave him an exceptionally wide knowledge of drugs and of how they were used in different cultures — both ancient and contemporary to his time.

This leaves only two qualities of note which were to have an immense bearing upon the progress of homoeopathy —his revolutionary and pedantic sides. We can profit from delving more deeply into these terms in order to gain the insights we need about Hahnemann as a man.

2. The Revolutionary

When we use the word revolutionary we might think of figures like Luther (1483-1546), Paracelsus (1493-1541) or Galileo (1564-1642), or in politics, such figures as Marx (1818- 83), Lenin (1870-1924), or Mao Dse Dung (1893-1976). Such figures appear to stand out of the main stream, to see things very differently, and to wish to change things a great deal, often suddenly. A revolutionary is bad news for the status quo; it is a person who causes trouble. Their actions stem from the fact that they see things others do not see and which trouble them so greatly, that they dare to state their view regardless of the consequences. This is certainly true of Luther, Galileo, etc and all the above figures. It is also true of Hahnemann.

In his case he was a straightforward and quite ordinary young doctor in the 1780s. His only trouble was that he could not get the system he had been taught (allopathy) to work very well, i.e. to generate cures. Even worse, he could not get it to work predictably, reliably or consistently.

> *"Hahnemann was so disillusioned with the state of medical practice and knowledge that, soon after his marriage in 1782, he totally refrained from practising medicine...so deep was his belief that the tools he had been given would do more harm than good."* [Danciger, 1987, p5]

And thus he gradually came to detest a system which he had previously adored. This troubled the fussy and pedantic, linguistic side of Hahnemann very greatly. He liked principles and systems; they form the very fabric of all languages —order, grammar, syntax, such things which can be relied upon in any language and which make it work along predictable lines. That appealed to his fussy, pedantic side, as it does to most linguists. It is akin to the fussy pedantry of musicians and mathematicians who also adore that principled, polished and predictable certainty of music and mathematics.

Being a great linguist also set him on the trail of finding out what other people in different times and cultures had done with drugs. This sets the stage therefore for all which came after. Searching in other cultures might provide him with answers to help him refine and improve the useless system of medicine he had been taught, so that it became more rational, more principled and more predictable. This was without doubt his starting point. We might say that this was the 'puzzle' which fate had pushed his way. It was also what most of his contemporary scientists were doing in other fields —polishing, refining, experimenting and establishing principles.

But being so fussy and methodical, Hahnemann was not put off easily. He searched other cultures and times for ideas in support of his desire to reform the irrational medicine of his day —the tool he had been handed but which did not work. He was originally a conservative and methodical man who did not want to fight the whole of medicine to prove a point —if he could avoid it. But once he had satisfied himself that allopathy really was useless —and fundamentally so —out of intellectual honesty he gave up the practice of medicine and amused himself with translation work.

Then, through carefully boiling allopathy down to its barest bones, he could see that it contained only three principles —using mixed remedies, using high doses and using contraries. Knowing through direct personal experience that these did not work, he was led to consider the opposite and deeply heretical principles of —single drugs, small doses and similars. For the next 30 years Hahnemann systematically investigated all three: first single drugs, then similars and finally small doses.

Although he started to use similar medicines around 1790, Hahnemann did not conduct the first experiments with dose reduction until the year 1798.

> 'We cannot fail to be struck by the sudden transition from the massive doses he prescribed in 1798 to the unheard-of minuteness of his doses only one year later, and we can but guess the causes for this abrupt transition.' [Dudgeon, 1853, pp395-6]

All his research up to 1798 was into single drugs and similars. After 1798 he began systematically to reduce dosage, and he continued experimenting with dosage (or tinkering, as some would call it) until his last days in Paris in July 1843, some 45 years later.

It is interesting historically that he called his new system homoeopathy, as it reflects what he did. Though he occasionally deviated from the other two principles, such as using material doses, even late in his career, and he even used some mixed remedies, yet he never compromised the law of similars, which forms the firmest bedrock of his system and which is why it is called homoeopathy or 'similar suffering'. The title reflects Hahnemann's care and love of accuracy in meaning.

It is always useful to remember that homoeopathy is a system of medicine entirely devised through experiment by one person. This single fact, so easy to miss or gloss over, is supremely important to our understanding and thus why an understanding of the man is the key to its history. Yet strangely, in its origin it was inspired as a systematic critique of a useless system —a system which did not work. He started with what was bad and which did not fit the facts, and decided to improve it. And that is just as revolutionary as Copernicus (1473-1543), Galileo and Luther. That is what I meant by a revolutionary.

3. The Fussy Pedant

I said his second quality was revolutionary and we can all see that side of him very clearly. Homoeopathy itself is most certainly a revolutionary form of medicine and it stands as abundant evidence in itself of the scale of his achievement.

The third feature of Hahnemann I have picked out is his methodical side. Now, while I would say that the two previous qualities were outstanding and mainly positive and beneficial in character, I must confess that I rank this third quality as outstanding but almost entirely negative in nature. A comment I must now try to justify and explore in greater depth.

A 'person of principle' is a person who follows guidelines assiduously and never varies. The philosopher Immanuel Kant (1724-1804) was just such a man. Yet a person of principle has a hard time in life, because it rarely conforms to their fussiness. It frustrates them when it is not as they want it to be. A person of principle is usually born that way —few I think would arrive at it through experience or choice.

I think Hahnemann was born that way as it is there from the start. To begin with, his fussy, methodical and painstaking nature was beneficial and positive, as it made him study hard, in great depth and to get right to the bottom of things. It probably forms the basis of his linguistic skills, for example. It also led him to ascertain the true nature of any problem in a detailed, systematic and accurate fashion.

Detail, accuracy and principle are the very hallmarks of such a mind, and Hahnemann possessed these qualities in abundance. But unfortunately for him (and for homoeopathy) these qualities all too often tend (in any of us) to degenerate and solidify into a rigid dogmatism; into a belief that so-called principles come before practice; to an insistence that you are right and everyone else is wrong; to petulent outbursts due to overexacting fussiness; and to the vilification of opponents. Which sadly is a pretty good description of what happened in Hahnemann's case.

So this side of Hahnemann and homoeopathic history —the two being welded together for so long —is almost entirely a trail of tears. And in my opinion, he was a fool to drag homoeopathy through the mud in the way he did and to give it the worst possible start imaginable. A big fool. None of it was necessary and most of it derived from his own excessively dogmatic, irrascible, reactive and really rather paranoid attitude towards others, most especially his closest and most devoted followers. Most of whom he unnecessarily upset and then accused of treachery. This negative side of him was very real and there is no use in our denying or ignoring it. In fact, it is vital to our understanding of the man and the early history of homoeopathy. It is also very regrettable, as he cast everyone into the role of enemy of him personally and of homoeopathy in general. That was foolishness of a high order, as it created a very troubled, combative and divisive start for homoeopathy, which it has never successfully shaken off.

Worse still, it set the tone for all later homoeopaths to emulate his bad behaviour and to be as hardline, bombastic and argumentative as he had been himself. It was a mistake to attack allopathy in the way he did and a mistake to try and change the rest of medicine. It was a futile, self-created battle which he had no hope of winning. It is still futile today and homoeopathy should seek dialogue and peaceful co-existence with allopathy, not argument and discord. The two systems will never merge and stem from entirely different views of the world. But no doubt to Hahnemann at the time, he must have felt that he had a good chance of creating a revolution for the whole of medicine. He must have thought that or else he would not have acted in the way he did.

When I say Hahnemann was hardline, dogmatic and dictatorial what I mean is that he allowed for himself the luxury of complete freedom of experimentation, but stifled the same trait in others. He enjoyed for himself the freedom to make changes or to change his mind whenever he felt like it (eg. the coffee theory) and to experiment continually, but he rebuked very severely anyone else who made small changes, voiced freedom of thought or mildly critical suggestions about homoeopathy. Such people were exposed to unbelievable ferocity from Hahnemann, amounting in fact to violent and unrelenting, scornful derision. The net result was that they ended up saying nothing, for fear of provoking such reactions from him. Thus he upset most of his closest followers at one time or another, usually over some trivial matter. Haehl and Bradford are packed with examples.

A good example is the argument he had with Schreter, Jenichen, Korsakoff and Boenninghaussen over their use of the higher centesimal potencies (ref Morrell, see also Haehl, vol 1, p32; Bradford, 1895, pp466-7; Dudgeon, 1853, p407-8). Hahnemann was opposed in principle to the higher potencies even though he felt at liberty to make actual use of them himself on several occasions, whenever the mood took him (ref Handley). It appears from incidents of this kind that he rather selfishly wanted to keep as his own every aspect of homoeopathy as a system, admitting no external influence from anyone, and jealously dismissing any interesting contributions made by others. He was violently opposed therefore in others to the very kind of freethinking and experimentation which he freely indulged in himself —which is at the very least unfair and bizarre.

In this sense therefore he looks like a 'control freak', quite unwilling to delegate the minutest particle of power and freedom to others. Homoeopathy was HIS baby and he seemed determined to keep it that way. That is the distinct impression one gets from reading accounts of these incidents in Haehl, Bradford and Dudgeon. The only reason Boenninghaussen managed to keep on such friendly terms with him was NOT by copying everything he said, but out of his immensely genial nature and his great love for Hahnemann.

> 'On the 20th of January last the genial and excellent old Dr C Von Boenninghausen died of apoplexy at the age of 79 years...' [Obituary, BJH, 1864]

Yet somewhat perversely, Boenninghaussen had

disagreed completely with Hahnemann for years about the higher potencies and used the 100, 200 and M potencies routinely for every case. He wrote many articles extolling their virtues. In effect they agreed to disagree and so remained on good terms and corresponded to the end. The articles (found in his Lesser Writings) are as follows:

The High Potencies, (1850)

Typhoid Fever and High Potencies, (1853)

Traumatic Ailments and High Potencies, (c1853)

The Advantages of the High Potencies, (1864)

Jenichen's High Potencies, (1867)

The Value of High Potencies, (1867)

The Use of High Attenuations in Homoeopathic Practice Cures of Animals with High Potencies, (1873)

Experience and the High Potencies (1846)

It is fairly obvious from incidents of this type that Hahnemann appears like a hypocrit, forbidding others to do what he himself was quite content to try out in private. And it is also obvious that this punitive, dogmatic and hardline side of Hahenmann came to be peculiarly crystallised in the tone and language of the Organon, which has been used by successive generations of homoeopathic zealots as a type of 'homoeopathic Bible'. A Bible they have willingly beaten the less faithful with at every opportunity. And the writings of most modern 'Classicalists' are just as arrogant and dogmatic in their insistence that the Organon contains everything there is to know about homoeopathy and Hahnemann.

MORE ON HIS CHARACTER

It is somewhat debateable and of interest to us, as to which of the two chief mental qualities was dominant or uppermost at different times in his long life. I have argued that his iconoclastic and revolutionary side was largely dominant, and I think there is a good case for stressing that aspect of his character, as it has been largely ignored hitherto, or played down as of no import. However, on closer inspection of his career, we can see that the linguistic, pedantic and meticulous side was dominant in his early life as a studious, bookish youth and at university. This side was also clearly the dominant influence when he wrote the Organon, and was probably what we might term his 'original state'. But once roused, his fearsome iconoclasm became very dominant, especially after he had become wholly disenchanted with allopathy and finally rejected it outright as a useless system. From that point forwards and for many years (c1785-1835) he was a violent polemicist against allopathy and just as violent a campaigner for homoeopathy. He spared absolutely no opportunity to denigrate allopathy, and in the strongest possible language. Which generated a lot of trouble for him.

> "Hahnemann...began openly to criticise the proceedings of his medical colleagues with inexorable severity...Besides this he protested against the practice at that time employed with the insane, whom the doctors and attendants treated as wildbeasts." [Jain, 1977, p3]

> "Thus it was that his independence became very obnoxious to the private physician of the recently deceased Emperor Leopold II of Austria, [this was in 1792] when Hahnemann openly charged him

> with being the cause of his death from the employment of excessive blood-letting in pleurisy." [ibid., p3]

This destructive (?) and experimental side to his nature knew no bounds during the middle period of his life and seems to strongly echo the turbulent career of Paracelsus. It is accurate to say that he flipped constantly from fussy pedant to revolutionary experimenter and back again throughout his long life, only later, in his Paris years, attaining a degree of less contentious tranquillity. Yet even then, in his maturity, we still find him busy experimenting, right to the end, trying out new ideas: devising the LM scale; using mixed remedies; prescribing for each presenting symptom (contrary to his own instructions in the Organon); opening every case with Sulphur; using olfaction; changing the dosage, even by the hour or less at times, like Clarke 50 years later —

> *'A keynote of Dr Clarke's work in homoeopathy was his catholicity... Clarke was one of the few homoeopaths who really practised what he said, "that there is a place for every potency, from the mother tincture to the highest, and the physician's skill consists in knowing which to choose and when."*
>
> *'Clarke had no hesitation. He would give remedies within extraordinary short range of one another; he would give one on top of another, and resort to different potencies. Mostly at that time he was giving fairly high potencies, 30s and 200s for chronic cases.'* [Dr John H Clarke, An Appreciation, BHJ, 1932, pp116-125]

And all the time (and in secret) Hahnemann was polishing his 6th Edition and distilling into it his new ideas.

Indeed, he seems at times to have tried the opposite of every maxim in the Organon, going out of his way to be a rebel against his own system. Why?

He must have hesitated a great deal over the 6th edition, unable to keep it up to date, never certain maybe, that he had finally captured in writing the elusive truth of his full system, and maybe never convinced that the world was ready (or able) to comprehend his final teachings. So, essentially, he was a strange mixture: a meticulous and perfectionistic pedant combined with a furious polemicist; with a willingness to experiment endlessly, in order to construct or fashion a system which worked and which worked predictably and along the lines of established principles. In other words, exactly what allopathy wasn't.

In that sense he was certainly a figure sublimely typical of the 18th century —a product of his times —like Goethe (1749-1832), Voltaire (1694-1778) and the Encyclopedists Rousseau (1712-78), Diderot (1713-84), etc, building up new ideas and grand systems based mainly upon personal observation and experiment and the rejection of past traditions and old dogmas (see Rogers, Russell, Tarnas).

He was also very like all his fellow 18th and 19th century scientists, who were also pioneers of experimentation, and who he admired so greatly. I think he really strongly yearned for their support and approval, if only for the sheer originality, vision and soundness of his work. And its rationality.

And because he never received their recognition, praise or adulation (which he certainly felt he deserved) that seems to have boiled up inside him and triggered his bitterly venomous and unrelenting onslaught against orthodoxy in general. A veritable 'blitzkreig' if ever there was one. Perhaps he never forgave them for abandoning him in his darkest hour of need. For their failing to recognise the importance of what he was doing and the 'root and branch' revolution he was creating for medicine. And fifty years after his death, allopathy finally started to reduce its doses, and to use single drugs instead of mixtures, just as he had first suggested, though he never got any credit for that.

THE PRAGMATIST

Another important aspect of Hahnemann's character which I have neglected to mention, and which certainly lies hidden in all of this, was his unfailing pragmatism, his ability to see that what works is of paramount importance in medicine. This was part of the 'good doctor' in him, no doubt. Medicine is an art and not a science, yet it must always produce results. It is not theory-led, but practice-led. Theory is fine, but does it cure the patient? This was constantly at the back of his mind. Thus he had the unfailing ability to grasp the massive importance of what works in practice and a willingness to abandon quickly and completely anything —everything —which did not work. To recognise and reject what was useless and move forward, then innovate again confident of eventual victory. When all was razed to dust, he would just start all over again. Remarkable quality. He never lost this shrewd pragmatism and optimism in the face of defeat, even though it contrasted so sharply with his more conservative, pedantic nature.

This is interesting and unusual psychologically. There are so many fussy and over- intellectual pedants who lack this skill, and probably as many practical innovators and experimenters who cannot write a clear account of what they do and why. Yet Hahnemann could do both and brilliantly and this was his ultimate strength: he combined in the one person very divergent qualities, rarely found together; qualities which were apparently cemented together by this extraordinary pragmatism. He had no truck whatever with ideas for their own sake, and was thus not really an intellectual in the ordinary sense, but only with 'ideas which work'. And ideas which work fired his entire being. And homoeopathy is above all else an idea which works.

PRACTICE

When we read of his practice and methods in the sources already mentioned and especially in Handley 1988, 1992 and 1997 (and also Adler, Michelowski et al), we can then more fully appreciate that the experimental side of his nature was very much in the driving seat for most of the time. And it is also clear that he often deviated widely from his own dictates as found in the Organon. In the final years in Paris, the old disputes and his deep dogmatism appear to have died-down, volcano-style, and he attains a quieter and more sage- like tranquillity, busy experimenting right till the end, and no doubt influenced a lot by Melanie.

It appears from Handley's studies that Hahnemann did all sorts of things in his Paris practice which previously in his writings he had expressly forbidden others to do. These can be summarised as follows:

1. Most cases are opened with Sulphur - some 90% of chronic cases. Sulphur was often repeated frequently in the early stages until symptoms of another remedy appeared and then that was given. Sometimes only Sulphur was used throughout.

2. He also prescribed for anything that came up in the course of treatment, e.g. some cough or symptoms of an acute nature.

3. He treated the return of old symptoms in the same way. In every case he regarded the return of old symptoms with delight and saw a new symptom as an indication of the next new remedy.

4. He also commonly used two remedies at the same time.

5. He frequently prescribed one remedy by mouth and another by Olfaction.

6. The LM's he used in many different ways and asserted that they—(a) could be repeated very frequently without aggravation or harm and (b). maintained continuous stimulation of the vital healing force. The LM's appear therefore to be mainly a product of his impatience with slow cases.

7. In his early days in Paris he mainly used 3, 6, 9, 12, 18, 24 and 30 potencies He then progressed to using the 200 and the 95. These remedies were often repeated frequently every day sometimes twice a day, or more up to a max of 6 times a day! He often used widely different potencies in the same case, going lower for acute conditions and higher for chronic work. He tended to use LM's for chronic and the centesimals for any acute symptoms that emerged.

8. He often repeated remedies very frequently. He abandoned the centesimal potencies mainly because of their power to produce aggravations. He suspected that the higher dilutions (above 30) would increase aggravations and he was very cautious about them. He used two remedies at once when he felt it necessary. He treated most symptoms as they came up.

These facts derive from close study of his Paris Casebooks (Krankenjournalen Pariser Praxis), and clearly reveal a very wide gulf between what he recommends to others in the Organon and what he himself did in practice. And this creates a real problem for homoeopaths today: which do we follow? The rebel, pioneer, experimenter and iconoclast: the discoverer of homoeopathy? Or the pedantic, fussy scholar who wrote the Organon? Which side more truly represents homoeopathy? Which did Hahnemann himself likely regard as his most prestigious and important gift to posterity? The Organon? Or his entire system of revolutionary medicine based upon clear principles? Some would urge us to choose one and some the other. Maybe we should embrace them both as the full Hahnemann.

THE ORGANON

To what extent Hahnemann succeeded in creating a set of workable principles is in fact somewhat open to question. The Organon is a complex work. Successive generations of homoeopaths have always had some difficulty with it and have grappled with its various translations and with variable success in actually copying the instructions of the Master. Yet it remains an obscure, dense and opaque piece of writing. But the most damning fact by far is that Hahnemann did not follow it very closely himself. This throws into doubt its value at all and therefore begs the question as to whether homoeopaths might be better off ignoring it completely and copying instead what he actually did in practice rather than what he wrote. The same criticism can be levelled at Kent, whose Lectures are merely a garbled and incomplete 'biblical commentary' to the Organon but mixed up with alien ideas from Swedenborg.

Many homoeopaths over the years have actually had the insight to abandon the strictures of the Organon and develop their own innovative and experimental forms of homoeopathy, just like the later Hahnemann. Examples include Burnett, Clarke and **Maughan** in Britain. Clarke in particular was very like Hahnemann as he used quick-fire, rapid succession, low potency homoeopathy with occasional use of higher potencies, occasional use of tinctures and occasional use of mixed remedies —just like Hahnemann himself, as portrayed in Handley's writings. All of these homoeopaths are in their own ways iconoclastic and experimental — practice-led rather than theory-led.

Thomas maughan

DEVIATION

The question inevitably arises as to why Hahnemann should have chosen to deviate from the Organon and practise on an experimental basis. The obvious answer to this question is both personal and practical —that he could not get the Organon system to work as well as he liked. Thus he deviated from it. An alternative view is that he just could not resist the temptation to experiment and tinker. This is unlikely as he was so methodical in everything he did.

His decision to deviate from his own principles as stated in the Organon must have been based upon practice. Everything else he did and revised was done to improve the practical value of his system. He never revised things on theoretical grounds alone. An example is his refusal to sanction any kind of spiritual views associated by Bonninghaussen, Schreter & Co with the higher potencies. He did not really hold 'spiritual views' about homoeopathy.

Two other important threads emerge about his deviation from the Organon. One is that as a teacher of others he may have inadvertently overemphasised to them the importance of theory over practice. There seems to be some mileage in this argument. Also, the history of homoeopathy since Hahnemann clearly shows that in different lands and continents, people have adapted his teachings and principles differently and devised various modes of practice, all with their own good track records. This also favours the idea that practical experimentation remains the dominant basis for homoeopathy rather than slavishly following an 'Organon of principles' as the Classicalists insist.

It also tends to dilute considerably the central and unquestioned importance of the Organon within homoeopathy to something approaching that of an 'historical relic', rather than the main text on the subject. A homoeopath can just as truly call him or herself 'Hahenmannian' to the degree by which they follow Hahnemann himself in practice, and especially through pioneering experimental work, as to the degree by which they pedantically follow the Organon. But as we have seen, these are wholly different things. As previously mentioned, relying on Kent as the basis for Classicalism also creates problems. Also, as Kent died in 1916 and the 6th Edition did not appear until 1922, it is clear that his Lectures inevitably give an incomplete view both of Hahnemann and of his system.

Thus Classicalism seems to be very largely an attempt to follow only one side of Hahnemann, the fussy pedant, and to downplay or ignore entirely his original, iconoclastic and experimental side. In this sense therefore classicalism is a myth which has dominated homoeopathy for too long. And which must be challenged if any progress is to be made.

DUDGEON

Dr Dudgeon should be especially commended because he stands out as one never afraid to criticise Hahnemann wherever he disagrees with what he sees as the excesses or deficiencies of his system. For example, the ludicrous Coffee Theory of chronic disease (On the Effects of Coffee from Original Observations (Leipzig, 1803) and listed in his Lesser Writings, pp391-410.), the Miasm theory (see Dudgeon, 1853, pp242-301) and the higher potencies (see Dudgeon, 1853, posology, pp391-446; mixed remedies pp486-91) — all of which he gives short shrift.

> '...Hahnemann himself alludes to the essay he wrote upon the action of coffee in 1803, where he had ascribed the production of a multitude of chronic diseases to the action of that all but universal beverage, and he confesses that he thinks he had ascribed an exaggerated importance and gravity to its use; since his discovery of psora as the cause of

> many chronic diseases, he is inclined to attribute to that agent the production of most of those affections he had imputed to coffee.' [Dudgeon, 1853, p259]

The point here is not that Dudgeon was necessarily right or wrong in these judgements, but that he shows such refreshing (and unique?) independence of mind in attempting to present to his audience a balanced and non-partisan view of homoeopathy. No other writer within homoeopathy, before or since, has shown such remarkable independence of thought. Instead, they all prefer to drool and slaver unquestioningly over Hahnemann, all of his ideas and the Greats, and to queue up slavishly, caps in hands, to heap their praises and devotions upon their revered Master.

This is the very tendency which Hahnemann himself so detested and fought against, just as Paracelsus had before him —burning the books of Galen and Avicenna in an attempt to wake his students up to new ideas. This drooling and sycophantic mentality is the cause of much mythologising and nonsense within homoeopathy down the years, and clearly stands in the way of our making any clear and objective assessment of the system as a whole. It is unnecessary in any case and prevents the subject gaining the social and medical acceptance it deserves.

The same mentality dominated the Middle Ages; gave the Pope and his Cardinals absolute and unquestioned power for centuries; gave kings and queens throughout history (and more recently communist dictators) the power to ride roughshod over their subjects and treat them with contempt; and which is still created and maintained today by weak people who cannot think for themselves and crave 'leaders' and 'heroes' to do it for them. Within homoeopathy it has been especially heaped upon Hahnemann and Kent, and to a degree which is quite sickening to behold. A cool and balanced assessment of these figures is impossible to obtain until this bloated and sugary sweet rhetoric of myths and legends is teased to one side and real facts and figures are actually examined.

We should remember that all the Greats of homoeopathy were first and foremost human beings like the rest of us, and we must strive to see them in a broader sweep, and resist this ludicrous tendency to overeulogize and mythologize big figures from the past or the present. A good example of this loathsome habit is Schmidt's claim that Kent saw over 18000 patients in a certain year (see his biography of Kent). Debates and divisions are not resolved through clinging to one position, but through open dialogue and experiment within an atmosphere of mutual respect from both sides.

HISTORICAL BACKDROP

There is another aspect relating to dogmatism and principles which also has an interesting historical thread. If the Materia Medica Pura was the 'what' of homoeopathy, then clearly the Organon was meant to be the 'how' and 'why'. Hahnemann was trying in the Organon to produce a list of clearly identified principles, aphorisms and guidelines through following which anyone could come (hopefully) to practice and understand his system. Yet it remains a mystery where the idea for such a grand work came from and whether in fact he had read some philosophical work which inspired him and which he might have used as a template.

Probably no other single event in the history of philosophy —and in the history of German philosophy —

was as important as the publication in 1781 of Kant's Critique of Pure Reason, which 'raised him to the foremost position among living philosophers.' (Rogers, p376). It placed him in the firmament of German Idealists for all time. At that very time Hahnemann was starting his 'systematic disenchantment' with allopathy and wondering, no doubt, if there would ever be found any clear 'guiding principles' for the practice of medicine.

It is my provisional hunch that it was Kant's work which inspired Hahnemann to write the Organon. He cannot really have failed to have seen it and probably read it. Rogers says '...for Kant, the truths of the intellect are subordinate to the truths of the practical will...scientific reason [has] the right to induce belief.' (Rogers, p398). Ideas which would most certainly have found fertile ground in the thinking of Samuel Hahnemann in the 1780s and 1790s. Indeed, we read in Hobhouse (p104-5) that Hahnemann liked Kant's writings and expressed this in a letter to von Villers.

Either way, Hahnemann clearly intended his Organon to become refined over time such that its principles could be amplified, clarified and updated, probably elevated eventually to the status of 'natural laws'. That he wrote six editions during his life might well be seen as good evidence of this tendency to revise and elevate. It is also true that this tendency to formulate natural laws was at that time very common, for example in Optics and Chemistry in particular, but also in natural science in general. And Hahnemann was keenly aware of all developments taking place in science, especially his beloved chemistry. Post-Enlightenment, it was a time of great systematisation of knowledge in all fields and the building up of grand systems for the first time.

Thus the Organon actually has two origins. First it was Hahnemann's personal idea to formulate his ideas and system of medicine into a series of aphorisms. To make it into a system of medicine based upon clear principles, which in his view allopathy certainly wasn't. This stemmed very largely from the dogmatic, fussy, high-principled and pedantic or Arsen alb side of his nature. Second, he had around him in the world, hosts of other scientists doing exactly the same thing in various other fields of endeavour. These include Michael Faraday (1791-1867), Joseph Priestley (1733-1804), John Dalton (1766-1844), Dmitri Mendeleyev (1834-1907), Antoine Lavoisier (1743-94) and Karl Scheele (1742-86) in Chemistry. Hahnemann is reported to have met Lavoisier in Dresden c1786 and also corresponded with him (Hobhouse, 1933, p59). In Botany there was Carolus Linnaeus (1707-78), in Zoology Georges Cuvier (1769-1832) and Jean Lamarck (1744-1829) and in Geology, Sir Charles Lyell (1797-1875). So the development of his ideas into a grand system was not only his own idea, but also part of a 'tide of the times' or 'zeitgeist'. Experimentation led to the establishment of principles and laws and so the fabric of science theory was built up c1700-1900 (see Russell, Rogers, Tarnas).

CLASSICALISM

The classicalists will probably reject most of what I have said as nonsense and also my main thesis. All I can do is to repeat the central and fundamental question: if the Organon truly represents the whole of homoeopathy then why did Hahnemann not practise according to it himself? I have explored in detail the possible reasons for that and I believe I have presented a reasonably sound and comprehensive analysis of the character of Hahnemann and the nature of his impact upon the development of homoeopathy —the two being almost completely inseparable. The Classicalists cling to a myth, the myth that the Organon is the whole of homoeopathy. As I have already shown, the Organon is NOT homoeopathy and this cuts away the central pillar which supports their view.

As I have also shown, he was first and foremost an experimenter, an empiricist and a dangerous medical rebel or heretic, just like Paracelsus before him —though far more rational and systematic. Though he did attempt to formulate a grand theoretical system of principles in the Organon (along Kantian lines) he could never shake off his deeply ingrained experimental tendency. And thus the Organon was never finished or fully updated and therefore does not represent the whole of homoeopathy, only one aspect. At best it shows only half of Hahnemann's full system.

THOMAS COOPER

We should now more confidently seek guidance on practice not in the Organon, but in Hahnemann's later practice, for a fuller view of homoeopathy. We can also look to others since Hahnemann who have pioneered interesting experimental work. These include Burnett, Clarke, **Cooper**, Bach, Maughan, etc in Britain and many others in Latin America and elsewhere. It also includes the provers like Jeremy Sherr and Madeline Evans. All

Thomas cooper

such work is within the experimental spirit of Hahnemann, though clearly at variance with the scholastic pedantry of his Organon side. The future development of homoeopathy should look more towards the experimental side of Hahnemann for any progress and new developments.

This essay was not composed as an attack upon Classicalism. That was not my express intention. It began as a new way of understanding Hahnemann and forming a clearer picture of what he was about. Nevertheless, it is true that the Classical position does place a lot of emphasis on following the Organon and is sceptical of 'late Hahnemann studies'. They also tend to dismiss any freethinking and experimentation as unHahnemannian and against the spirit of homoeopathy. As I have tried to show, this is a threadbare argument. After upsetting them so much, the best I can do to try and win them over is to say that the Organon and the rebelliousness and experimentation both have an equal claim to be regarded as the main aspects of Hahnemann himself. Thus homoeopathy must reflect both those elements in order to be truly Hahnemannian. Currently it does not have that balance and tilts too far towards Organon-inspired classicalism and pedantry.

CONCLUSIONS

The central and most baffling question remains why Hahnemann chose to deviate from the dictates of his own work, the Organon. And this of course, raises other questions we must address. To have deviated from it implies, historically, that he had gone too far (or too early?) in the direction of his contemporary scientists and philosophers in attempting to formulate a grand system of natural laws. And, that far from being a true system at that stage, it was in fact deficient, incomplete and imperfect in some respects. Why else would he abandon its directions? If the Organon was so wonderful, so complete and so perfect, as Classicalists would still have us believe, then why did he continue to experiment right up to the end? How can you revise and extend that which is already perfect? We can only conclude from this fact that he could not resist the temptation to revise and improve something that WAS imperfect and unsatisfactory in some important way which he perceived, and probably only he perceived.

If this were not the case, then it all becomes very confusing for a serious homoeopath who wishes to be as Hahnemannian as possible. Which edition should he or she follow? And which translation?

This line of argument also ties in with three other aspects of the late Hahnemann. Firstly his refusal to publish the 6th edition of the Organon and Melanie and then her daughter clinging on to it for so long —to 1921 in fact. Secondly is the argument he had about the high potencies, of which he strongly disapproved vocally, even though he used them occasionally in his last years in Paris. Thirdly, there is his development of the LM scale of potencies. If everything was so complete, then why go and create an entirely new scale of potencies that followers had no knowledge of and which would lead to further confusion? All of these factors collude to strongly imply that Hahnemann was still experimenting and to have been such, he must have been unhappy about certain aspects of his system as published up to 1843. To believe otherwise is clearly to ignore a lot of evidence.

'*I have been fascinated to discover the amount of experimentation and ad hoc solutions to which*

> *Hahnemann resorted...what is interesting, however, is to see how often he broke his own rules, as do all creative people.'* [Handley, 1997, p15]

There is also another problem. This relates to the main aspects of his personality. That he was still 'tinkering around' in his last years also suggests that he was mainly an experimental person, rather than the pedant we have seen. Thus it implies that again the classicalists have got it wrong. From his failure to act more decisively in his final years, this implies that he did not consider that the Organon stood supreme over practice and experimentation. If he did think that then he would have taken steps and found the time (made the time) to update and publish a 6th or even a 7th edition in those final years. If the Organon WAS his main work, as Classicalists suggest, then why did such a determined and energetic man not find the time to publish all his final ideas?

That he neglected to do that implies that his thoughts were elsewhere — for example on further experimentation and continual revision of technique in practice. This also implies psychologically, therefore, that in the last analysis his experimental urge was always by far the more dominant and uppermost in his mentality and not the pedantic side which composed the Organon. And thus again we are led to conclude that the classicalists have got it wrong and misinterpreted his intentions by choosing to overemphasise the central importance of the Organon as written dogma 'carved in stone', rather than experimentation. In doing so they have missed the true Hahnemann and thus missed the true homoeopathy.

May be the Organon was merely a venture or experiment in ideas for Hahnemann and which he later became disenchanted with in some way and he may have dithered over its actual importance? We shall never know the answer to that. Towards the end he may also have realised the deep dichotomy in his thinking and realised that the pedant was in truth the smaller part of him and that what he really liked to do was tinker around and experiment with ideas that work. Maybe that sums up Hahnemann better than anything else. If so, then the Organon really does appear like a beached historical relic of little lasting value and the Paris Casebooks therefore take on immense new significance. In which case they should at long last be revealed in toto to the homoeopathic world for the jewels of insight they must contain about his final ideas.

At last, and 200 years after Hahnemann's 'first footprints on fresh sand', Rima Handley has published her long studies of the Paris Casebooks. But will the homoeopathic world actually sit up and take notice of their contents? And make the necessary adjustments to their beliefs? Or will they continue to prefer a thundering silence and the same old spats over dogmas in the Organon? In my view, that would seem now to be the real challenge for modern homoeopathy and the true legacy of the life and work of Samuel Hahnemann. Do homoeopaths wish to be united under a single banner? Or to remain as the bickering mess we see before us today?

Thomas Skinner

CONFUSION OVER HAHNEMANN'S SMALL DOSES

Crete

Because of the confusion in the letters to this article, I present a series of quotations from reputable sources which convey the essence of how Hahnemann came upon and developed the whole technique of making small doses. Those wishing further detail can consult the texts here cited. Apologies for length.

'When Hahnemann first announced cures of diseases by extremely small doses of medicine, his statements were received with incredulity and ridicule...Hahnemann's appeal to the medical profession to test the new method and publish results to the world was met by active opposition. He was forbidden to practice and was driven from his home by relentless persecution....[even though] the use of the infinitesimal dose in homoeopathy was the outcome of experience...'

'[The] principle of the infinitesimal dose [is]...an outrage to human reason.'

"...the doctrines of potentiation and the infinitesimal dose has always been the central point of attack upon homoeopathy by its enemies."

'In the United States, regular physicians...found Hahnemann's theories absurd and incredible. Reasoning that no one in his right mind could believe such arrant nonsense, they concluded that homoeopaths must be either knaves or fools.'

"Hahnemann claimed that a dilution as minute as 1/500,000th of a grain or even 1/1,000,000th of a grain, could be effective...to orthodox practitioners, who in many cases prescribed drugs by the spoonful, Hahnemann's ideas were ridiculous."

"Hahnemann pointed to...classical literature to demonstrate that his discoverey was known to writers of antiquity and was essentially rediscovered by him. He also recognised that his doses would be considered ludicrous by physicians accustomed to heroic therapy."

"Hahnemann argued that skeptical regular physicians should not concern themselves with the logic of homoeopathy, but rather look at the results."

"Most regular physicians regarded their homoeopathic colleagues first with skepticism, then with incredulity, and finally with bitter hostility."

"Hahnemann's final views and practice in regard to the dose were arrived at gradually, through long years of careful experiment and observation."

"Many before Hahnemann, from Hippocrates down, had glimpses of the law [of similars], and some had tried to make use of it therapeutically; but all had failed because of their inability to properly graduate and adapt the dose."

"Hahnemann's idea at first was simply to reduce the "strength" or material mass of his drug, but his passion for accuracy led him to adopt a scale, that he might always be sure of the degree of reduction and establish a standard for comparison."

"He soon discovered that large doses were very undesirable in ascertaining the effects of drugs [on the healthy person]."

"The more he experimented with the proper homoeopathic doses, the smaller the dose he recommended."

"His discovery of the principle of potentisation came about gradually as he experimented in the reduction of his doses, in order to arrive at a point where severe aggravations would not occur. Gradually, by experience, he learned that the latent powers of drugs were released or developed by trituration, dilution and succussion."

"Hahnemann...perplexed by the aggravations resulting from ordinary doses, seeking to find a dose so small that it would not endanger life and desiring to accurately measure his degree of dilution so that he might repeat or retrace his steps, invented or adopted the centesimal scale..."

'Under certain conditions he found, perhaps to his surprise, that instead of weakening the drug he was actually increasing its curative power. In reducing the density of the mass he perceived that he was setting free powers previously latent, and that these powers were the greatest and most efficient for their therapeutic purposes...'

"This reduction [in dose] was apparently due to Hahnemann's observation that medicines administered in substantial amounts according to the law of similars caused severe aggravation of symptoms."

"His chief endeavour was obviously to establish a theory of dosage."

"From [1796] onwards he selected remedies from the standpoint of similarity, still administering, however, fairly large doses."

"...in 1798...he still prescribed 8 grains of Ignatia and China in quantities of ½-1 grain..."

"In his essay announcing the discovery of a new therapeutic principle, published in 1796, no allusion is made to any doses different from those in ordinary use...and in his writings up to 1801 nothing is to be found to lead us to suppose that there was anything exceptional in his mode of employing drugs..."

"In his early years of practice Hahnemann used doses comparable to those of his colleagues...in 1799 he first announced the principle of the infinitesimal dose, and after 1800 his dose sizes were gradually reduced."

'We cannot fail to be struck by the sudden transition from the massive doses he prescribed in 1798 to the unheard-of minuteness of his doses only one year later, and we can but guess the causes for this abrupt transition.'

"In 1799 he suddenly announced without particular explanation very small and so-called infinitesimal doses."

"It is in his little work on Scarlet Fever, published in 1801, that we have the first forebodings of an unusual mode of preparing the medicines...the dose of Opium there recommended...is very small compared with the ordinary dose...the object of this dilution was to diminish the power of the medicine chiefly...for patients of very tranquil disposition..."

"For the cure of the first stage of Scarlet Fever [published in 1801] the dose of Belladonna prescribed was only the 432,000th part of a grain of the extract, a quantity intermediate betwixt our 2nd and 3rd dilution."

"He gave her the one four hundred and thirty-two thousandth part of a grain of Belladonna, with the result that in about twenty four hours she became well...in Hufeland's Journal, 13.2, January 1801, he published 'On Small Doses of Medicine in General and of Belladonna in Particular'...and supports his doses of Belladonna previously given."

"...the question of doses. Remarkably enough he even passes over them in silence in his first Materia Medica, which appeared in 1805..."

"...Materia Medica Pura...there are accurate statements in the second volume appearing in 1816...Arsenicum is recommended in 12th, 18th and 30th dilution; Hahnemann gives preference to the 30th..."

"The year 1817 saw the publication of the third volume of the Materia Medica Pura...China 12, Asarum 12 or 15..."

"...from 1824 to 1827...he gradually increased the dilution of remedies."

"Hahnemann himself felt in 1829, the urgent necessity of a limit in potentisation and declared the ultimate degree of dilution to be the 30th centesimal potency."

"In the year 1829 Hahnemann came upon the strange idea of setting up a kind of standard dose for all curative remedies...this was to be the 30th centesimal."

"...1/1,000,000 of its original strength. This constituted the third centesimal dilution; Hahnemann recommended the thirtieth dilution."

"The materialistically minded [homoeopaths] restricted themselves to the crude tinctures and triturations, or the very low dilutions, ranging from 1x to 6x...another small class of metaphysical tendency used only the very highest potencies, ranging from the two hundredth to the millionth..."

"The efficiency of homoeopathic potencies is not to be determined by calculation, but by actual trial upon the living organism."

'In the Organon, however, he stated that trituration and succussion release the 'spirit-like power' of the medicine - which is compatible with his assumption that medicines act through their spiritual [geistlich] or dynamic impact upon the organism.'

'He...[advised] ...that the liquid medicine, having been made up, should be slightly succussed between each dose...'

'Only very occasionally is a succussion of the container of the liquid specified...this appears to be a succussion of the stock bottle, or main container, rather than of an intermediate glass.'

'But with time there emerges ever more clearly the view that, by shaking and trituration, a uniform mixing, dilution and weakening of the medicinal substance is not all that is achieved; on the contrary, the material part of the medicine is thereby more and more eradicated and as a consequence the spiritual part of the medicine [not perceptible to human faculties] is released and extraordinarily increased. This is dynamization...be possible to increase the power by succussion; the more the medicine is succussed when prepared, the stronger its effect...'

'...in regard to the most appropriate number of succussions he altered his opinion repeatedly within a few years.'

'By trituration and succussion, he says, the medicinal power of medicines may be increased almost to an infinite degree. Hence we are warned against succussing our succussive dilutions over-much.'

'Whilst in the earlier periods of the growth of his system he merely tells us to shake the bottle, to shake it strongly - to shake it for a minute or longer - he afterwards tells us that much shaking increases the power of the medicine to a dangerous extent, and therefore only two shakes must be used for each dilution. Latterly, however, he again loses his dread of shaking, and after once more appointing ten shakes for each dilution as the standard, he becomes more liberal and allows twenty, fifty, or more shakes, and half a dozen shakes to the bottle before each dose of the medicinal solution. Again, whereas in one place he says that the shaking is the only agent in the dynamization...in another he alleges that dilution is essential to the dynamizing effect of succussion, and that all the rubbing and shaking in the world will not dynamize an undiluted substance.'

"...in preparation the vial had to be 'succussed'. A simple dilution was not sufficient; the vial containing the medicine had to be struck against a leather pad a number of times."

"It is highly probable that during such dynamization...the material substance eventually dissolves completely into its individual spirit-like essence and that its crude state can be regarded as actually consisting only of this spirit-like essence, as yet undeveloped."

'Homoeopathy is opposed to the use...of drugs in physiological doses...it depends for all its results upon the dynamical action of single, pure, potentised medicines, prepared by a special mathematico-mechanical process and administered in minimum dose.

"...he would then prescribe this drug in a small dose. In some patients the symptoms at first increased before there was any response. He then tried giving progressively smaller and smaller doses. He always advocated giving the smallest dose necessary to help the patient...he evolved a method of mixing, diluting and shaking which he called succussion..."

"He was well aware that some of the remedies in their most concentrated form were highly poisonous and he had, therefore, successively reduced the size of the dose. Experimenting in this way he found that not only was the effectiveness maintained, but even increased, when the dose was infinitesimally small."

"...it was not long before Hahnemann's persistent experimentation revealed that dilution and succussion of remedies somehow rendered them more effective..."

'Yet today in retrospect homoeopathy merits a more favorable consideration for its ultimate influence upon the field of medicine. First, along with others, it forced the conventional practitioners to give up the harmful and obsolete practice of bloodletting and the use of calomel. Second, it proved to be the stimulus which led orthodox medicine to improve medical education.'

■

HUNTER, HAHNEMANN AND THE ORIGIN OF HOMOEOPATHY

'Hahnemann was not the first to try drugs on the healthy organism. Anton Stoerck, on June 23 1760, rubbed fresh Stramonium on his hands to see if, as the botanists said, it would inebriate him. It did not, and he then rubbed some in a mortar, and, sleeping in the same room, got a headache. He then made an extract, placing it on his tongue. He wished to know if the drug

study of portrait of a girl-by the dutc artist, Frans Hals - 29 June 1999

could be safely used as a remedy. Stoerck says that if Stramonium disturbs the senses and produces mental derangement in persons who are healthy, it might very easily be administered to maniacs for the purpose of restoring the senses by effecting a change in ideas. Crumpe, an Irish physician, tried drugs on the healthy, and published a book in London on the effects of Opium in 1793, three years after the first experiments of Hahnemann. Hahnemann refers in the 'Organon' to the Danish surgeon, Stahl, who says: 'I am convinced that diseases are subdued by agents which produce similar affections.' [Organon, 4th edition, New York, p.91].' [Bradford, p.42 1st edition]

This essay predominantly consists of a discussion about the constituent elements of a formative process Hahnemann was engaged in between 1782-1798, in his first formulation of homoeopathy.

'From 1782 until 1796 Hahnemann earned a meagre living through work as a translator, writer and chemical researcher...' [Nicholls, p.11]

The origin of homoeopathy contains a number of problems. Homoeopathy is not a single dogma, but consists of four central features which, when defined and clearly understood, distinguish it completely from eighteenth century allopathy. These are single drugs, provings, minute doses and the law of similars. Many have pondered upon the processes and events which caused Hahnemann to choose these principles. This essay attempts to do precisely that.

The minute dose was in fact the last development of the four and derived entirely from Hahnemann's experimentation. Therefore, we do not need to explain that as an aspect of the central problem we are addressing here about origins. It comes in later as a secondary development. The same can also be said about single drugs, the use of which can be explained mostly from Hahnemann's penchant for simplifying things, like most Enlightenment thinkers of his day:

> 'Then let us...agree to give but one single, simple remedy at a time, for every single disease...' [Are the Obstacles to Certainty and Simplicity in Practical Medicine Insurmountable?, 1797, in Lesser Writings, p.320]

> 'Hippocrates sought the simplest from out an entire genus of diseases...and gave single simple remedies from the then scanty store...' [Are the Obstacles to Certainty and Simplicity in Practical Medicine Insurmountable?, 1797, in Lesser Writings, p.321]

> 'Dare I confess, that for many years I have never prescribed anything but a single medicine at once, and have never repeated the dose until the action of the former one had ceased....and always a simple, never a compound remedy...' [Are the Obstacles to Certainty and Simplicity in Practical Medicine Insurmountable?, 1797, in Lesser Writings, pp.321-2]

> '...wise nature produces the greatest effects with simple, often with small means...more frequently with one alone, we may restore to normal harmony the greatest derangements of the diseased body...' [The Medicine of Experience, 1805, in Lesser Writings, p.469]

He had long railed against the weird mixtures of the apothecaries as being an outdated, essentially harmful, uncurative and unscientific approach, and thus again, the problem of the origin of homoeopathy is not really pivotal around the origin of the use of the single drug:

> 'His next article was 'Are the Obstacles to Certainty and Simplicity in Practical Medicine Insurmountable?' [1797]. In it he argues in favor of simple, careful methods...at this time Hahnemann was habitually depending on the single remedy at a time for every single disease, and says in this essay that it has been a long time since he has given more than one remedy at a time. He also prescribed according to the law of similars. He was in the habit of preparing and dispensing his own medicines independent of the apothecaries.' [Bradford, p.59; p.51 of 1st edition]

> 'Hahnemann was the first to raise his voice against the compounding of prescriptions, holding that the effects of compounds on disease could never be known precisely.' [Coulter, Vol. 2, p.335]

Thus we are left with two central problems which he faced at the beginning, and which do deserve greater attention: the law of similars and the proving.

I have argued before [see The Proving, Potentisation and The Law of Similars [Resonance, USA, June 1998]; From Poisonings and Provings to Holism [Similia 11.2, Australia, Dec. 1998]] that the proving derives very largely from reaching a position of having abandoned allopathic practice completely and then wanting to know in detail the precise therapeutic action of a single drug. This forms the crux of

Hahnemann's problem right at the start of his search and is a fair account of the position he found himself in. How can one determine the action of any single drug, if one has already abandoned the dictates of signatures and tradition? It seems like a conundrum which is impossible to solve. The only way is to test drugs on the healthy, which is what he did. If you combine this knotty problem with Hahnemann's obsession throughout the 1780s with poisons and their effects [see below], then it is possible to show that some experimentation on his part with mild self-poisonings using single drugs was more or less inevitable at that point in time. That arguably forms the basis for his discovery of the proving as a technique. Added to which are the influences of von Stoerck, and others, already alluded to in quotation.

> 'Hahnemann's dose reduction made possible the systematic use of poisons in medicine. While this had been recommended by von Stoerck and others, it could not be practised as long as large doses were considered necessary...the homoeopathic pharmacopoeia later used dozens of the most powerful poisons: Belladonna, Aconite, Arsenic, Strychnine, Rattlesnake...' [Coulter, pp.403-4]

Essentially, it came down to a straight choice between signatures and provings:

> 'There is, afterall, an important difference between the selection of a medicine on the basis of its ability to reproduce, in a healthy person, the symptom complex manifested in a patient, and the selection of a medicine on the basis of some physical resemblance between it and the organ affected...' [Nicholls, 1988, p.8]

Thus having dealt with three out of the four, we have now narrowed down our search into the origin of homoeopathy to a single question, which concerns his discovery of the law of similars. This also forms the basis for the name 'homoeopathy' a word carefully chosen by 'Hahnemann the linguist' to most accurately portray the central, most essential and most dominant feature of his system: the use of drugs based upon similia similibus rather than upon the ancient Galenic principle of contraria contrariis, which forms, then as now, the basis for allopathy: cure by opposites, using mixed drugs in high doses and selected upon the basis of signatures and trial and error rather than provings.

Regarding mixed drugs, Hahnemann's instinct left him in no doubt:

> 'Sophistical whimsicalities were pressed into the service...from these ancient times came the unhappy idea, that if sufficient number of drugs were mixed in the receipt, it could scarcely fail to contain the one capable of triumphing over the enemy of health...' [Aesculapius in the Balance, 1805, in Lesser Writings, p.420-1]

Hahnemann's scornful view of Galen is also painfully apparent:

> 'But not long after them came Claudius Galen...the torch and trumpet of general therapeutics, a man more desirous of inventing a subtle system than of consulting experience. Disdaining to learn the powers of medicines by instituting experiments, he gave the bad example of generalizing and framing hypotheses.' [On The Helleborism of the Ancients, 1812, in Lesser Writings, p.592]

The Origin of Homoeopathy

The law of similars was mentioned by Hippocrates [see Lesser Writings, p.460] and occasionally by other medical writers in history, but it seems never to have been regarded as a dominant healing principle.

> 'In the Hippocratic text 'Of The Places In Man', probably written around 350 BC, the writer holds that the general therapeutic rule is 'contraria contrariis curentur' but notes 'Another type is the following: through the similar the disease develops and through the employment of the similar the disease is healed'.' [In Nicholls, 1988, p.16]

It was revived for a brief time by Paracelsus before it sank back into obscurity. Thus it does seem exceptional that Hahnemann stumbled upon it and elevated it into the central principle of his new homoeopathic system. Therefore, in order to understand the origin of this most central aspect of homoeopathy we need to more clearly delineate his method of working. It is notoriously difficult to accurately recreate the situation of a long-dead person, let alone their thinking and the evolution of an idea, but we must at least try.

Though it is true to say that Hahnemann in the 1780s was 'groping in the dark' nevertheless we are right in saying that it was a partially illuminated darkness. It seems that there are certain things he had already ruled out of his search, and certain things he had already ruled in. For instance, he had more or less ruled out all the four central pillars of Old Physick: signatures, large doses, mixed drugs and contraries, which he at least suspected of being bogus. Once he had clearly identified these four principles [which happened around 1783], then from that point forwards, we might conclude that he conceived their opposite principles, at the outset, to be worth investigating more thoroughly: i.e. provings, small doses, single drugs and similars.

Well, it is a neat idea, but the known facts simply do not support the notion. If he had conceived a four-fold grand system early on, based simply upon some principles the exact opposite to those of allopathy, then we could surely expect to find him reducing his doses and conducting provings much earlier than he did? His first proving is likely to have been conducted in 1790 and he did not reduce doses significantly and in truly potentised form until 1799.

> 'In his early years of practice Hahnemann used doses comparable to those of his colleagues: 5-50 grams of Antimony, 20-70 grams of Jalap Root...his 1796 Essay mentions 'moderate' doses. In 1799 he first announced the principle of the infinitesimal dose, and after 1800 his dose sizes were gradually reduced...' [Coulter, p.400]

> 'We cannot fail to be struck by the sudden transition from the massive doses he prescribed in 1798 to the unheard-of minuteness of his doses only one year later, and we can but guess the causes for this abrupt transition.' [Dudgeon, 1853, pp.395-6]

He was still using material doses as late as 1798. That is 8 years after his Cinchona bark proving and thus at least two elements of homoeopathy [the proving and small doses], could not have been formulated at an early stage [even in his mind] in some grand plan in the 1780s. It clearly does not seem to suggest, therefore, a system formulated in one piece at an early stage in response to an early rejection of allopathy's four principles.

> '[After the first proving] Hahnemann waited some time before giving vent to these ideas... 'The Essay on a New Principle'...did not appear until 1796. And a further fourteen years passed before the first edition of 'The Organon' appeared...' [Nicholls, p.10]

Rather, it seems to signify a piecemeal approach, a slow elaboration, probably derived from 'groping in the dark', great uncertainty and a surprisingly slow evolution in his thinking and experimentation. It suggests that his ideas meandered around somewhat, and also that the first proving of 1790 might not have been such a great illumination to him as is commonly supposed by us now looking back. If he had nurtured a grand plan preconceived at an early stage, then why did he wait so long and delay his experiments? Surely he would have pursued quickly, and with vigour, a systematic investigation much earlier than he actually did? That certainly characterised his general approach to most matters.

The fact that he did not do that but meandered around for at least 8 years, quite strongly implies that he was no nearer conceiving homoeopathy as a full system at an early stage. Thus it seems clear that homoeopathy as a full system was not hit upon in one go, but that its four main tenets were unravelled quite slowly and haphazardly in a gradual and piecemeal fashion.

As well as not knowing precisely which principle of homoeopathy he came to solidly embrace at what time or in what sequence, nor do we know in what order Hahnemann definitely relinquished the 4 dogmas of Old Physick. We can merely guess these things from what he said at various stages. But we do know that he detested high doses of drugs from an early stage [see quote below from Lesser Writings, pp.747-9], and that he railed against mixed drugs in general:

> 'I have no hesitation in asserting that whenever two medicines are mingled together, they almost never produce each its own action on the system, but one almost always different from the action of both separately - an intermediate action, a neutral action, - if I may be allowed to borrow the expression from chemical language.' [Are the Obstacles to Certainty and Simplicity in Practical Medicine Insurmountable?, 1797, in Lesser Writings, p.320]

Afterall, these facts comprised the main reasons that he abandoned allopathic practice [on his move to Dresden in the Fall of 1784; see Cook, pp.46-7 and Bradford, p.36] in the first place. He also bemoaned, from an early stage, the use of signatures as 'an absurd and fabulous folly':

> 'I shall spare the ordinary school the humiliation of reminding them of the folly of those ancient physicians who, determining the medicinal powers of crude drugs from their signature, that is from their colour and form...but I shall refrain from taunting the physicians of the present day with these absurdities, although traces of them are met with in the most modern treatises on materia medica.' [Examination of the Sources of the Common Materia Medica, 1817, in Lesser Writings, p.670]

> '...the mere suppositions of our superstitious forefathers, who had childishly enough asserted certain medicinal substances to be the remedies of certain diseases, merely on account of some external

> resemblance of those medicines with some...[signature], or whose efficacy rested only on the authority of old women's tales, or was deduced from certain properties that had no essential connexion with their fabulous medicinal powers...'
> [On the Value of the Speculative Systems of Medicine, 1808, in Lesser Writings, p.502]

All this therefore probably implies that he begrudgingly tolerated the contraria principle much longer than most homoeopaths today would care to imagine, i.e. for virtually all the 1780s. Finally, we can add that in the same period of time [1782-99] he published numerous papers on Chemistry and Medicine in the journals, and translated into German over twenty large medical texts from English, French, Latin and Italian, plus a growing number of original essays on homoeopathy [for lists of these publications see Bradford, pp.515-21; and Haehl, Vol. 2, pp.511-15]. Thus he had other reasons to be seeming to make such slow progress.

Once he had completely abandoned mixed drugs and signatures then he was forced to contemplate how to determine what the action of a single drug is upon the healthy organism. This forms the central and most pivotal event in the development of homoeopathy, in my view, as it shows a major turning point in his thinking. We can now focus on this central problem. At that point in his knowledge Hahnemann must have found himself gazing at several rivers of thought converging before him. As we pointed out above, in order to determine the action of a single drug you either have to follow tradition and signatures or you do what? What other means is there to find out except by giving it to the sick? Thus he faced two choices: give the drug to the sick or to the healthy. He was averse to the former, as it proves so hard to distinguish the symptom elements of the illness from the effects caused by the drug.

'The dispute as to whether the brooklime [Anagallis arvensis] and the bark of Misletoe [Viscum album] possess great curative virtues or none at all, would immediately be settled, if it were tried on the healthy whether large doses produce bad effects, and an artificial disease similar to that in which they have been hitherto empirically used.' [Essay On a New Principle for Ascertaining the Curative Powers of Drugs, 1796, in Lesser Writings, pp.269-70]

Another stream of ideas flowed from his deep interest in poisons, which reveal the effects of drugs upon the healthy. For example, his publications: On Arsenical Poisoning, 1786; The Complete Mode of Preparing The Soluble Mercury, 1790; On The Best Method of Preventing Salivation and The Destructive Effects of Mercury, 1791; What Are Poisons? What are Medicines?, 1806.

'All other substances which excite antagonistic irritability and artificial fever check intermittent fever, if administered shortly after the attack...all bitter plants excite, in large doses, some artifical fever, however small, and thus occasionally drive away intermittent fever by themselves.'[Bradford, p.49]

'Hahnemann very carefully argues the question of the new law; he adduces many results of poisonings by drugs, gives his experiences in the uses of medicines...and records the symptoms that certain medicines produced on himself and others.' [Bradford, p.58]

If the effects of poisons on the healthy can be delineated in such detail, then why not the effects of any drug at all? Thus at least two forces were pushing him in the same direction towards the first proving. Yet another important event also pushed him along the same path: the side-effects of high doses, especially of mercurials for Syphilis became a central problem of his early practice. He knew that Mercury could cure Syphilis. He had a mercury preparation named after him [Mercurius solubilis Hahnemannii] which also shows how much interest he took in the treatment of that condition.

Dr. John Hunter (1728-93)

It is at this point also that the work of the English surgeon, **John Hunter** [1728-93], becomes an important influence upon Hahnemann. Coulter suggests [p.356-7] that Hahnemann gained some insights into the tenet: 'what will cause can cure' from reading Hunter's work on the Mercurial treatment of Syphilis:

> 'This new approach [i.e. the proving]...was inspired by the writings of the profoundly original and pathbreaking Scottish physician, John Hunter [1728-1793].' [Coulter, p.356]

Hunter had worked on venereal diseases and later published texts on that subject [e.g. A Treatise on the Venereal Disease, Longmans, London, 1837]. Hahnemann referenced Hunter's work in his early work on Syphilis published in 1786 [Instructions for Surgeons on Venereal

Diseases, Leipzig, 1789; see Cook, p.51; Gumpert, p.58]:

'Although the translation of Cullen's treatise appears to have been a crucial turning point in Hahnemann's thought, he was neither the first to have suggested the simile - as he admitted - nor was its presence entirely absent from his own thinking prior to 1790. John Hunter's essay, 'Treatise on the Venereal Diseases', in which he observed the effects of venereal inoculation, seems to have been influential. Certainly, Hunter's work is mentioned by Hahnemann in his own publication of 1789, 'Instructions for Surgeons'...and indications of the subsequent direction of Hahnemann's ideas, realised in the 'New Principle' essay of 1796, may be found here.

One of the most immediate precursors of Hahnemann was Anton von Stoerck [1731-1803] who, in the late 1760s, suggested the treatment of diseases with poisons according to the principle of similars....since Hahnemann had studied medicine under **Joseph von Quarin** at Vienna, who in turn had studied under von Stoerck, one of the more proximate sources of Hahnemann's thinking is perhaps indicated here.' [Nicholls, 1988, p.12; see also Bradford, p.50]

Dr. Joshph Von QUARIN

'...the parallels between the two works are striking. To Hunter is thus due a share of the credit

for Hahnemann's discovery of the drug proving.'
[Coulter, p.356]

The important line of Hahnemann's reasoning here must be teased right out into the open, as it reveals quite clearly how the observations he made were suggestive of what later became elevated into important homoeopathic principles.

He knew that Mercury can cause as many symptoms as it can cure and that the higher the dose the more aggravated are the symptoms it produces. This taught him the curious and sensitive relationship between toxic and therapeutic action. Thus we can safely conclude from this the line of reasoning which must have trickled through Hahnemann's mind when observing such events. He must have realised that crude doses in general are bad because they produce unwanted aggravations and iatrogenic diseases [side-effects]:

> 'The mischievous effects of...overloading them with strong unknown drugs, will be perfectly obvious...every medicine is a disease-creating substance, consequently every powerful medicine taken day after day...will make healthy persons ill...long-continued doses of strong allopathic medicines...[leads to] the establishment of permanent alterations of our organisms...that is not capable of being cured and removed by any human art...for which there is and can be no remedy on earth, no antidote, no restorative medicines in nature.' [Allopathy: A Word of Warning To All Sick Persons, 1831, in Lesser Writings, pp.747-9]

Yet he also knew that Mercury in small doses could greatly improve or even cure Syphilis. Thus he must have conceived from such observations the thought that the most similar medicine [what he called a 'specific' but not meaning the same as a specific in medicine] has a special and unique power.

He was the first to see a polarity principle operating in relation to dosage. Thus for Merc and Syph, for Bell and Scarlet fever and also for Cinchona and Malaria. This revealed that the specific drug [i.e. the most similar or homoeopathic to the patient] has a very special power over its similar disease [patient]. Small doses cure while large doses aggravate. What he next had to do was to experiment with crude doses of ANY drug to see what they could produce in the healthy. Poisons are special, and stand out from all other drugs, by virtue of their strong power to produce symptoms. Indeed, the 'power to produce symptoms' can in fact be regarded as the guiding aphorism which led Hahnemann ['torch and trumpet'] to the realisation that poisons held an important key to solving his central problem about similars and the action of the single drug. It is this very axiom which I think must have droned through Hahnemann's mind continuously like a loud mantra. Again we see, all roads led him to the proving, i.e. experiments with mild self-poisonings. The purpose? His purpose was to settle for once and all, unequivocally and without the use of signatures, what the therapeutic action of a single drug is.

But to deliberately write him off as merely yet another 'system-builder' in medicine is to woefully misapprehend the man, and his work:

'After all, Hahnemann had cast homoeopathy in substantially the same eighteenth century mold that had given shape to the systems of Cullen, Brown

> and Rush...homoeopathy offered an unambiguous example of extreme rationalism informing a dogmatic system of practice with dire consequences.' [Warner, pp.52-3]

> 'Thus Hahnemann reduced most conditions to the itch and most treatments to the like cures like theory and the high dilution formulas, somewhat as Dr. Still would later reduce all pathologic processes to spinal conditions and all therapeutic practice to spinal manipulations.' [Shryock, 1966, p.171]

That he thoroughly detested medical systems of ideas and speculations is very apparent in all his writings:

> 'There was now the influence of the stars, now that of evil spirits and witchcraft; anon came the alchymist with his salt, sulphur and mercury; anon Silvius, with his acids, biles and mucus...our system-builders delighted in these metaphysical heights, where it was so easy to win territory; for in the boundless region of speculation every one becomes a ruler who can most effectually elevate himself beyond the domain of the senses.' [Aesculapius in the Balance, 1805, in Lesser Writings, p.421-2]

He also edged closer to settling the question of dosage. All this work also explained to him the fundamental nature of what similar really means. And also in this he found the primary and secondary or 'biphasic action' of drugs too:

> '..close inspection of the action of medicinal substances on the healthy led to a major discovery–
>
> the biphasic action of drugs.' [Coulter, p.363; see also Nicholls, p.78]

Thus we can begin to see that all of this research and experimentation in the 1780s and 90s led him to contemplate and grapple with all these profound and unresolved aspects of medicine. He could also address the problem of the similarity between a drug and its disease. The fact that Bell and Scarlet fever and Merc and Syph resonated with each other so well and so profoundly allowed him to see that the law of similars as formulated by the doctrine of signatures, though imperfect, was perhaps closer to the truth afterall and capable of being forged into an infinitely more precise and workable therapeutic weapon against disease than contraries ever could. In some manner therefore he must have sensed the superiority of the law of similars. Arguably, it was only through his deep and sustained contemplation of the notion of similars and poisonings which led him finally to his 'home port' of the proving technique.

Indeed, in the period in question, Hahnemann seems to have been pretty well assailed on all sides by many difficult and unresolved medical problems at the same time as to make his task so much more difficult, and this, probably explains the relatively slow pace of his progress between 1782 and 1799. Like a military commander besieged and fighting on several active fronts at the same time he could only devote a small amount of his time, energy and intelligence to any one problem at a time. In short, this meant that he was flooded out with too many questions to solve to allow him the time to disentangle them quickly into some kind of meaningful framework. It really is a testament to his inventive genius that he did settle all these complex problems in less than two decades. Only when we today contemplate the vast size of the homoeopathic materia medica, our relatively detailed and exhaustive knowledge of each drug and all the information in the Organon about drug actions, can we fully appreciate the staggering achievement of Hahnemann.

At that early stage he had no materia medica at all, worthy of that name, and stood at the base of what would soon become one of mountainous proportions. For example, how was he to know that the symptom phenomena he had observed with Cinchona, Mercury and Belladonna also applied to all other drugs? He had no way of knowing if the production of symptoms in the healthy was a principle applying to all drugs. Only after he had proved tens of drugs was he able, confidently and unambiguously, to declare that the proving seemingly was a universal and immutable principle. Very gradually he solved all these complex, profound and mutually entangled problems, to create an entirely new medical system founded solely upon experimentation and sound principles - the very things which eighteenth century allopathy was woefully devoid of, being in fact a mass of warring factions:

> 'Physiology...looked only through the spectacles of hypothetical conceits, gross mechanical explanations, and pretensions to systems...little has been added...what are we to think of a science, the operations of which are founded upon perhapses and blind chance?' [Aesculapius In the Balance, 1805, in Lesser Writings, pp.423-6]

> '...because they placed the essence of the medical art, and their own chief pride, in explaining much even of the inexplicable...this was the first and great delusion they practised upon themselves and on the world. This was the unhappy conceit which, from Galen's time down to our own, made the medical

art a stage for the display of the most fantastic, often most self-contradictory, hypotheses, explanations, demonstrations, conjectures, dogmas, and systems, whose evil consequences are not to be overlooked...'
[*On the Value of the Speculative Systems of Medicine, 1808, in Lesser Writings, pp.489-90*]

Thus all these considerations reinforce the impression we have made regarding the remarkable nature of Hahnemann's achievement. What is remarkable about him is that in the same period of time he managed to identify and distance himself from the 4 fundamental principles of Old Physick, to formulate and develop the principles of homoeopathy, to investigate the primary and secondary actions of poisons and drugs and to investigate the polarity principle of dosage [see Coulter, pp.363-7]. He thoroughly tested and established all of these four aspects of his search. And he did all these things entirely on his own. He was the only person to do this. Only through thoroughly immersing himself in all of that could he confidently emerge from it at the end both with a full practical system of therapy in his hands that worked as well as one which rested upon a firm bedrock of clear principles. Homoeopathy as a working system was the child of his practical experimentation, while the Organon sprang into life from his investigation of the theoretical principles of medicine in general, both of which he had researched pretty exhaustively between 1782 and 1799. The fact that he had read so widely of other medical writers and translated so many important texts into German, demonstrate the seriousness and great learning he brought to his task:

'*Let it be borne in mind that he was a thoroughly well-posted physician, skilled both in theory and* practice, better read in the various notions of the medical books of the time than most of his fellows.' [Bradford, p.35].

■

HAHNEMANN'S DEBT TO ALCHEMY

Crete 23-4-2000

Samuel Hahnemann denied any link whatsoever to Paracelsus and any link to medieval alchemy as sources of his ideas or techniques. This article examines a range of evidence which suggests otherwise.

INTRODUCTION

Homoeopathy has a range of clearly traceable origins, but chiefly began as a reaction against the Heroic overdrugging, bleeding and cupping of 18th century medicine. Even here though, the reaction was chiefly against the inefficacy rather than the barbarity of those methods per se. The medical approach of homoeopathy can be traced back to some of the theoretical ideas of medieval alchemists like Albertus Magnus [1193-1280], Agrippa von Nettsheim [1486-1535], and especially Theophrastus Paracelsus [1493-1541]. It also contains elements from the early Greeks, especially Hippocrates [468-377BC] and also Thomas Sydenham [1624-1689]. Yet it is not until the work of Hahnemann that all these separate threads were combined to form the homoeopathic system of medicine as we know it. As the name implies, its key feature is the use of the similars principle [*similia similibus curentur*] rather than the use of opposites [*contraria contrariis*] in disease.

> "...a pattern emerges of ideas, influences, cultural realities and historical momentum behind his discoveries..." [Danciger, 1987, p.1]

The question has often been asked did Hahnemann copy Paracelsus? The answer is 'yes' in the sense that he used the law of similars and knew that others in medicine [including Paracelsus] before him had also used it. The answer is 'no' in the sense that what Paracelsus used was not homoeopathy in the Hahnemannian sense, because Paracelsus did not conduct provings and nor did he, as far as we know, attenuate the dose. These latter two techniques were developed exclusively by Hahnemann and form unique components of the homoeopathic system which he created. However, Paracelsus did, apparently, do something with dosage and did use small doses compared with his medical peers. Like Hahnemann, he also detested complex mixtures of drugs and tended to use a smaller compass of drugs than most of his peers. He also elied heavily on the healing power of natue to take up the work once his dose was exhausted:

> 'I write short prescriptions, not forty to sixty ingredients. I prescribe little and seldom...'
> [Paracelsus, Sieben Defensiones, in Coulter, Vol. 1, p.348]

Paracelsus can thus be regarded as Hahnemann's most 'homoeopathic' predecessor, as he is the most famous physician before Hahnemann to make extensive clinical use of the law of similars.

> "Paracelsus felt that diseases should be classified as diseases of lead, silver, gold, Saturn, moon, sun or some other substance according to the cosmic patterns that correspond to and activate them."
> [Whitmont, 1980, p.10]

As far as we know Paracelsus did not conduct provings of drugs in the Hahnemannian sense, but he was very interested in their poisonous effects, and he seemed to perceive the same link that Hahnemann made, between the toxicity and the therapeutic action of a drug. Paracelsus did, however, do something unusual with remedy preparation. Perhaps he glimpsed but dimly the underlying principle which Hahnemann was later able to clarify in much greater detail. Yet even Paracelsus used contraries and was not reliable or consistent in his approach.

> '[Paracelsus's]...next step would have been to administer metals and minerals in a systematic way to healthy persons [as had been suggested by Galen]. This step was in fact taken by Samuel Hahnemann, the founder of homoeopathic medicine, possibly

> through inspiration from Paracelsus.' [Coulter, Vol. 1, p.442]

Hahnemann undoubtedly knew of and built upon the work of Paracelsus. But it is the size and extent of his debt that is difficult to quantify. Some [e.g. Danciger, 1987 Gutman, 1978] have suggested that Hahnemann's debt to Paracelsus was great, that he was a member of Western Esoteric traditions [or drew heavily upon them] and that he was very familiar with the metaphysical views of his near-contemporary, Goethe [1749-1832], Western Esoteric traditions like the Freemasons, Knight's Templar and the Rosicrucians. This may be stretching the point somewhat, as Hahnemann himself goes no further than mentioning Hippocrates as using the law of similars. Similar points are made by Neagu [1995] and Bradford [1895].

It is peculiar that Hahnemann never mentions that medical rebel and doyen of similars, Paracelsus. Perhaps he felt that Paracelsus was too controversial a figure to be linked with his new therapy. He was also complex and contradictory. He may have felt that accusations of plagiarism would have been made against him. It is well known that Hahnemann was a lifelong Freemason, and perhaps he was under a vow of silence about the influence of Paracelsus and other Esotericists on his new system of therapy.

Perhaps Hahnemann discovered similar ideas to Paracelsus but entirely via a different route, through his own experimentation and research and thus wished to stress the originality of his own work. This important aspect of influences upon the early Hahnemann, is discussed in depth in Haehl, 1922, [Vol. 1, p.11 & pp.21-24, & Vol. 2, pp.9-10]

Hahnemann's Debt to Alchemy

in which he specifically rejects any link with Paracelsus. Yet this remains a somewhat unconvincing viewpoint.

It is very difficult to know with certainty to what degree Hahnemann leaned upon Paracelsus. He left behind little evidence of any substantial interest in occultism or mediaeval medicine, so it is more likely that he devised homoeopathy partly through practice and partly through his own mind just thinking things through. And for that there is abundant evidence right through his life - he had a brilliant, searching and restless inventiveness to his mentality. He was very perceptive and very original in almost everything he did.

PARACELSUS

Some people say that Paracelsus had done much the same thing as Hahnemann some 250 years previously. This is a claim we need to look at more carefully. It is not quite true that Paracelsus had done the same thing. Paracelsus had certainly criticised allopathy both at a theoretical level and as a method, and he adopted and stressed a range of unorthodox ideas (e.g. law of similars), but unlike Hahnemann appears to have done all that emotionally, irrationally, chaotically and unsystematically

- which was his way. A way that was peculiar to him and valid for him - and a way that is still valid for some. But he failed to articulate any clear, rational or well-reasoned alternative to allopathy. Much of what he wrote is very obscure and contradictory and can in no way be regarded as a tidy medical system with a consistent and rational philosophy. Moreover, it is mostly understandable and of interest now in the light of Hahnemann and homoeopathy which came later. So it was not a clear system that predates homoeopathy as a well-argued and rational ideology. It was a mixed bag. If it had been a clear system it might well have been adopted more widely. The fact that it wasn't is one piece of evidence against it.

It might more realistically be seen as 'a preparation for Hahnemann', a clearing of debris, levelling of ground and the building of basic foundations for homoeopathy. But it never went any further than that. It was a foundation for a new house, that was never actually built. There were no walls, no rooms and no roof. On a theoretical or ideological level it is perfectly true that Paracelsus predates Hahnemann and forms a sound basis of ideas upon which Hahnemann built his 'house of homoeopathy', but it is misleading to then say that Hahnemann copied Paracelsus or that he derived homoeopathy from Paracelsan medicine. In a sense he did do that. In another sense he just made parallel discoveries (mainly through direct insight and experiment) and built up a system with strong similarities to Paracelsus. His system was built up chiefly through experiment based upon some ideas from Cullen and Paracelsus, amongst others, and from his critique of allopathy. But it is oversimplistic and misleading to say that homoeopathy was first produced by Paracelsus and then perfected by Hahnemann.

It probably is true that Hahnemann magicked the 'white dove' of homoeopathy out of the 'black hat' of Paracelsan medicine, but it is very much Hahnemann's white dove and not that of Paracelsus. I stress this point at some length because it has been an oft-repeated claim, even in his lifetime, that Hahnemann was a copier and imitator of Paracelsus - a charge he vigorously denied. If it was true he might have admitted it. That he denied it repeatedly indicates that it was probably more of a coincidence. That he became angry at these accusations does show that he may have been denying something. Of course, to those who swim in the wider river of history of ideas it is difficult to deny some link between Paracelsus and Hahnemann - they are profoundly similar people - and Hahnemann knew about Paracelsus in depth, but that does not inevitably mean that there is a strong causal link between them.

Hahnemann's link with Paracelsus was again emphasised in a paper given at the recent Stuttgart Conference on the History of Medicine [April 1995] by Dr. Michael Neagu, about the history of homoeopathy in his native Rumania [Geschichte der homoopathie in Rumanien]. The post that Hahnemann took in Transylvania at the beginning of his career [1777-79], as a cataloguist to the medical library of a patron, Baron Samuel von Brukenthal, at Sibiu is crucial, because that library in which he spent two years, contained one of the largest European collections of original works by mediaeval alchemists and physicians, including a large collection of works by Paracelsus. It also contained the esoteric *Medicina Spagyrica Tripartita* [1648] of Jean Pharamond Rhumelius [c.1600-c.1660], which Neagu describes as '*a fundamental esoteric work, relying on the principle of similia similibus curentur.*' [p.25 of his paper; p.259 in Dinges, 1996].

The story goes that Hahnemann could not fail to have been inspired by the contents of that collection and probably picked up some therapeutic ideas while there, if only unconsciously. Neagu goes on to add that one of Hahnemann's direct disciples, Honigberger, '*was a speaker of the Rumanian language and had practised homoeopathy in all three Romanian principiates.*' [p.25]. Nevertheless, we might say, this still does not prove that Hahnemann read these works, had any interest in them or obtained ideas from them. But it does indeed seem highly likely that here we find a strong influence which had previously been dismissed or even underplayed, and one of profound importance to Hahnemann's later development.

As Close [1924, p.215] suggests:

"*Many before Hahnemann, from Hippocrates down, had glimpses of the law [of similars], and some had tried to make use of it therapeutically; but all had failed because of their inability to properly graduate and adapt the dose.*"

"*Paracelsus was also a firm believer in the doctrine of signatures, and in illustration of it explained every single part of St. John's Wort [Hypericum perforatum] in terms of this belief...the holes in the leaves mean that this herb helps all inner and outer orifices of the skin...the blooms rot in the form of blood, a sign that it is good for wounds and should be used where flesh has to be treated.*" [Griggs, 1981, p.50]

Leaning heavily, as some might suggest, upon the pioneering work of Paracelsus, he proved and introduced many minerals, metals and acids into the materia medica such as Silica, Calcarea carbonica, Sulphur, Acidum nitricum, Aurum, Cuprum and Argentum, Kali bichromicum, etc. These substances were generally regarded as medicinally inert before the provings of Hahnemann. He also greatly improved the medical knowledge and usefulness of several conventional drugs [through proving them] such as Carbo vegetabilis, Mercury, Arsenic and Sulphur.

Perhaps he deliberately wished to dissociate himself from Paracelsus. The truth is, of course, that Hahnemann was in many respects a second Paracelsus, but he felt he had to hide this fact.

> 'Karlsbad 5 May 1820
>
> ...nobody is allowed to practise by Hahnemann's method...but now Prince Schwarzenberg, very ill and probably incurable, has confidence in **this new Theophrastus Paracelsus** and begs for leave of absence from the Emperor to seek a cure across the border.' [Letter from Goethe, quoted in Haehl, Vol. 1, p.113]

Both mercilessly derided their medical contemporaries, rejected the medicine in which they were trained, used small doses and emphasised the law of similars.

> '...the heathen teachers and philosophers, who follow the subteleties and crafts of their own inventions and opinions. Such teachers are Aristotle, Hippocrates, Avicenna, Galen, and the rest, who based all their arts upon their own opinions. Even

if, at any time, they learnt anything from Nature, they destroyed it again with their own fantasies, dreams, and inventions, before they came to the final issue. By means of these, then, and their followers, nothing perfect can be discovered.'
[Paracelsus, Concerning the Spirits of the Planets, p.4]

Both became deeply enchanted by chemical experiments. Both made extensive use of poisons, minerals, acids and metals. Both also obtained brief university teaching posts, but got sacked after abusing their position, 'indoctrinating' their students, castigating the medical system of the day and teaching heretical forms of medicine. How similar to each other can you get? And both were thoroughly castigated by their orthodox brethren. The following could just as esily have been said by Hahnemann, and with equal truth:

'After leaving university he practised medicine along traditional lines, but gave up in disgust after discovering that he was only harming his patients:

'I found that the medicine I had learned was faulty, and that those who written about it neither knew nor understood it. They all tried to teach what they did not know. They are vainglorious babblers in all their wealth and pomp...[Paracelsus in Das Buch Paragranum, quoted in Coulter, Vol. 1, p.346]

Their biggest difference, perhaps, is that Hahnemann used purified drugs, while Paracelsus tended to use unrefined natural products. Likewise, Paracelsus loved Alchemy, astrology and mysticism, while Hahnemann appears to have loathed all three. Paracelsus was a real problem for Hahnemann about whom he must have thought a great deal: how to shake himself free? Yet he never mentions him in all his writings. One reason is obvious: guilt by association, which had to be avoided at all costs.

> 'Let it be borne in mind that he was a thoroughly well-posted physician, skilled both in theory and practice, better read in the various notions of the medical books of the time than most of his fellows.'
> [Bradford, p.35]

The point here, of course, is that Hahnemann was far more widely read than any other doctor of his day. He knew medical history intimately. Indeed, some of his works contain references in Greek, Latin and Arabic from authors before the Christian era [e.g. *On the Helleborism of the Ancients*, Lesser Writings, Jain Edition, pp 569-617]. He translated medical works from English, French, Italian, and Latin. His linguistic skills were truly astonishing. Of course he knew about Paracelsus, but he chose to keep quiet. It cannot be a coincidence that he put people off the trail leading to Paracelsus by never even mentioning him. The two systems of therapy are unmistakably similar. It is amazing that he is never mentioned. Indeed, many of the metals, acids and minerals in use in 18th century medicine, and later proved by Hahnemann, were actually introduced into medicine originally by Paracelsus, including Mercury, Arsenic, Sulphur, Tin, Lead, Gold, Iron, Copper and Salt.

> 'Paracelsus...[introduced]..a number of mineral remedies...iron, saltpetre, ammonia of sulfur [liver of sulphur], bicarbonate of soda, sufuric acid, and red and black pulvis solaris [mercurial and antomonial compounds]...[and] he appears to have added several new one: flower of sulphur, calomel,

blue vitriol, and other zinc, copper, arsenic and lead compounds...' [Coulter, Vol. 1, p.350]

Nor can it be a coincidence that Hahnemann proved and installed in his materia medica the seven metals of ancient alchemy: Aurum, Argentum, Cuprum, Hydrargyrum, Ferrum, Stannum and Plumbum. These seven metals form the absolute core of alchemical theory and practice [see Pelikan]. And in recent years Sol, Luna and Venus have also been proved and brought into use by alchemy-inspired homoeopaths.

HAHNEMANN'S DENIALS

As we have seen, Hahnemann denied any link with alchemy.

> 'And when the idea of the relations of similarity between illness and medicinal effect flashed upon Hahnemann in 1790, he had no suspicion that Paracelsus had similar ideas. When Trinks, from his own narrative, pointed out to Hahnemann whilst visiting him in Koethen in 1825, that the main features of homoeopathy were to be found in Paracelsus, Hahnemann replied that was unknown to him. In a letter to Stapf, Hahnemann refused very definitely and with some indignation to be associated with Paracelsus's fantastic and none too seriously written 'Will o' the Wisp', as had been suggested by Professor Dr. C. H. Schultz.' [Haehl, Vol. 1, pp.273-4]

> 'In 1825 Trinks...made the personal acquaintance of Hahnemann, whom he visited in Koethen. On this occasion he is said to have pointed out that the principles of homoeopathy are to be found in

Paracelsus. Hahnemann replied that, until that moment, he had known nothing of it.' [Haehl, Vol. 1, p.425]

Although Hahnemann denied any association with Alchemy and persistently denied that he had copied Paracelsus or borrowed anything from him in the formulation of homoeopathy, nevertheless, there do remain some baffling aspects about homoeopathy which can probably best be contextualised by assuming some form an underlying link to alchemy, and with which we can safely assume he MUST have been familiar, both from his early travels and teachings in Transylvania [with von Bruckenthal] and also from his vast reading of medical history.

The main problem areas can be delineated as follows:

calcination

distillation

sublimation [to make Ammonium carb.]

which were used by SH in the preparation of certain weird remedies e.g. Hepar sulph and Causticum. There seems to be no other credible explanation of where he got these techniques from or why he used them for making such peculiar remedies.

ALCHEMICAL TECHNIQUES IN HOMOEOPATHY

Clear evidence of Hahnemann's detailed knowledge of alchemical techniques lies scattered here and there throughout his writings, especially in his mode of preparation of certain remedies. Extracts now follow. Let us begin by considering some of Hahnemann's own instructions for the mode of preparation of some of the elite members of his materia medica.

AMMONIUM CARBONICUM:

'The salt obtained from equal parts of sal-ammoniac and crystalline carbonate of soda, triturated together and sublimated at a moderate heat..' [Chronic Disease, Vol. 1, p.231]

CAUSTICUM:

'Take a piece of freshly burned lime of about two pounds, dip this piece into a vessel of distilled water for about one minute, then lay it in a dish, in which it will soon turn into powder with the development of much heat and its peculiar odour, called lime-vapor. Of this fine powder take two ounces and mix with it in a (warmed) porcelain triturating bowl a solution of two ounces of bisulphate of potash, which has been heated to red heat and melted, cooled again and then pulverised and dissolved in two ounces of boiling hot water. This thickish mixture is put into a small glass retort, to which the helm is attached with wet bladder; into the tube of the helm is inserted the receiver half submerged in water; the retort is warmed by the gradual approach of a charcoal fire below and all the fluid is distilled over by applying the suitable heat. The distilled fluid will be about an ounce and a half of watery clearness, containing in concentrated form the substance mentioned above, i.e., Causticum; its smells like the ley of caustic Potash...' [Chronic Diseases, Vol. 1, p.559]

HEPAR SULPHURIS CALCAREUM:

'A mixture of equal parts of finely powdered, clean oyster shells and quite pure flowers of sulphur is kept for ten minutes at a white heat in a hermetically closed crucible and afterwards stored up in a well-corked bottle. To develop its powers, it is treated like other dry drugs in order to potentize it to the higher degrees, according to the directions at the end of the first volume.' [Chronic Diseases, Vol. 1, p.762]

KALI CARB:

'Half an ounce of purified tartar, moistened with a few drops of water, is pressed together into a ball, which is rolled up into a piece of paper and allowed to dry; then it is brought to a red heat between the glowing charcoal of a grate [or of a draught furnace]. It is then taken out, laid in a porcelain saucer and covered with a linen cloth; it is allowed to attract moisture from the air in a cellar, which causes the alkaline salt partially to deliquesce, and, if allowed to stay there a few weeks, it will deposit even the last trace of lime. A clear drop of this preparation is then triturated three times with 100 grains of sugar of milk...' [Chronic Diseases, Vol. 1, p.805]

Such examples can be multiplied many times and it would be pointless to do so. The gist is that he was aware if and used alchemical techniques. The above highlighted terms are certainly central to alchemical techniques and it therefore seems ridiculous to continue to deny any link between homoeopathy and alchemy when such obvious links exist between these techniques as used by Hahnemann in homoeopathy and their obviously central position within alchemy.

Here are some extracts of alchemical texts for comparison:

> 'Preparation of corals to restrain menstruum and profluvium...make a mixture, reduce by calcination through the fourth grade of reverberation for 12 hours or more; afterwards reduce by ablution with water and plantain.' [Paracelsus, Alchemical Medicine, 1987, p.20]

> 'Concerning magnet...it has virtue for wounds and ulcers...of magnet...of calyx of eggs...set in layers in a crucible. Place in a fire of reverberation a day and a night. Extract and it will be prepared...' [ibid., p.22]

> 'Concerning silver, the virtue of silver obtains in complaints of the cerebrum, the spleen, the liver, and in the retention of profluvium...arrange in layers and reduce to the fourth grade of reverberation for 24 hours...' [ibid., p.32]

Though Hahnemann may not have intended to carry into his new system any of the ideas of alchemy, there seems little doubt that several of its techniques did get carried in, intentionally or otherwise. Indeed, he seems to have taken many of the techniques of alchemy, dumped the theories and used the techniques to prepare his new remedies, chosen on the basis of the law of similars.

We are now in a position to examine briefly what these techniques were and how they are similar to homoeopathic techniques.

On top of the previous material it is also true that certain links with alchemy can also be delineated in relation to the following techniques which are central and unique to the homoeopathic system:

law of similars

minute doses

succussion

trituration

potentisation

The following quotation material supplements the material above drawn from homoeopathy and supports the notion that Hahnemann used some alchemical techniques in his preparation of homoeopathic remedies. He must therefore have been knowledgeable about alchemy and his denials were probably designed to conceal his knowledge. There are seven central pocesses in alchemy. These are 1. calcination or roastin; 2. dissolution; 3. separation; 4. conjunction; 5. fermentation; 6. distillation; and 7. coagulation.

> **1.** *"CALCINATION is the first of seven major operations in the alchemy of transformation [and]...involves heating a substance in a crucible or over an open flame until it is reduced to ashes. In the Arcanum Experiment, Calcination is represented by sulfuric acid, which the alchemists made from a naturally occurring substance called Vitriol. Sulfuric acid is a powerful corrosive that eats away flesh and reacts with all metals except gold.*
>
> ***Physiologically**, the Fire of Calcination can be experienced as the metabolic discipline or aerobic*

activity that tunes the body, burning off excesses from overindulgence and producing a lean, mean, fighting machine.

In **Society**, the Calcination is expressed in the careers of revolutionaries, conquerors, and other warriors who try to overthrow the status quo."

2. "**Chemically**, it is the dissolving the ashes from Calcination in water. In the Arcanum Experiment,"

3. "**Separation** is the third of the operations of transformation in alchemy....it is the isolation of the components of Dissolution by filtration and then discarding any ungenuine or unworthy material. In the Arcanum Experiment, Separation is represented by the compound sodium carbonate, which separates out of water and appears as white soda ash on dry lakebeds. The oldest known deposits are in Egypt. The alchemists sometimes referred to this compound as Natron, which meant the common tendency in all salts to form solid bodies or precipitates.

Physiologically, Separation is following and controlling the breath in the body as it works with the forces of Spirit and Soul to give birth to new energy and physical renewal. ...

In **Society**, Separation is expressed as the establishment of clans, cities, and nationalities."

4. "**Conjunction** is the fourth of the seven operations of alchemy...it is the recombination of the saved elements from Separation into a new substance. In the Arcanum Experiment, Conjunction is

symbolized by a nitrate compound known as cubic-saltpeter or potassium nitrate, which the alchemists called Natron or simply Salt. Blue-colored Natron acid (aqua fortis) was made by mixing potassium nitrate with sulfuric acid and was used to separate silver from gold. The inert residue precipitated from the acid during the reaction like a child being born....

Physiologically, Conjunction is using the body's sexual energies for personal transformation....

In **Society**, it is the growth of crafts and technology to master the environment."

5. "**DISTILLATION** is the sixth major operation in the alchemy of transformation...it is the boiling and condensation of the fermented solution to increase its purity, such as takes place in the distilling of wine to make brandy. In the Arcanum Experiment, Distillation is represented by a compound known as Black Pulvis Solaris, which is made by mixing black antimony with purified sulfur. The two immediately clump together to make what the alchemists called a bezoar, a kind of sublimated solid that forms in the intestines and brain. ...

Physiologically, Distillation is raising the life force repeatedly from the lower regions in the cauldron of the body to the brain (what Oriental alchemists called the Circulation of the Light), where it eventually becomes a wondrous solidifying light full of power. ...

In **Society**, the Distillation experience is expressed as science and objective experimentation..."

Calcination: Roasting; Conflagration; Reduction; Trituration

Distillation: Potentizing; Exaltation; Cohobation; Multiplication

Above Quotation material from 'Operations of Alchemy' on a website Oct. 1999

HAHNEMANN'S LABORATORY WORK

Hahnemann's interest in chemistry is legendary, but few know where he studied it on a daily basis when in his twenties. Gumpert tells us:

> 'But the sole consolation of Hahnemann's existence in Dessau [1779-83] was his daily visit to the apothecary, Haeseler, in whose laboratory he could continue his study of chemistry.' [Gumpert, p.26]

> 'The more definitely Hahnemann passed into oblivion as a doctor, the greater grew his reputation as a writer on medical subjects. Orders for translations poured in on him from Leipzig.' [ibid., p.58]

> 'Day after day, he tested medicines on himself and others. He collected histories of cases of poisoning. His purpose was to establish a physiological doctrine of medical remedies, free from all suppositions, and based solely on experiments.' [ibid., p.92]

> 'Medicine tests [provings] constitute one of the most critical points of Hahnemann's teachings. This grandiose attempt to acquire unhypothetical medical experience was outwardly justified by the complete lack of objective methods of investigation

and experimental systems in those days...[Hahnemann had] the courage to break away from hypotheses and systems...' [ibid., p.122]

'When he left Hermannstadt [now Sibiu in Romania], at the age of 22 years, he was master of Greek, Latin, English, Italian, Hebrew, Syriac, Arabic, Spanish, German, and some smattering of Chaldaic...here he was unwittingly preparing himself for his great future.' [Bradford, p.28]

Nor is it true that Hahnemann gave up medicine because he 'was unable to earn a living' from it [Bradford, p.36].

'Had he wished he could have remained in Gommern [1781-84], for means for his ample living were assured. According to the statements made by his contemporaries and by himself, he had become disgusted with the errors and uncertainties of the prevalent methods of medical practice, and wished earnestly, to seek for some better method. He reduced himself and his family to want for conscience sake.' [Bradford, p.36]

He moved to Dresden in the autumn of 1784:

'He did not practise medicine, but devoted himself to his translations from the French, English and Italian. He also pursued with renewed zeal his favourite, chemistry.' [Bradford, p.37]

By around 1784, Hahnemann very reluctantly and very sorrowfully gave up the practice of medicine. At least this allowed him to channel his energy and time into translating chemical and medical treatises from English, French and Italian into German. This gave him a bit of an income, and also stimulated his further investigations of drugs, poisonings and diseases, and gave him more time for historical research into actual medical cases in various languages.

> 'Thus he arrived at the decision to give up his practice "and to treat scarcely anyone else medically, so as not to injure him" and to occupy himself "merely with chemistry and writing"...'
> [Haehl, Vol. 1, p.267]

Taken together, these changes which Hahnemann made in his life, provided him with the opportunity he needed to devote a lot of his time, to reading, writing and thinking. We also know that he conducted chemical experiments in the laboratory of his father-in-law, Herr Haesler, the apothecary in Dessau, and step-father of his first wife.

> 'But the sole consolation of Hahnemann's existence in Dessau was his daily visit to the apothecary, Haesler, in whose laboratory he could continue his study of chemistry.' [Gumpert, p.26]

The time he spent in Dessau afforded him a welcome opportunity of pursuing his chemical research in the laboratory of the 'Moor Apothecary Shop' - work which was so significant for his pioneer activities in medicine. [Haehl, Vol. 1, p.265]

> 'Hahnemann devoted himself entirely to chemistry and writing, according to his own admission. He puts chemistry first. In this science he was self-taught. He had never received any definite course of instruction in the subject or possessed a laboratory except during his stay in Dessau (1781), where he had found a suitable place in the Moor Apothecary

> *Shop for his experiments and probably also an occasional tutor in the person of the Apothecary Herr Haesler.'* [Haehl, Vol. 1, p.268]

Apart from the loss of his medical practice, which seems to have become an agony his conscience would not allow him to prolong, he now placed himself in a more favourable position for making some fundamental medical discoveries.

It is clear from the sheer mass and volume of these translations, that Hahnemann must have been one of the best read physicians of his day and certainly therefore, a person well-placed to observe and criticise some of the wilder absurdities of the medicine of his day, which had indisputably become a veritable mass of conflicting theories, not one of which had been tested by experiment, but merely composed as an exercise in rhetoric and then used to further the career of its inventor:

> *'At this period there was a complete anarchy in the domain of therapeutics. Theories Hippocratico-vitalistic, Galenic, Mathematical, Chemical, Humoral, Electro-Galvanic, formed an inextricable tissue of variable opinions. Hahnemann had abstained from a search for therapeutical indications in this mass of hazardous theories. He had adopted a simple medication partly expectant, that corresponded more fully with his ideal of the art of healing.'* [Rapou 'Histoire de la doctrine medicale Homoeopathique, Paris, 1847, quoted in Bradford, p.34]

Hahnemann utterly despaired at the irrational nature of the medicine of his day, and its learned professors in the university medical schools, who he felt did more harm than good through their quarrelling:

> 'No learned brains could unravel the skein of hypotheses and theories which entangled the professors and set them all at odds...the words of an arrogant and incomprehensible professorial language were in themselves without results, but the application of those same professors' erroneous deductions killed thousands of men and women. There were no experiments, there was no painstaking research; there were only odd and eccentric systems which were exalted into dogmas, without any possibility of testing senseless methods of treatment.' [Gumpert, p.15]

Hahnemann abandoned medical practice for fear of its harmful effects and through a profound dissatisfaction with its dismal clinical results. He thus became paralysed into medical inactivity through a profound uncertainty about the usefulness of its main techniques and with what he was going to do with the rest of his life. His apparently stop-gap solution to this problem was both intelligent and deeply pragmatic: keep translating to earn a living and given time some truth might just emerge out of a terrible darkness.

> 'The future looked very dark to the honest seeker after truth. He had lost his faith in medicine. Of this time he writes: 'Where shall I look for aid, sure aid? sighed the disconsolate father on hearing the moaning of his dear, inexpressibly dear sick children. The darkness of night and the darkness of a desert all around me; no prospect of relief for my oppressed paternal heart.' [Hahnemann in Hufeland, Lesser Writings, p.513, quoted in Bradford, p.51]

In effect, therefore, he used his translations as a platform from which first to probe the depths of allopathy, and then later, to launch into massive and sustained attacks against it. That was by no means his starting position, but it was certainly how things ended up. No wonder, then, that he never flinched in his furious arguments with allopaths after 1806: he had probably seen and rehearsed all their arguments during his translations and had already demolished their positions point by point. He had in fact attained a state of renewed medical certainty, which others interpreted as stubborn arrogance. He can only have attained this through his translations, backed up by his experiments.

'He now saw full well that he must not look to his medical brethren for assistance in his great aim, but he did not despair; on the contrary, this very opposition of his colleagues made him more resolute in his determination to carry out his plans alone, or with what casual assistance he could procure from non-professional friends.' [Dudgeon, 1853, p.181]

Thus his translations gave him an unparalleled insider's knowledge of the 'enemy camp' and uniquely prepared him for every future battle. Like a brilliant military commander, he knew intimately all their weapons and how they would be used. As a result, they stood before him entirely disarmed. The only weapon they had left was contempt, which they rained down upon him without mercy.

It seems fairly clear that by 1806 Hahnemann had emerged from that 'darkness', and returned from that lonely 'desert', having answered this same question entirely to his own satisfaction, and found in the homoeopathic system of his own making, the 'sure aid' and the 'relief' his heart had yearned for. And at a deeper level, creating homoeopathy would seem to have closed another circle of his life, one which had started thirty years before, in the wild mountains of Trannsylvania, while working as a young man, at the start of his career, for his beloved Patron:

> '[In 1777] he carefully catalogued Baron von Bruckenthal's immense library of books and rare manuscripts. It was during the quiet, scholarly days, in the secluded library at Hermannstadt [Sibiu], that he acquired that extensive and diverse knowledge of ancient literature, and of occult sciences, of which he afterwards proved himself the master, and with which he astonished the scientific world.' [Bradford, p.28]

SUMMARY

We must now try to give a summary of this whole matter. When Hahnemann gave up the practice of medicine on his move to Dresden in the fall of 1784 he did so with a heavy heart and considerable bitterness. He felt he had been defeated by a system which, in spite of his most devoted efforts, failed to cure. And he felt betrayed by a profession founded upon an illusion. Prior to his transition into a literary career, he had spent much time at the house of his father-in-law, Herr Haesler, the apothecary in Desau. Indeed, he is reported to have visited him on a daily basis to undertake chemical experiments in his laboratory, over what must have been at least a two year period.

Having had no formal training himself in chemistry and having never owned a laboratory of his own, we can assume that these frequent visits to Haesler's laboratory were very important to him. We can only guess as to the nature of the experiments he conducted there. But it is my contention that he learned there the practical operations and techniques of alchemy, about which he had read in depth in the library of von Bruckenthal in 1777-9. It is also my contention that he satisfied himself sufficiently with these techniques to become highly competent in their execution and that later, in preparing some homoeopathic remedies, he used many of the same alchemical techniques. There would seem to be no other convincing explanation for the observations we have made on this matter presented in this essay.

How else could he have become so thoroughly familiar with these techniques other than via von Bruckenthal's exhaustive library? Where else could he have personally practised them to such a high level of competence, but in Haesler's laboratory? How else can we explain where he obtained these methods from, but through prolonged study of alchemical texts and through personal experimentation? It is not possible, in other words, for Hahnemann to have adopted and used these techniques of remedy preparation without a thorough knowledge of alchemy as a system and for him to have applied these techniques so competently without considerable personal experience in their use. Thus, he must have applied the techniques of alchemy personally, in order to have so thoroughly known the methods for preparing such remedies as Hepar sulph and Causticum, for example.

I think we have gathered here sufficient evidence in support of the above thesis, and I also think we have given a sound and convincing account of this whole matter. Hahnemann probably failed to mention alchemy and Paracelsus quite deliberately, thinking that in a more scientific age such as his, no-one would know enough about such dusty old matters to notice the hidden links. And when Trinks and others brought up this topic he simply denied all knowledge of it, saying he knew nothing about Paracelsus or alchemy. A very inconvincing performance for a man so well-informed and so well-read about every virtually aspect of medical history and a man so accomplished in chemistry.

■

HAHNEMANN & OTHERS ON THE SUCCUSSION OF MEDICINAL FLUIDS, ETC.

Dream of Egypt, 1995

> 'His keen interest for chemistry and pharmacy, completely underestimated by so many of his colleagues, became of great service to Hahnemann in his later work.' [Haehl, vol. 1, pp.268-9]

Homoeopathic remedies are not only diluted but also succussed. As the physical nature of homoeopathic remedies is still unknown, so the precise role which succussion plays in the process is a mystery. The origin of succussion as a process also remains obscure.

It has been mentioned before that the idea for first using succussion was based upon the jostling of medicinal liquids in bottles when riding on horseback. In the past this idea has been derided and dismissed. But it might in truth have some small basis in fact. Quite inadvertently, while looking for something else entirely, I chanced upon the following about succussion:

> 'In the Organon, however, he stated that trituration and succussion release the 'spirit-like power' of the medicine - which is compatible with his assumption that medicines act through their spiritual (geistlich) or dynamic impact upon the organism [321, d].' [Coulter, vol. 2, p.403]

> For this reason Hahnemann warned against shipping the liquid remedies over long distances, since they receive 'an enormous number of additional succussions during the transport, and they are so highly potentized during a long journey that on their arrival they are scarcely fit for use, at least not for susceptible patients, on account of their excessive strength, as many observations go to prove' (Lesser Writings, 736 *) Fortunately for suffering

humanity, the dry pills were not affected in this way (ibid., 766 **)

Note 321. Hahnemann, Organon, Sec. 269, 270.

* ' It is only in this form [i.e. dry pills] that the homoeopathic medicines can be sent to the most distant parts, without any alteration of their powers, which is impossible to be done in their fluid form; for in that case the medicinal fluid, which has already been sufficiently potentized during the preparation (by two successions at each dilution), receives an enormous number of additional successions during the transport, and they are so highly potentized during a long journey, that on their arrival they are scarcely fit for use...' as stated by Coulter above. [Lesser Writings, pp.735-6]

** 'The supposition of our author that dry globules that have been impregnated with a certain degree of development of power can be further dynamized and their medicinal power increased in their bottles by shaking, or carrying in the pocket, like medicinal fluids further shaken, is not borne out by any fact and will appear to me incredible until it is supported by proper experimental proofs.' [Hahnemann, Lesser Writings, p.766]

Stuart Close says this about potentisation:

'Under certain conditions he found, perhaps to his surprise, that instead of weakening the drug he was actually increasing its curative power. In reducing the density of the mass he perceived that he was setting free powers previously latent, and that these powers were the greatest and most efficient for their

> *therapeutic purposes...' [Close, 1924, The Genius of Homoeopathy, p.216]*

Furthermore, in his last years in Paris, Hahnemann frequently instructed patients to shake their liquid doses in the bottle before their daily dose, thus enhancing or reinvigorating their medicinal power. Or to stir vigorously with a spoon in the glass.

> *'He...[advised] ...that the liquid medicine, having been made up, should be slightly succussed between each dose...' [Handley, 1997, In Search of the Later Hahnemann, p.131]*

> *'Only very occasionally is a succussion of the container of the liquid specified...this appears to be a succussion of the stock bottle, or main container, rather than of an intermediate glass.' [ibid., p.131]*

> *'...it was stated that he should...shake the glass of water ten times and then put the contents into another glass, taking a teaspoonful from there mornings and evenings...one teaspoonful from this was to be put into a glass of water, this was to be shaken well...the glasses of water were to be thrown away each evening.' [Handley, p.133]*

In an essay titled *'Hahnemann's Doses of Medicines'*, dated 1844, and published in his **Lesser Writings**, Boenninghausen gives us Dr. Croserio's account:

> *'Hahnemann at all times used only the well known small pellets...moistened with the 30th dilution...he would dissolve one or at most two in eight to fifteen tablespoons of water and a half or whole tablespoonful of French brandy in a bottle and thoroughly shake it up. Only one tablespoon of this*

solution was put in a tumblerful of water, and of this latter the patient would take only a coffeespoonful until he observed some action.' [Boenninghausen, p.212]

'From correspondence with Boenninghausen and conversations with Everest, it is clear that in the final years of his life, Hahnemann considerably diverged from his earlier methods of dilution.' [Haehl, vol.1, p.325]

A similar account is given in Handley, 1997.

'He never prescribed two different remedies, to be used in alternation or one after the other...'[ibid., p.213]

But Handley says he sometimes did, especially by olfaction.

'Hahnemann in the last years of his practice seemed to devote his whole dexterity to continually diminish the doses of his medicines. On this account he in the last years frequently contented himself to allow his patients to smell of the medicine...in chronic diseases he would in no case allow the patient to smell at the medicine oftener than once a week, and would give nothing but sugar of milk besides...by your constant correspondence you have had abundant opportunity to appreciate his rare powers of observation...' [ibid., p.213]

Most of this is already well known.

'...he potentized in the last years all his medicines with many, at least with 25 strokes.' [ibid., p.215]

'But with time there emerges ever more clearly the view that, by shaking and trituration, a uniform mixing, dilution and weakening of the medicinal substance is not all that is achieved; on the contrary, the material part of the medicine is thereby more and more eradicated and as a consequence the spiritual part of the medicine (not perceptible to human faculties) is released and extraordinarily increased. This is dynamization...be possible to increase the power by succussion; the more the medicine is succussed when prepared, the stronger its effect...' [Haehl, 1922, vol.1, p.324]

'...in regard to the most appropriate number of succussions he altered his opinion repeatedly within a few years.' [ibid., p.326]

As usual, Dudgeon makes some very informative, but also some very critical remarks about succussion:

'By trituration and succussion, he says, the medicinal power of medicines may be increased almost to an infinite degree. Hence we are warned against succussing our successive dilutions overmuch.' [Dudgeon, p.346]

'So fearful is he of increasing the medicinal potency of a medicine by shaking it too much, that he earnestly deprecates the practice of carrying about medicines in the liquid state, as the mere shaking of walking or driving will, he alleges, increase their potency to a dangerous extent.' [ibid., p.347]

'Whilst in the earlier periods of the growth of his system he merely tells us to shake the bottle, to shake it strongly - to shake it for a minute or longer - he *afterwards tells us that much shaking increases the power of the medicine to a dangerous extent, and therefore only two shakes must be used for each dilution. Latterly, however, he again loses his dread of shaking, and after once more appointing ten shakes for each dilution as the standard, he becomes more liberal and allows twenty, fifty, or more shakes, and half a dozen shakes to the bottle before each dose of the medicinal solution. Again, whereas in one place he says that the shaking is the only agent in the dynamization...in another he alleges that dilution is essential to the dynamizing effect of succussion, and that all the rubbing and shaking in the world will not dynamize an undiluted substance.' [ibid., pp.349-50]'*

All these quotations also illustrate the manner in which Hahnemann believed that succussion was more important in creating potency than mere dilution. He seemed to believe that by violent shaking some subtle medicinal power, derived from the kinetic energy of shaking, was imparted into the liquid. And it was this subtle force which he believed to be the true healing power of the remedy.

■

HAHNEMANN & HOMOEOPATHY FROM ROMANTICISM TO POST-MODERNISM

When Dr Samuel Hahnemann [1755-1843] died of bronchitis in Paris in July 1843, few people were told of his death, and the funeral, in driving rain at Montmartre, was only thinly attended. His coffin was inscribed 'Non inutilis vixi' - I have not lived in vain.

The following short account hopes to clarify and illuminate the changing nuances of attitude towards homoeopathy, from its humble origins in Saxony, and the intellectual milieu that created Hahnemann, tracking shifting attitudes since the mid-19th century and so through to the modern era of homoeopathy's dramatic revival on all continents.

At his passing, many doctors must have heaved a sigh of relief that a rather unedifying chapter of medical history was finally drawing to a close. Yet, his homoeopathic system of medicine became the darling of the fashionable classes throughout Europe. Like Mesmer before him, it was Paris, which had given him a thriving medical practice, and made him, and his young second wife, rich and famous. Hahnemann treated patients from all social classes, including the virtuoso violinist Paganini, and some minor British aristocrats. Though he occasionally went to the Opera with his fashionable, artist wife, generally speaking he lived a quiet, unassuming life, oblivious of the delights on offer in the capital of the 'beau monde'.

Homoeopathy had been taken up by doctors all over Europe, was exported to Russia, India, South America and USA, where it especially thrived, becoming the preferred medical system of royals and aristocrats everywhere. Along with other complementary therapies, homoeopathy today is back on the medical map once more; having undergone a resurgence in public interest, it now flies under a pluralist, post-modern banner, which challenges the entrenched reductionist orthodoxy of medical modernism.

ORIGINS

In the origins of homoeopathy, several diverse currents and ideas can be seen to converge. A humble pottery painter's son from the porcelain town of Meissen, Hahnemann indulged a passion for experimentation and chemistry, eventually rejecting the medicine in which he had been trained, as bogus, ineffective and bereft of rational principles. Being also a gifted linguist, he was fortunate in having translation work to fall back on in the 1780s after the severe disappointments of his first medical practice.

Abandoning medical practice and moving to Dresden

in 1784, he became an official translator of medical and scientific texts for the Dresden Economic Society. Between 1777 and 1805, he translated into German over 20 large texts from the Italian, Latin, English and French.

Hahnemann became bitterly disappointed with the medicine of his day and resolved to elucidate the fundamental causes of its errors. While translating texts, he studied case histories in the literature and collected evidence in an effort to establish some sound principles for the actions of drugs. He became famous for the copious and highly learned footnotes and annotations he inserted into his translations, making them more sought after than the originals. Correcting numerous points of fact and interpretation, he clearly relishing putting his extensive knowledge to good use in this task. That they grew in length and disputatiousness as time went on, can be judged from his translation of the 'Thesaurus Medicaminum' in 1798, where he exhorts the reader in a preface to 'kindly burn this useless book'.

FROM SIGNATURES TO POISONS

Like other scientists of his day, he remained hopeful that genuine medical principles would eventually be found. Fearlessly iconoclastic, he rejected the 'doctrine of signatures' as forming any kind of rational basis for the selection of drugs. Having held sway for many centuries, this unquestioned dogma pretended that the shape and colour of a plant could accurately reveal its general therapeutic properties. It was to be the first medical icon that Hahnemann fractured, ridiculing it as 'a preposterous folly'. Further research inspired him to attack two other favoured doctrines: mixed drugs and high doses.

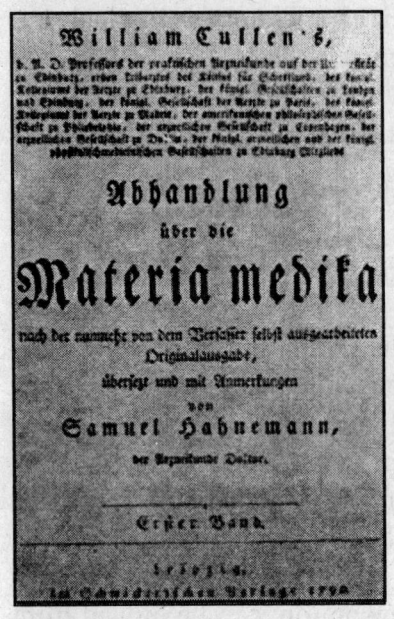

Through his reading, he soon became fascinated by poisonings, entertaining the notion that the toxic action of a drug more surely reveals its therapeutic properties. In this notion, he came close to a view expressed by Shakespeare, in Romeo and Juliet, when Friar Lawrence chose the plant from which to make Juliet's sleeping potion: "Within the infant rind of this small flower, Poison hath residence, and medicine power". Fastening hard to this principle, Hahnemann soon found abundant evidence for it in the medical literature. A literature not only of six north European languages, but being also fluent in Arabic, Greek and Hebrew, he soon accessed previously untapped streams of medical knowledge. While translating William Cullen's 'Materia Medica' in 1790, Hahnemann was led to make experiments testing drugs on himself. It was these mild self-poisonings of drugs ['provings'] that spawned homoeopathy, which is embodied in the phrases: 'law of similars' or 'like cures like'.

DRUG EXPERIMENTS

From his iconoclastic attitude he was to reap a bitter harvest of trouble, as much from apothecaries as from other doctors. Hunted down wherever he went as a loathsome medical heretic, his growing family were forced to endure a peripatetic existence for many years. He settled for a time in Dresden and later in Leipzig, obtaining a brief teaching post in the university medical faculty, until his deviant views got him sacked for 'corrupting the young' - a similar charge that had so abruptly terminated the teaching career of Paracelsus three centuries earlier. The two lives carry many important similarities.

The testing of drugs on the healthy, which might almost be called the first ever drug trials, became a foundation stone of homoeopathy, from its inception. Certainly, this reflected Hahnemann's insistence that only through scientific experiments and mass trials can the truth about the nature and actions of drugs in health and disease be finally settled. Having deliberately laid to one side centuries of entrenched dogma and superstition about drugs, in preference for experimentally demonstrable facts, homoeopathy can therefore claim to be the first evidence-based system of medicine. It also reflects Hahnemann's upbringing, steeped as it was in the pervasive spirit of the French Enlightenment.

In spite of all this rationalism, and empiricism, it is not hard to find woven into the fabric of homoeopathy several concepts closer to Romanticism. These include the infinitesimal doses, a form of vitalism [healing power of nature] and the idea that medical similars [similia similibus] will always triumph over opposites [contraria contrariis]. Thus, in Hahnemann we can discern a clear rejection of the entrenched dogmas of Claudius Galen [2nd century founder of contraries] in preference for the views of clinicians like Paracelsus [1493-1541, doyen of similars]. By drawing equally upon the scientific and the romantic traditions, Hahnemann assembled a very motley crew of concepts and techniques that reflect the late 1790s obsession with conflicting ideas - Enlightenment rationalism and the empiricism of experimental science, both so beloved of the French, combined with ancient, almost mystical ideas of the spirit of minute doses and the innate healing power of the body. Such 'nebulosities' arguably reveal some influence by German Romantic thinkers, like his contemporaries Goethe [1749-1832], Kant [1724-1804] and Schiller [1759-1805].

MIXED INFLUENCES

Drawing heavily on no-one directly, he was clearly in tune with the 'zeitgeist' or spirit of his times. Many European thinkers were still obsessed with science and the concept, associated with Newton and Descartes, that all phenomena can somehow be explained through experimentation and the material concepts of the machine. Such a reductionist impulse had already made a thoroughgoing rejection of vitalism and organicism in preference for chemistry and mechanics. Yet, with the rise of Romanticism - a Counter-Enlightenment - the smouldering, intense, and mainly German, rejection of materialism and industrialism, signalled a revival of such pastoral notions as the sanctity of life, the pervasive presence of God in the world and a precious regard for human life. These largely incompatible world views lived side by side at that time and still endure in homoeopathy.

As well as being dominated by pioneering experimental scientists like Lavoisier, Priestley and Scheele, this was also the great age of Wordsworth, Blake, Byron and Keats, not to mention Beethoven, Constable and Turner. Blake eloquently encapsulated the passionate Romantic rejection of machines and Newton when he wrote: 'A Robin redbreast in a cage, puts all Heaven in a rage'. The 'cage' being Newton's 'universe as machine'. Thus, in Hahnemann, we can see opposing elements of late 1790s philosophy conjoined. He drew heavily on both traditions, outrightly favouring neither, and thus rendered homoeopathy ambivalent towards each.

Hahnemann ignored virtually every tumultuous contemporary development in philosophy, in economics and in politics. Battles seemed to rage, conquerors came and went, whole philosophies erupted and had their day, while he blinked not an eye. He steadfastly focused upon his one chosen task, living through some of the most exciting events of history, oblivious of and making no comment upon Napoleon, the Battle of Leipzig [1813], the American Revolution [1776], the French Revolutions [1792, 1830] and the philosophies of Kant and Hegel.

NINETEENTH CENTURY

What probably made homoeopathy so thrilling in the 19th century, is the way it was taken up by people who mattered - the rich and influential. It is no exaggeration to say, that it went through all the European royal and aristocratic families like a forest fire, becoming a social phenomenon. It became the preferred medical system of the Kings of Prussia and Saxony, and later of Wurttenburg. This popularity soon spread to Austria [where it was later banned], Poland, Russia and Italy, where it was popular among those rich Englishmen embarking on the Grand Tour.

Its English origins can be traced to Naples via Dr Frederick H F Quin [1798-1878] and the Earl of Shrewsbury, who frequented Naples and brought homoeopathy back with them to Britain in the 1820s. Quin first encountered it through a Dr Neckar, an Austrian army physician then resident in Naples. The causes of homoeopathy's popularity with the rich are not hard to see. Compared to barbaric conventional methods, like bleeding and purging, it was an extremely benign and gentle system of therapy - water and sugar pills - and it had gained a reputation for being efficacious against epidemics like cholera, typhus and scarlet fever.

Homoeopathy soon became a thorn in the side of conventional medicine, which it attacked with unrelenting ferocity, and which failed repeatedly to halt the spread of this 'medical heresay'. It also engendered a revolution in conventional medicine, which, unable to justify its own methods, gradually began to reduce the doses of drugs in use, to terminate the unpopular use of bleeding, purging and blistering, and to employ simpler drugs rather than the complex mixtures in vogue in 1800. By 1900, the entire edifice of conventional medicine had been radically transformed, partly through advances in science [mostly drug chemistry] and partly driven forwards by the sustained and corrosive critique alternative therapies were making of its ineffective and dangerous 'Heroic Methods'.

The entire 19th century saw the battle-lines in medicine drawn between 'conventional' and 'alternative'. Only with the political legitimation of scientific medicine by the 1858 Medical Act, did the popular healing sects finally become legally pressured into decline and seem outdated. Becoming a true profession after 1860, medicine barred entry to the unqualified, and though it declined to outlaw quackery entirely, it strongly suppressed deviance within its own ranks.

MODERN TIMES

That is not to say that sectarian healers all went away and the story ended there; far from it. Homoeopathy, herbalism, osteopathy and nature cure trickled on as a 'medical underground' movement, occasionally emerging from the darkness of marginality, to mount fierce attacks on orthodoxy, and continuing to attract the loyal patronage of royals and aristocrats. Even though they were deviantised by the orthodox, these marginal healers continued to play a minor part in the medical scene through the 1930s and into the 1960s. Though interest in them had certainly declined, they still succeeded in attracting clientele; in England, homoeopathy has enjoyed unbroken royal patronage since about 1900. During the late 1960s, when 'alternatives' of all kinds became fashionable once again, with a renewed flowering of Romanticism, their revival seemed assured. All these systems of healing are now popular as never before, and so an age of medical pluralism, reminiscent of the 1840s, is made manifest.

It seems that deviance performs a useful function in all professions, holding up the mirror of caricature to the orthodox and so, through friction, generating an impulse for change and innovation. From contact with its opposite, orthodoxy is challenged, put on the defensive, and hence has to garner inspiration for change and renewal. That is just as true today as in the 19th century, and has, above all, been a dominant theme of the 20th. The current revival of these diverse healing systems is fundamentally post-modern in character - challenging the right of any fundamentalist, monistic hegemony to assert a 'single medical truth' or to elevate itself in rank above any other medical modality. Pluralism has become king and this inspires change. As

Aristotle insisted: 'Everybody has something to add to the truth.'

Due to the sheer popularity of these healing methods, modern medicine is being forced once more to scrutinise its own principles and methods, not to say its social niche, and to decide how this strangeling might become more comfortably accommodated. As in the 1840s, so at the start of the 21st century, history is repeating itself. As we are now finding, the silver plate on Hahnemann's coffin still seems apt, he did 'not live in vain'.

■

THE SECRETIVE HAHNEMANN AND THE ESOTERIC ROOTS OF HOMOEOPATHY

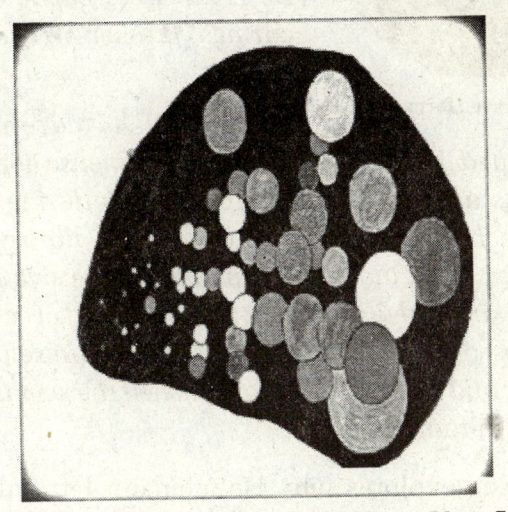

Plato is absorbed into the realm of pure Ideas, 7
Dec 2001 - Peter Morrell

"Not a single founder or follower of any of the medical systems could or...would dare to carry out

his system faithfully and vigorously into practice, without doing the greatest injury to patients." [**Lesser Writings**, 1808, 497]

"In an eight years' practice, pursued with conscientious attention, I had learned the delusive nature of the ordinary methods of treatment, and from sad experience I knew right well how far the methods of Sydenham, and Frederick Hoffmann, of Boerhaave and Gaubius, of Stoll, Quarin, Cullen, and De Haan were capable of curing." [**Lesser Writings**, 513]

Boerhaave Herman

"[In 1777] he carefully catalogued Baron von Brukenthal's immense library of books and rare manuscripts. It was during the quiet, scholarly days, in the secluded library at Hermannstadt, that he acquired that extensive and diverse knowledge of ancient literature, and of occult sciences, of which he afterwards proved himself the master, and with which he astonished the scientific world." [Bradford, 28]

This essay explores why Hahnemann left only scant hints about where he obtained his medical ideas and what major historical influences impinged upon his formulation of homoeopathy.

To summarise Hahnemann's life in the early 1780s would be a compelling and very worthwhile task, primarily because it was undoubtedly the major turning point in his life, and from which sprang his burning desire to reform medicine and so become, like Paracelsus before him, a "*medical Luther,*" [Temkin, 16]. Despondent is not really a word strong enough to describe how he felt at that point in time, about to abandon in disgust, as he was, the practice of medicine [Dresden, 1784 - Bradford, 36-7], which had been his life's love and ambition and into which he had poured all his energy, his life and his soul.

Yet, even this summary does not really convey the true extent of his problems. Having been trained in the medicine of the day, he had applied himself most diligently to its practice at the bedside, only to be rewarded by severe disappointment at every turn by a system that seemed to be utterly useless, unpredictable and downright harmful to patients.

How could any honest man of conscience and good moral character such as he, hold his head high and look his fellow in the eye armed only with such a desultory, damaging and inefficacious tool to treat the sick? He just could not stomach what to him amounted to a form of deceit against his fellow human beings. He was temperamentally quite unsuited to deceive his patients and 'calm their fears' when he knew full-well that most treatments on offer were useless: "*...he was not more clumsy or stupid than other doctors; he simply lacked that power to shuffle off responsibility which enabled them to face every failure,*" [Gumpert, 43]. His conscience for those who entrusted themselves to his care "*was more and more troubled,*" [Haehl, I, 267]. Having married in Dec 1782 [Bradford, 36] and his first child [Henriette] having been born in 1783 in Gommern [Haehl, I, 30], he could not bring himself to 'bleed and purge' his own dear children:

"But children were born to me, several children, and in course of time serious diseases occurred, which, because they afflicted and endangered the lives of my children - my flesh and blood - caused my conscience to reproach me still more loudly, that I had no means on which I could rely for affording them relief." **[Lesser Writings, 512]**

It is probably true to say that quite apart from concern for his growing family, Hahnemann had four great forces gestating inside him at that time, struggling for power and dominance in his thinking and comprising the main elements of his dilemma. The first force was his training in Old Physic, with which he was by now so bitterly disenchanted because of its woeful inadequacy as a medical system [Haehl, I, 22, 40; Bradford, 42].

The second force was the esoteric tradition of arcane medicine and mysticism, parts of which he had undoubtedly glimpsed in his studies in Sibiu [Hermannstadt] in 1777-9 with Baron Samuel von Brukenthal [1721-1803; the rich Patron who had saved him from ruin by paying for his last year of study to gain his MD at Erlangen, and who had initiated him into the Freemasons in October 1777 [Bradford, 27] only three days after his arrival in Transylvania [Haehl, I, 22]. Apart from acting as his physician, he also repaid his debt to Brukenthal by cataloguing his library [websites: http://www.verena.ro/

Samuel von Brukenthal

brukenthal/library. - latter in Romanian] over the best part of two years.

We read in Haehl, that while in Sibiu, Hahnemann *"spent most of his time arranging his patron's extensive private library,"* [Haehl, I, 23], which "counts about 280,000 books; the most precious collection is represented by the 386 incunabula (Thoma de Aquino, Opus praeclarum quarti Scripti, Mainz, 1469; Breviarum croaticum, 1493; Petrarca, Triomphi, 1488; Schedel's Chronicals (2,000 woodcut illustrations), Nürnberg, 1493; De mirabilibus mundi by Solinus C. Iulius, printed in Venice in 1488; Strabo's Geography, Rome, 1473; Pliniu the Older's Natural History, Venice, 1498; Boccacio's and Petrarca's works and so on)."

Dr Michael Neagu, in his history of Homoeopathy in Rumania [Geschichte der Homöopathie in Rumänien, 1995], discusses the significance of the position Hahnemann took as cataloguist to the library of Brukenthal at Sibiu [north-west of Bucharest], because the library contains a large collection of original works by mediaeval alchemists and physicians, including, for example, the 'Medicina Spagyrica Tripartita' (1648) of Jean Pharamond Rhumelius [c1600-c1660], which Neagu describes as *"a fundamental esoteric work, relying on the principle of 'similia similibus curentur',"* [Neagu, 25; Dinges, 259]. This otherwise forgotten yet important aspect of influences upon

Jean Pharamond Rhumelius

the early Hahnemann, is also discussed in Haehl, 1922, [I, 11 & 21-24, & II, 9-10].

Neagu's main point is that Hahnemann could hardly have failed to be inspired by the contents of that Library and probably picked up some therapeutic ideas while there, if only unconsciously. Neagu goes on to add that one of Hahnemann's direct disciples, Honigberger [1794-1869], *"was a speaker of the Rumanian language and had practised homoeopathy in all three Romanian principiates,"* [Neagu, 25]. Although this does not conclusively prove that Hahnemann read these works, had any interest in them or obtained ideas from them, yet it does match other aspects about him, as explored here, touching as it does upon an unresolved problem about the origins of homoeopathy, which Hahnemann himself was consistently unwilling to discuss.

The third force that pushed him on was undoubtedly science and experimentation, with which, as a means of proof and to dispel superstition, he was deeply enchanted. Having a strong experimental bent himself and a yearning to dabble in chemistry, he greatly admired figures like Priestley [1733-1804], Lavoisier [1743-94] [Haehl, I, 32; Bradford, 38] and Berzelius [1779-1848; Dudgeon, xxi].

> *"But the sole consolation of Hahnemann's existence in Dessau [1779-83] was his daily visit to the apothecary, Häesler, in whose laboratory he could continue his study of chemistry."* [Gumpert, 26]
>
> *"The time he spent in Dessau afforded him a welcome opportunity of pursuing his chemical research in the laboratory of the Moor Apothecary Shop — work which was so significant for his*

> *pioneer activities in medicine." [Haehl, I, 265]*
>
> *"Hahnemann devoted himself entirely to chemistry and writing, according to his own admission. He puts chemistry first. In this science he was self-taught. He had never received any definite course of instruction in the subject or possessed a laboratory except during his stay in Dessau (1781), where he had found a suitable place in the Moor Apothecary Shop for his experiments and probably also an occasional tutor in the person of the Apothecary Häesler." [Haehl, I, 268]*

However, this chemical interest could also be interpreted as a means for him to test some of the alchemical insights he had derived from secret study of arcane medical texts. Consider, for example, *Hepar sulph* and *Causticum* that require overtly alchemical procedures like calcination and distillation for their preparation [**Chronic Diseases**, I, 559, 762; Bradford, 152]. It does not seem unreasonable to suppose that he acquired some practical experience and instruction in alchemy from Häesler.

Finally, the fourth great force at work in him, and which dominated his thinking at this time of crisis, was his study of the medical past through his great skill as a linguist and as the translator of diverse scientific and medical treatises from Latin, French, and English into the German language:

> *"[In 1784]...he translated Demarchy's 'The Art of Manufacturing Chemical Products' from the French. It was an elaborate work in two volumes, to which he made numerous additions of his own." [Gumpert, 34].*

Yet, Hahnemann, *"driven by his own inward dissatisfaction, eked out only a scanty living by means of translations,"* [Haehl, I, 262]. As a measure of his great energy, he *"published during this period [1790-1805] over 5,500 printed pages - original work, essays in medical journals, and translations, among these were works of fundamental importance, which deserve special attention,"* [Haehl, I, 48]. During the period from 1777 to 1806, he translated 24 texts from other languages into German. All but six of these translations were made during the 1780's and 1790's, when he was conducting various chemical experiments.

Recognising *"the insufficiency of medical science,"* [Haehl, I, 33], and *"disgusted with the errors and uncertainties of the prevalent methods of medical practice,"* [Bradford, 36], it was probably his *"growing disgust for the medical fallacies of the day,"* [Bradford, 43], and while *"searching for some reliable basis upon which to resume practice,"* [Coulter, II, 311], that forced Hahnemann back within himself to study the medical past and to reconsider some of those strange medical ideas which he had first encountered in von Brukenthal's great library in Sibiu - allegedly the greatest collection of arcane medical texts in Europe. [Neagu, and website], and study of which had made him *"master of occult sciences,"* [Bradford, 28]. How else can we explain his behaviour? When the tried and tested has failed us, then we cast around within the sphere of the known, and even into the sphere of the unknown, to find a replacement set of ideas and methods. This is by no means an unreasonable viewpoint, and explains much.

"After I had discovered the weakness and errors of my teachers and books, I sank into a state of

sorrowful indignation, which had nearly altogether disgusted me with the study of medicine." [Opening lines of Aesculapius in the Balance, *1805, in* **Lesser Writings**, *410, Jain Edition]*

In essence, circumstance forces anyone who has lost everything to reconsider in greater depth those things they had previously and perhaps impulsively cast aside as useless. Discovering the abject failure of orthodoxy, and being rendered bereft of any medical philosophy at all, must have inspired Hahnemann to reinvestigate the old systems with a fresh and more attentive spirit. He was thus impelled to indulge the other three passions to a much greater extent: reading and translating, conducting chemical experiments and reviewing those ideas and methods from the arcane world.

In somewhat wearily embarking upon this new path, prepared for him by Destiny and *"his conscience,"* [Bradford, 36; Haehl, I, 47], Hahnemann must soon have found himself the inheritor of a range of complex problems issuing from the medical past, which prevented him from taking up medical practice. These also barred his way to further progress because they were simply unsolved riddles, age-old problems that each of his illustrious predecessors had failed fully to solve: such fundamental matters as similars vs. contraries; mixed vs. single drugs; large or small doses; vitalism vs. mechanism. In his reading, Hahnemann soon laid bare a complex web of contrasting opinions amounting to a veritable war-zone of debate. Sydenham [1624-89], Hoffmann [1660-1742] and Boerhaave [1668-1738], had their views, which, though rising to prominence in the 17th and 18th centuries, did not enjoy universal acceptance by all the medical profession. They represented the ascending mechanical and materialist school, which portrayed the body as little more than a machine.

This age of medicine can be seen as an age dominated by the machine. Just as the first sciences were concerned with mechanics, the laws governing the movement of physical objects, so too in the 1500s and 1600s the main focus is upon the physical body itself, its dissection, drawings of the organs and the machine-like conception of blood flow, the mechanics of muscle action and the pneumatic principles of breathing. The anatomical work of Harvey [1578-1657] and Vesalius [1514-64], Boyle's work on gases, and the drawings by Leonardo [1452-1519] are therefore very typical advances of this period. We might realistically conceive these advances to be the 'medical analogues' of the machine cosmology of Newton [1642-1727], Copernicus [1473-1543], Galileo [1564-1642] and Kepler [1571-1630], and probably reflect an excessive *"admiration for the triumphs of the sciences since Galileo and Newton,"* [Berlin, 1996, 28].

This age also sought to displace all those previously dominant magical and religious elements in medical conceptuality, and what had become a *"period of conformity...mechanical, and in the end meaningless, through mere repetition... the blankest patches in the history of human thought...a great and arid waste,"* [Berlin, 1996, 74].

The supernatural fabric of medieval medicine gradually became abandoned and dismantled and so fell into neglect, to be replaced by the new passion for 'mechanism' extolled by figures like Hoffmann and Boerhaave. What happened in medicine certainly reflected things happening, and conceptual shifts taking place in the natural sciences and philosophy. Mechanics dominated everything at that time.

Sydenham, for example, who had very much set this impulse going, ruthlessly stripped disease of any deeper philosophical relevance to the life of the patient as a being, made individuality inconsequential, and regarded any disease as merely another example of an infection by some noxious external agent that has invaded the patient for no particular ethical or spiritual reason. No special meaning was to be attached to any disease. He *"applied his objective investigations to both the treatment and to the description of diseases. Divesting himself of much medieval tradition, he approached therapeutic problems in a relatively empirical manner,"* [Shryock, 12].

He *"turned to methodological empiricism,"* [Warner, 44; King, 1970] and gave credence to the view that a disease was a real entity separate from the patient [Porter, 230]. Sydenham also *"converted Bacon's neo-Platonic 'form' into a wholly new concept - the specific disease'..."* [Coulter, II, 2, 180]. He viewed diseases as *"clear and distinct entities ripe for taxonomy,"* [Porter, 307]. *"...the description of a disease as an entity. This latter meaning prevailed with Thomas Sydenham,"* [Temkin, 28]. Sydenham also misinterpreted Paracelsus about the physical nature of morbific particles of contagion, echoing the view of Fracastoro [1478-1553; Veith, 505], and so spawned the basis for the modern Germ Theory of disease.

"Where the ancients had seen an inseparable connection between the patient and his malady, Sydenham saw in the patient certain pathological symptoms which he had observed in others and expected to see again...he distinguished between the

sick man *and* the illness, *and objectified the latter as* a thing in itself. *This was a new outlook, an ontological conception of the nature of disease which was eventually to prove of the utmost significance." [Shryock, 13, my emphases].*

Like Sydenham, Hahnemann also revered Bacon as the founder of the inductive scientific method [see Close, 1924, 15, 27-8, 248-9].

Then, by contrast, there were those full-blooded vitalists like Paracelsus [1493-1541], van Helmont [1577-1644] and Stahl [1660-1734], who held a more esoteric stance, believing that each disease carries a special spiritual aspect as well as its obvious physical attributes. Like homoeopaths such as Kent [1849-1916], they rejected the outer physical aspects of disease as being the true realm of disease causation, believing the organism to possess an inner 'spiritual body' or 'vital force' - "...*Van Helmont's Archeus, Stahl's Animal Soul...*" [**Lesser Writings**, 1808, 490; Haehl, I, 284] - that heals and coordinates during health, but which also harbours the root causes of sickness, and what van Helmont called "...*exogenous agents...that irritate the Archeus...*" [Pagel, 428]. In the **Organon**, when writing about the vital force, Hahnemann even *"uses phrases that might have been Stahl's own,"* [Haehl, I, 284].

Unlike Sydenham, van Helmont correctly interpreted Paracelsus that contagion occurred by a *"spiritual Gas,"* [Pagel, 1946, 436] that invades the *Archeus* and so creates sickness. Contagion had always been viewed as a spiritual process and never physical. These ideas also resurfaced with homoeopaths like Kent, who denounced *"the bacteria doctrine,"* and *"the molecular theory,"* in favour of a position of unbridled vitalism, declaring that *"We do not take disease through our bodies but through the Vital Force," [Kent, **Lesser Writings**, 1926].

> "...the old school of medicine believed it might cure diseases in a direct manner by the removal of the [imaginary] material cause..." [**Organon**, 4]

> "These [allopathically conceived disease entities]...were all idle dreams, unfounded assumptions and hypotheses, cunningly devised for the convenience of therapeutics...the easiest way of performing a cure would be to remove the material, morbific matters..." [**Organon**, 7]

The eighteenth century then surrendered itself completely to a period of unrestrained speculation and quite absurd medical theorising, about which Hahnemann was profoundly contemptuous:

> "...metaphysical, mystical, and supernatural speculations, which idle and self-sufficient visionaries have devised..." [**Lesser Writings**, 1808, 491]

> "...vapoury theorising...word-mongers...system-framers and system-followers...framed for show, for a make-believe, and not for use... [**Lesser Writings**, 1808, 497-8]

> "...the state of the body has only been viewed through the spectacles of manufactured systems..." [Lesser Writings, 1808, 499]

> "...we were fooled by the natural philosophers....their whole conception - so unintelligible, so hollow and unmeaning, that no clear sense could be drawn from it." [**Lesser Writings**, 1808, 494]

> "...inflated bombast, passing for demonstration, abounding in words, but void of sense - all the antics and curvets of the sophists...perfectly insufferable."
> [**Lesser Writings**, 1808, 492]

> "This...made the medical art a stage for the display of the most fantastic, often most self-contradictory, hypotheses, explanations, demonstrations, conjectures, dogmas, and systems, whose evil consequences are not to be overlooked..."
> [Hahnemann, 1808, 489-90]

It was customary, even up to the end of the 19th century, for medical students to be taught all previous systems of healing, and have their heads *"crammed with theories and systems,"* [Haehl, I, 24]: *"Even the student was taught to think he was master of the art of discovering and removing disease, when he had stuffed his head with these baseless hypotheses...leading him as far as possible away from a true conception of disease and its cure,"* [**Lesser Writings**, 1808, 490]. In *"the eighteenth century, the opinions of these men were still matters of vital concern,"* [Temkin, 1946, 15], and knowing *"the various systems of the time was a matter of necessary orientation for the doctor,"* [Temkin, 1946, 16]. Indeed, Greek and Latin authors *"were still read and interpreted in the medical faculties of the universities in the early nineteenth cnetury,"* [Temkin, 22]

Being something of *"a student of ancient history,"* [Bradford, 150], Hahnemann, in his insistent probing, dislodged problems flowing from both medical traditions, and thus became the inheritor of a mass of conflicting views and techniques, which circumstance more or less forced him to pick his way through in order to make sense of the medicine of his day. Making very slow progress along what was a crooked, thistle-strewn and rocky path towards his construction of a new system, which worked in practice as well as having a sound underpinning rationale of coherent ideas, such was the mountain Hahnemann had chosen to climb, as he trudged along a bitterly lonely and perilous track, illuminated at times, and but dimly, only by the bright lamp of his inner hope.

Earning only a *"meagre living through work as a translator, writer and chemical researcher..."* [Nicholls, 1988, 11], Hahnemann was a lonely figure in the 1780s, and seems to have been more or less paralysed by the uncertainty of his position. It was doubtless this paralysing fog of uncertainty that had eventually forced him to abandon medical practice completely [Bradford, 37]. *"Hahnemann at this time, 1790, was poor,"* [Bradford, 47]. His *"struggle with poverty,"* [Haehl, I, 34] reduced him to the merely passive role of a scholar of the medical past and a translator of medical texts; *"his translation work gave him meagre support...in the year 1791, poverty compelled him to move from Leipzic to Stotteritz,"* [Bradford, 51]. *"He reduced himself and his family to want for conscience sake,"* [Bradford, 36]. But to what extent how being reduced to penury by lowly translation work [Haehl, I, 262], affected his sense of self-worth or pride in being a doctor, and for which he had worked so hard, is an interesting point. It is highly likely that his pride was hurt, because *"Hahnemann entertained a high conception of the physician's dignity...[and a] justifiable pride in his calling,"* [Haehl, I, 278].

Two features particularly stand out in all this that are most remarkable. Firstly, in all his writings he rarely mentions by name the great figures of the medical past, who were creators of vitalist medical systems and his greatest forebears, and who had laid out the very foundations upon which homeopathy would be built. Mention of these figures is so scant as to be conspicuous by its virtual absence in all his writings.

It is especially suspicious that Hahnemann only fleetingly mentions Stahl, Paracelsus or van Helmont by name, who truly were his greatest forebears and it is mostly their ideas and connected problems, which he inherited and was able to solve, update and push forwards. It is therefore very hard to explain why a man so saturated in every medical theorist and practitioner of the past, and possessed of such an encyclopaedic knowledge of systems ["He used 861 quotations from 389 books in his essay on Arsenic." Bradford, 40, 93; see also Haehl, I, 97], should then remain so silent about those to whom his own system owes so much.

Stahl's system involved a vital principle that he called the 'anima', which was the *"Hippocratic 'physis' to which Stahl added the attributes of Paracelus' 'Alchemist' and van Helmont's 'Archeus'..."* [Coulter, II, 229]. Stahl made it clear that he regarded the Anima as a vital principle, because it *"directs and controls the organism and its struggle against harmful environmental influences,"* [Coulter, II, 231] and which *"protects it in health and cures it when diseased,"* [Coulter, II, 232].

> "Paracelsus's system...was a rude form of homoeopathy...but it was not equal in value to Hahnemann's system..." [Dudgeon, 1853, 14]

In what is a clear reference to his deeper knowledge of Paracelsus, Hahnemann talks of: *"...the old mystic number* three...triplicity, presented a miniature of the universe [microcosm, macrocosm]...explained to a hair's-breadth..." [**Lesser Writings**, 490]. Hahnemann's medical outlook, "*like that of Paracelsus, was shaped by his early life...the parallels between their careers, as between their medical doctrines, are striking,*" [Coulter, II, 306].

Yet, when Dr. Trinks, in 1825, asked him directly about Paracelsus, he replied "*that it was unknown to him,*" [Haehl, I, 274], claiming he knew nothing about "*the great heresiarch,*" [Temkin, 1946, 18], claiming never to have read a single word he had ever written or to know anything about his medical system. "*In 1825 Trinks...pointed out to Hahnemann that the principles of homoeopathy are to be found in Paracelsus. Hahnemann replied that until that moment, he had known nothing of it,*" [Haehl, I, 425]. In a letter to Dr Stapf, "*Hahnemann refused very definitely, and with some indignation to be associated with Paracelsus's fantastic and will-o-the-wisp...[theories],*" [Haehl, I, 274], having had "*no suspicion that Paracelsus had similar ideas,*" [Haehl, I, 273]. These denials amount to outright lies and clearly reveal how determined Hahnemann had become to conceal his true sources. It is utterly inconceivable that Hahnemann knew nothing about Paracelsus. Goethe even refers to Hahnemann as "*this new Theophrastus Paracelsus,*" [Haehl, I, 113].

Van Helmont

"Like Paracelsus and van Helmont, he was disillusioned with the prevailing ideas and retired from practice to think out a new approach," [Coulter, II, 310].

Yet, he only once mentions Stahl, "*the founder of vitalism*," [Veith, 505-6], and van Helmont [Lesser Writings, 1808, 490], who were undoubtedly two of the greatest builders of vitalist medical systems, and both holding views remarkably concordant with his own. How can such a broad confluence of medical ideas reasonably have been coincidental? Their views on such central matters as the life force and miasms come so astonishingly close to those of Hahnemann that it is quite simply impossible for such a well-read and articulate physician like Hahnemann to claim any ignorance of their names or their medical views. Van Helmont's 'Archeus' and Stahl's 'anima' [Temkin, 1946, 22; Haehl, I, 284] are virtually identical to Hahnemann's life-force and perform exactly the same function within the conceptual fabric of these three medical systems.

The second remarkable feature is that Hahnemann also remained very tight-lipped about his esoteric studies with von Brukenthal in Sibiu in the late 1770s and because of which he was a lifelong Freemason and an active member of a Masonic lodge in every town wherever he lived [Haehl, I, 23], and which was a subject to which he was "*inwardly greatly attracted*," [Haehl, I, 255]. Haehl claims he was always "*a good Mason*," [Haehl, I, 119, 253]. This again seems to reveal some hidden, undisclosed aspect of the man, about which he also remained silent. Given that he had such a brilliant mind, such exceptional reasoning and debating skills, such linguistic gifts [Haehl, I, 10-15, 34-35; Bradford, 28, 94] and such rare, subtle and profound skills as a thinker and observer [Haehl, I, 250-2], it is hard to imagine why he chose not to write about the great medical problems of the past with which he must undoubtedly have struggled and in which he was daily immersed between say 1780 and 1800. Thus again we are forced to conclude that Hahnemann deliberately chose to stay silent on all these pertinent matters.

What were truly *"wilderness years"* [Coulter, II, 348], the 1780s and 1790s were entirely devoted to one grand struggle: the gradual demolition of his old views, a steady formulation of the new and a long and complex process of mental metamorphosis, sifting, analysis, reflection and experimentation, a movement from darkness towards light, *"a state of complete internal revolution,"* [Haehl, I, 48] that finally led him to the triumphant realisation of his dreams and that gave slow and painful birth to homeopathic medicine, rising like some Phoenix out of the ashes of his bitterly disappointing early years of medical practice and his long years of study. Having been to Hell and back, he returned like a prodigal: strengthened, renewed and undeterred:

> *"He could only wait for the moment, as inevitable as the Day of Judgement, which would see him revealed as the apostle of a pure and true doctrine of medicine."* [Gumpert, 59]

Having solved the two greatest riddles in medical history - the relationship between the drug and the disease/patient, and the dose-dependent relationship between the toxic and therapeutic actions of drugs - he was determined to tell the world what his answers were – the proving and potentisation of single drugs.

> "Men of authentic genius are necessarily to a large degree destructive of past traditions. Great philosophers always transform, upset and destroy. It is only the small philosophers who defend vested interests, apply rules, squeeze into procrustean beds." [Berlin, 1996, 70]

> "He sought to discover the specific relations of certain medicines to certain diseases, to certain organs and tissues, he strove to do away with the blind chimney-sweeper's methods of dulling symptoms." [Gumpert, 99]

> "He struck deadly blows...first...that the doctor should prepare his own medicines; second...the administration of small doses; and, third, he was a most passionate opponent of mixed doses that contained a large number of ingredients." [Gumpert, 96]

> "...employment of the many-mixed, this pell-mell administration of several substances at once...these hotch-potch doses..." [**Lesser Writings**, 1808, 498]

Yet, in this other sense about which we speak, this unusually garrulous and articulate Hahnemann, so often given to *"raging like a hurricane,"* [Haehl, I, 98], or ranting *"like the old prophets,"* [Haehl, I, 33], has consistently and mysteriously failed to tell the world where his ideas came from or in which particular brood-chamber they had long fermented, or finally been hatched. He declined to reveal whom he had drawn on the most and what the true antecedents or roots of homoeopathy were. As we have seen, on all these points, he remained conspicuously silent and cloaked himself only in denial, obfuscation, and a profound and uncharacteristic reticence.

There seems little point, therefore, in denying the facts. Hahnemann did have intimate knowledge of these great figures and their grand medical conceptions, but he deliberately chose never to mention them. This somewhat baffling and monumental silence therefore raises the inevitable question of why a man with such detailed knowledge of all these matters, refused to discuss or to lay out before his contemporaries an honest account of the true origins of his new medical system; a point we shall presently examine.

Two passages in his writings, especially revealing his deeper knowledge of medical history and systems, occur in the essays *'On the Helleborism of the Ancients'* [1811], and *'Aesculapius in the Balance'* [1805], which can be read in his **Lesser Writings**, pp.569-616, and pp.419-26 respectively. Other useful comments he makes about medical systems can be seen in his *'On the Value of the Speculative Systems of Medicine'* [1808] and *'On the Great Necessity of a Regeneration of Medicine'* [1808], in **Lesser Writings**, pp.488-505, and pp.511-21 respectively.

Another important secret of Hahnemann is revealed in his choice of drugs to admit into his new materia medica. One feature that distinguishes homoeopathy quite markedly from other medical systems is the large number of mineral drugs it employs. In **The Chronic Diseases**, for example, of the 48 drugs listed, 35 are minerals, 12 from plants and only one from an animal source [*Sepia*]. Thus, over 70% are of mineral origin. Hahnemann showed almost as strong a love of minerals, metals and acids, dozens of which appear in his materia medica, as his great forebears Paracelsus and van Helmont, who believed that minerals are blessed with greater potency as healing agents, because they are so ancient and take so long to form in the fabric of the earth, in comparison to most plants [Coulter, II, 48-9]. Again, Hahnemann never mentions them.

Similar notions were applied to metals, gems and other crystalline minerals, which were conceived to be the purified products of a slow maturation process, an alchemical form of gestation or distillation in the earth's crust, again imparting extreme healing potency upon them. While Hahnemann may not have shared these precise views, nevertheless the parallels are striking. It is of more than passing interest that his drug preferences disclose a heavy reliance on alchemical preconceptions, pointing to deeper knowledge of his own on such matters, but about which he never overtly speaks.

Paracelsus so loved minerals that he even preferred to augment plant tinctures with the ash from the burned plant, forming what he called a 'spagyric' remedy. This reflected his belief that the mineral component of a plant has especially strong healing powers, without which the tincture is an incomplete healing agent [Coulter, I, 350, 413, 421, 443; II, 51]. Again, this reflects a strong preference for mineral drugs, and also the notion that the unique life-force of each plant specially concocts a subtle blend of minerals from the soil, which becomes sealed with the 'spiritual imprint' of the plant's life-force. These ideas and techniques also found transmission through Goethe [1749-1832] to Rudolph Steiner [1861-1925] and sprouted in his anthroposophical medicine [Hill, 29], where similar techniques are still employed.

All such arcane knowledge, Hahnemann could easily have accessed - and very probably did - in the many esoteric medical and alchemical texts in Brukenthal's great library in Sibiu, and which he had spent "*a year and nine months,*" [Bradford, 28] cataloguing. Indeed, it would be remarkable if he had not absorbed such ideas. Even the potentisation process could originally have been devised as a method to liberate and concentrate the 'healing spirit' [*Archeus*] of a substance, and thus seems strangely parallel to Paracelsan and alchemical techniques, though admittedly dressed up in a more scientific garb. In which case, fire, time, trituration and succussion therefore seem to be those sole and Promethean alchemical agents capable of transforming and purifying any substance and concentrating its 'spiritual imprint'. Such is and was 'medical alchemy'.

All things considered, therefore, it is very hard to believe that Hahnemann, such a well-read [Bradford, 35, 93] and inquisitive man himself, was not aware of these facts. Especially when we consider his immensely detailed knowledge of the various previous systems of healing [**Lesser Writings**, 420-3; 488-505; Bradford, 93-4], "*his extraordinary knowledge of medical history,*" [Haehl, I, 97], or when considering his linguistic skills [Bradford, 28, 94], his translation work, and his librarianship and alchemical studies in Sibiu with von Brukenthal. All of these are bound to have brought him into intimate contact with such arcane details of these previous healing systems, some points of which must have been rubbed off and been retained in "*his extraordinary memory,*" [Haehl, I, 277] from 5-6 years earlier. Quite simply, he must have known all these things, yet he never once mentions them.

Furthermore, anyone knowing homoeopathy intimately, and especially the metaphysical ideas of giants like Kent, if they then turn to any serious study of the works of van Helmont, Stahl and Paracelsus, they will not fail to be impressed, if not amazed, by the numerous strong parallels begirdering all these vitalistic medical systems. As systems of ideas on the nature and causes of disease, of how the organism is thought to function, on the life-force, the most likely remedies and their modes of selection and preparation, then it becomes apparent that the parallels between them are so numerous and striking to ever be regarded as coincidental.

However, even if he knew them as intimately as seems likely, that still does not mean that Hahnemann simply sat down and copied them all wholesale. Rather, it seems more likely that he will have received abundant inspiration just from contemplating them. Copying those basic principles that chimed best with his own thoughts and medical experience - similars and single drugs, for example - he could then pick up and extend them further through experiment. Proceeding exactly in such a manner; he could then build up a corpus of likely ideas, to inspire his experiments and guide his choice of drugs. Much like rich veins, he could go back to these systems repeatedly to draw fresh inspiration.

As we have seen, it is well nigh impossible that he was ignorant of these systems and probably read them in detail in their original Latin and German, [Haehl, I, 250; Bradford, 28, 94].

Though he felt obliged to strip these systems bare of their astrology and theology, their supernatural garb, with which he had little patience: *"...metaphysical, mystical, and supernatural speculations, which idle and self-sufficient visionaries have devised..."* [**Lesser Writings**, 1808, 491]; *"...now the influence of the stars, now that of evil spirits and witchcraft..."* [**Lesser Writings**, 1805, 421]. In an especially contemptuous blast, Hahnemann even questions how *"old astrology was to explain what puzzled modern natural philosophy..."* [**Lesser Writings**, 490]. *"The majority of elite men and the medical establishment no longer valued astrology by the early 18th century and it ceased to occupy a central place..."* [Gouk, 317]

Yet, what is left is still strikingly similar to homoeopathy in respect of small doses; single drugs; many metals, acids and minerals; miasms as taints [disease images] contained in the life-force [*Archeus* or anima]; that the internal disease-causing factors predominate as true causes and must be neutralised by internally-employed medicines, often singly, in small, widely-spaced doses; and that a resonance or sympathy pertains between the malady and the remedy; that like cures like; and that the true image of a sickness/person matches in detail the image of the correct drug. There is broad agreement on all such central matters. And Hahnemann must have known this.

True to their times, Van Helmont and Paracelsus did, however, lean far more heavily upon alleged spiritual, astral and theological causes of disease: the *"blas of the stars,"* [Coulter, II, 200] while Hahnemann typically gives only 'defects in the life force', which allows 'susceptibility' to act as the generalised 'template' upon which acute and chronic maladies can then establish themselves. Homoeopathy, like all other vitalist systems, respects the obvious physiological holism and vitalism of the body, and always seeks to strengthen its innate healing power or vital force [Haehl, I, 64, 284, 289]. This approach does not deny, but embraces, the subtle differences between individual cases of a disease, and reaffirms that disease and patient comprise inseparably dual aspects of one united biophysical continuum. Disease is viewed as a 'dynamic derangement of the life force' [Close, 1924, 37-8, 74].

> *"The organism is indeed the material instrument of life, but it is not conceivable without the animation imparted to it by the instinctively perceiving and regulating vital force..."* **[Organon,** *para 15]*

> *"Let it be granted now...that no disease...is caused by any material substance, but that every one is only and always a peculiar, virtual, dynamic derangement of the health..."* **[Organon,** *Introduction, 10]*

Hahnemann was less keen to explore the psychological or psychic causes of sickness and he seems to play down the significance of such factors. Moreover, in homoeopathy, that still remains a more or less blank sheet even to this day.

Having resolved in his own mind the importance of his own work, gave him greater confidence, even in adversity: *"the...very opposition of his colleagues made him more resolute in his determination to carry out his plans alone, or with what casual assistance he could procure from non-professional friends,"* [Dudgeon, 1853, 181]. This might also suggest that he knew his own system was the best, because he knew intimately everything else that was on offer, and none of which worked in practice: *"In an eight years' practice, pursued with conscientious attention, I had learned the delusive nature of the ordinary methods of treatment, and from sad experience I knew right well how far the methods of Sydenham, and Frederick Hoffmann, of Boerhaave and Gaubius, of Stoll, Quarin, Cullen, and De Haan were capable of curing,"* [**Lesser Writings**, 513].

We must accept that Hahnemann had his own reasons for ploughing a lonely furrow [see Haehl, I, 255], for not even mentioning the figures and systems of the past - a rich seam, which he must have gone back to repeatedly to quarry ideas and inspiration, and forming a vague template on which to build his homoeopathic system. As he does occasionally refer to those past *"system-makers,"* [Lesser Writings, 1808, 497-8] he disagrees with, such as Cullen [1710-90], Brown [1735-88], Hunter [1728-93], Galen [c.130-201], Boerhaave and Hoffmann, who he mostly repudiates [especially Galen - e.g. **Lesser Writings**, I, 421, 592], are we therefore entitled to presume that he deliberately neglected to mention those with whom he shared a broad measure of agreement?

Leaving all this information undisclosed could have been devised for two reasons - to leave the trail 'cold' for the inquisitive, and to give homoeopathy the cleanest possible start in life as a brand new medical system, seeming to be complete unto itself and rooted solely in experiments that he had personally conducted, and possessed of medical principles, he had personally uncovered. Although this account is probably more true than false, it is still a shame that Hahnemann seemed too darned secretive and too proud [his egotism, Haehl, I, 256] to acknowledge his considerable debt to a small clutch of important medical predecessors, whose ideas and methods contain so much that is common to homoeopathy. Such massive similarities between these systems must have been known to Hahnemann - probably in detail - and must have richly informed his formulation of homoeopathy.

Clearly, Hahnemann seemed eager to sever homoeopathy completely from its arcane roots and to deny that it had any spiritual or theological connections at all. In stripping these ancient systems bare of all their supernatural and magical elements, what is left is largely homoeopathy. It is only when we look at figures like Kent that all such hastily ejected theological material comes back to the fore:

> "You cannot divorce medicine and theology. Man exists all the way down from his innermost spiritual to his outermost natural" [Kent, **Lesser Writings**, 641]

Implicit to Kent's view is the notion that no matter how much Hahnemann - or anyone - tries to hide, deny, suppress or stamp out the spiritual, supernatural and theological in medicine, it has a strange habit of finding some means of expression, bubbling back to the surface. And so homoeopathy will always re-establish its true connections and re-grow its true roots. The very things that Sydenham ejected from medieval medicine - in 'divorcing medicine and theology' [Veith, 502] - and which Hahnemann seems also to have discouraged, are as truly real links to homoeopathy as ever. These links cannot be separated for too long and will yearn for, find and grow back to each other naturally like severed roots of the same plant.

Probably in order not to validate the rampant spirituality and Romantic philosophy of his day, Hahnemann did not wish homoeopathy to be associated with the vitalist systems of the past, choosing instead to 'cover his tracks'. In an age like his so dominated by science, would he have wished to see homoeopathy associated in any way with magical, religious or supernatural tendencies? He probably feared that any such links, if ever they were made explicit, would be a retrograde step, that could seriously impede its acceptance within wider medicine, that might smear his reputation as a scientist, or to offer even vague support for such nebulous ideas would somehow cast him in a bad light. That I think gives a fair account of this fascinating but highly convoluted matter.

Hahnemann's vociferous attitude towards allopathy meant that he did indeed regard *"the old overthrown philosophy...as a mass of superstition and error."* [Berlin, 1996, 62], as *"...a chaotic amalgam of ignorance, laziness, guesswork, superstition, prejudice, dogma, fantasy..."* [Berlin, 1979, 163] or *"...casual impression, half-remembered, unverified recollections, guesswork, mere rules of thumb, unscientific hypotheses,"* [Berlin, 1996, 41]. And its antiquated corpus of ideas as little more than *"...metaphysical and theological explanations unsupported by...evidence, conducted by methods the opposite of rational, the happy hunting ground of bigots and charlatans and their dupes and slaves,"* [Berlin, 1979, 133].

Wherever the true origins of homoeopathy might lie hidden within previous healing systems, we can definitely say that with his most genuinely original contributions - the proving and potentisation - Hahnemann had effectively modernised and rekindled the previous vitalist systems, which, like long-silent and broken machines, he had fixed and which now hummed sweetly into new life. Had not this been his sole aim all along? Was this not indeed a revolution in medicine?

Haehl's assessment therefore looks more accurate afterall: *"Medicine has nothing in the whole course of her history which in any way approaches the accomplishment of this man...[Hahnemann was]...primarily a champion - and indeed the most brilliant champion - of internal remedies, the imperfections and manifold unfruitfulness of which he undertook to metamorphose..."* [Haehl, I, 274-5]. And the reasons now seem clearer too: *"The task of the great philosophers who break through the orthodoxy is to sweep away the painstaking edifices of their honourable but limited predecessors who...tend to imprison thought within their own tidy but fatally misconceived constructions,"* [Berlin, 1996, 72].

■

HAHNEMANN'S USE OF POTENCY OVER TIME

Pencil Sketch of a rusty old boiler at a disused green marble quarry on the southern tip of Iona in western Scotland, 1979 - Peter Morrell

It is possible to track in detail and thus reveal clearly the evolution of Hahnemann's prescribing habits and his move away from the crude and therapeutically disappointing doses he used at the commencement of his career, towards the higher potencies he used at the end of it.

Repeatedly, Hahnemann states that the underlying purpose of the dynamization process that he initiated is not in any way metaphysical or spiritual (as frequently claimed, for example, by Kentians), but is purely pragmatic and medical - i.e. to reduce the aggravations caused by similar medicines when used in crude doses, and thus to obtain medicines which are both gentle and effective. Furthermore, this engagement with pragmatism never left him and entirely dominated his approach to medical theory and practice throughout his life.

This is confirmed by reference to the stark facts of homoeopathic development - the use of similars came first and dose reduction second. He first started to employ 'similar' medicines around 1790 and 8 years later began to experiment with gradual reductions in dosage. As a physician, he clearly became increasingly satisfied with the results of using dynamised medicines, because he continued to use them in preference to material doses until the end of his long life. As is well known, he never ceased from campaigning against the crude doses and barbaric methods of `heroic medicine'. It appears that he developed the potentisation system in order to produce a reliable and consistent dosage system for drugs, that combined ensured medicinal action with a minimum of aggravation. At that time there was no such standard dosage system within allopathic medicine, and nor were the massive doses in use without considerable ill-effects.

The methods used in this study avoids idle speculation and focuses instead upon clearly identified historical data. It is inductive rather than deductive, in that it commences with no particular a priori theory to prove or disprove. It addresses neutrally the stark facts, as far as they can be ascertained. It is evidence-driven rather than theory-driven. It involves recording every specific potency and year that is mentioned about the person in question. A database is then compiled which covers the range of potencies and the range of years. This is then placed into a Computer Spreadsheet - in this case Supercalc 5 - and the data converted into bar-charts. The data can also be manipulated, condensed, averaged, re-arranged and analysed in various ways. In the case of Hahnemann, the sources of the data include his Chronic Diseases and Lesser Writings, Dudgeon's Lectures on Homoeopathy, Bradford's Life and Letters of Hahnemann, Haehl's Samuel Hahnemann, His Life and Work and Trevor Cook's Samuel Hahnemann, the Founder of Homoeopathy.

After initially compiling the data it immediately became apparent that far from being random, it contained clearly defined patterns. In fact, the data fell into quite distinct bands or phases that form a sequence and reveal development. These phases can be chronologically identified as follows:

1784 TO 1797

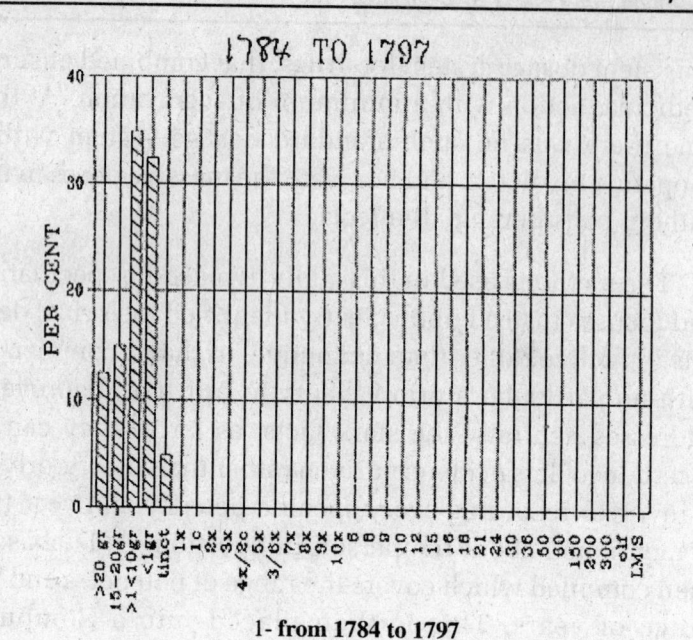

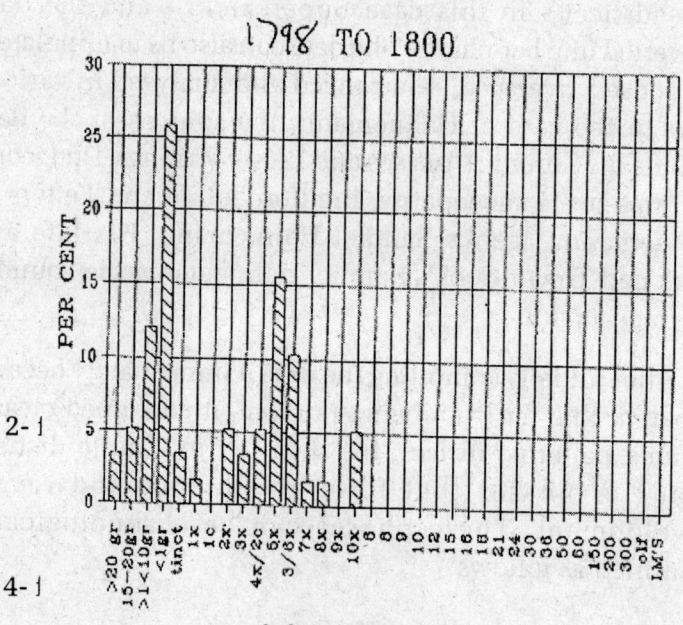

1- from 1784 to 1797

1798 TO 1800

2- from 1789 to 1813

4- from 1814 to 1819

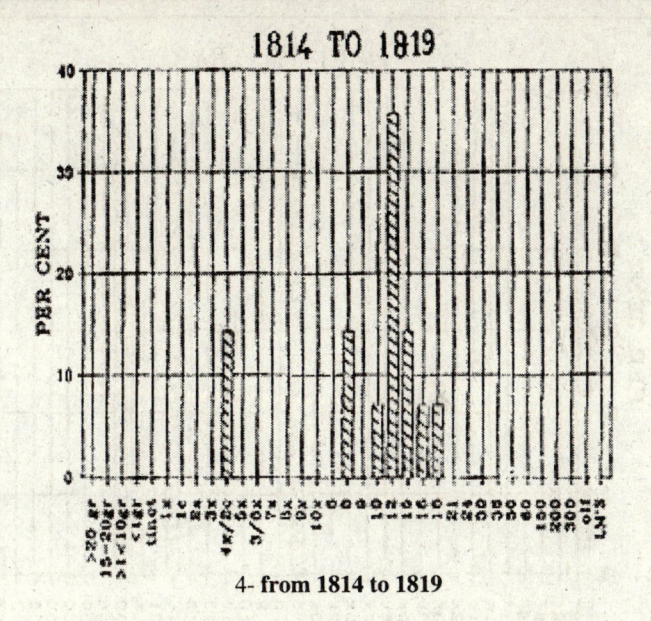

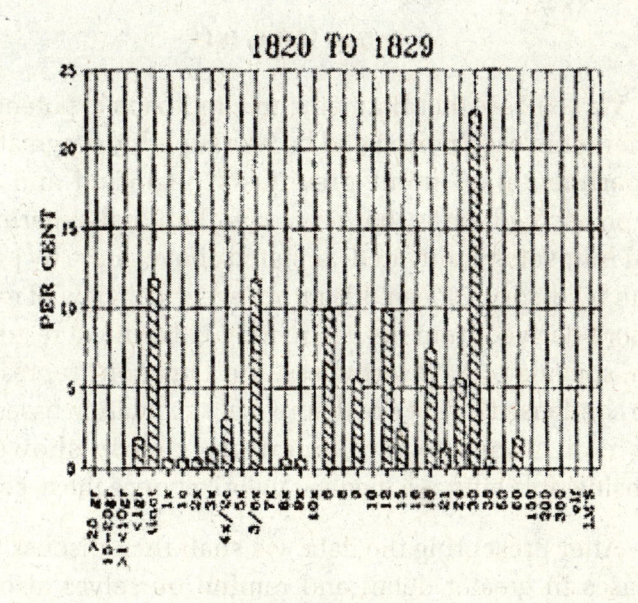

5- from 1820 to 1829

1830 TO 1843

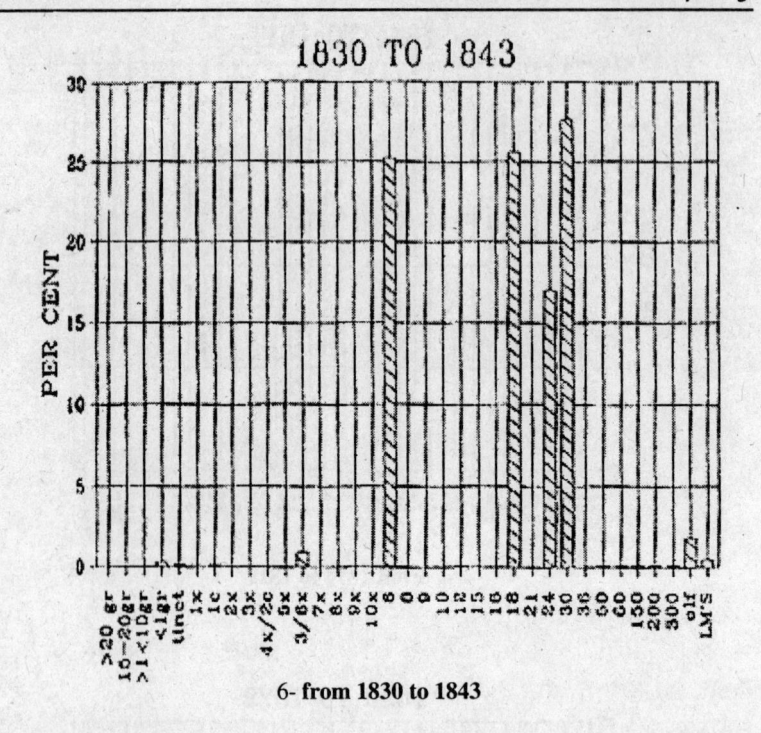

6- **from 1830 to 1843**

We shall see that Hahnemann's approach to potency was different in each period and he was superbly pragmatic and experimental. A point previously neglected and worth emphasising here is that he was an habitual experimenter and innovator, motivated, as stated above, more by practice than by theory. Indeed, his rather sceptical view of medical theory derived from his desire for good clinical results, not idle speculation. Nevertheless, the 'Organon', representing the condensed essence of theoretical speculation based upon his continuous experimentation, clearly showed his considerable gifts as a medical theorizer once the need arose.

After presenting the data, we shall then discuss the six phases in greater detail and remind ourselves also along the way, of some of the places, things and published works

Hahnemann was involved with at each stage. In this way we shall hopefully begin to see his prescribing habits placed against the broader context of his life.

CAUTIONARY STATISTICAL NOTE

The usual problem applies to this data and the conclusions derived from it. As with all statistical work, the patterns revealed and the conclusions they indicate are entirely based upon the samples of data used in the study. This cannot be over-emphasised. If the samples are too small or prove to be untypical in some respect, then the patterns, their significance and conclusions are entirely provisional.

This work is based on a smallish sample and not on Hahnemann's numerous casebooks held in Stuttgart. Clearly, this work is useful and interesting for the time being, but it may require dramatic revision in the future once a complete study has been undertaken of the entire Hahnemann Casebooks (Krankenjournalen). For this reason I would caution against getting too excited about the patterns or conclusions.

Having said that, however, I do believe this is a useful piece of research and paves the way for similar but more exhaustive studies in the future. It is also quite often the case - though not inevitably so - that the overall pattern and general trend contained within large data is still revealed even in a small sample. I strongly suspect this will be the case here.

THE DATA

In its crude form, the data is presented in Table 1. This is extracted from the following pages of the works cited.

Bradford p73, p93, p156, 186, 192,284, 367, 369, 398, 453-61; Haehl vol 1, pp115, 140, 141-2, 175, 181, 241, 311-329, 462-473; vol 2 p428 re medicine chests; Dudgeon p392-407 & p408; Chronic Diseases pp ; Lesser Writings pp ; Cook pages. It is noteworthy that Hahnemann approvingly mentions the occasional use of mixed remedies and the use of higher potencies like 60, 150 and 200 (refs). But predominantly he uses 6c to 30c and single drugs.

As can be seen from the accompanying bar-charts, the data was initially re-classified into groups, which, for convenience, correspond roughly to the patterns seen in the data over time. Thus the crude doses were re-classified into the following categories:

dosesover 20 grains;
doses of 10-20 grains;
doses of 1-10 grains;
doses of less than 1 grain.

These were followed by mother tinctures where specifically cited by Hahnemann. All other potencies appear just as listed in the above texts, with the exception that 4x and 2c and 3c and 6x appear together in the tables as one item respectively. In the early work (c1788-89) 'equivalent potencies' have been used which are based upon the complicated dilutions of drugs Hahnemann was experimenting with at that time. Clearly, in the strictest sense these were dilutions of drugs rather than potencies.

PRELIMINARIES

A few preliminary remarks can be made before we descend into the detail of each phase. We can clearly identify the first appearance of each potency mentioned. Again, these dates are provisional rather than definitive, as they may require revision in the light of more evidence in the future.

Firstly, we can see that he started to conduct the very first experiments with dose reduction in the year 1798. This includes 2x, 4x and 2c. In 1799 he began to reduce the dose further, using 5x, 6x, 3c and 8x. In 1800 he begins to use 10x and in 1803 12c appears for the very first time. In 1805 the 18th centesimal dilution appears, which was to prove one of the most consistently favourite potencies that he used throughout his long career. There is then a long gap in new developments, but in 1814 8c, 15c and 16c all make their first appearance in his writings. In 1816 30c makes its first appearance and this remained for all intents and purposes his most extensively used and most highly recommended potency of all time. Another one of his favourite potencies, 24c, was one of the last, first appearing in his writings in 1821.

Further developments include the first mention of 6c in 1819 and the first mention of 60c in 1824. In 1830 he first mentions Olfaction as a means of drug administration and this remained a very popular method with him until the end of his life. Again, he was motivated entirely by gentleness combined with effectiveness. Unfortunately, very few others shared his enthusiasm for it and it has been neglected ever since. However, there was a Glasgow lay homoeopath of the 1930's called Jack Short who used it on a regular basis. I am indebted to the retired homoeopathic pharmacist, John Pert for this valuable piece of information.

Finally, in 1838 the LM potencies make their first appearance. It is also interesting to point out that

Hahnemann never specifically mentions 3x, one of the most popular potencies of the last century, and still widely used on the Continent and in the Tissue Salts of Schuessler. Nor does he make great use of the now popular 6c before 1820, though he used it extensively in the last period of his career (1830-43).

COMMENTS UPON THE BAR-CHARTS

The data presented in these bar-charts forms a unique and fascinating insight into Hahnemannn's use of potency. They form a series of 'snapshots' of his avowed prescribing habits.

Potency	To 1797	To 1800	To1813	To1819	To1829	To 1843
1-20gr	62.5	20.7	0	0	0	0
<1 gr	32.5	25.9	0	0	1.86	0.26
2x	5	3.45	0	0	11.8	0.13
4x	0	5.17	6	14.3	3.11	0
6x	0	10.3	22	0	11.8	1
6	0	0	0	0	9.94	25.2
9	0	0	6	0	5.59	0
12	0	0	2	35.7	9.94	0.13
18	0	0	6	7.14	7.45	25.6
24	0	0	0	0	5.59	17.0
30	0	0	0	0	22.4	27.7

First Phase

This runs from 1784 to 1797. Sample size is 40 and is 32.5% doses of 1 grain or less, 12.5% over 20 grains.

Second Phase

This runs from 1798 to 1800. Sample size is 58 and is centred 25.9% less than 1 grain with 25.8% of 5x or 6x.

Third Phase

This runs from 1801 to 1813. Sample size is 50 comprising chiefly 22% 3x and 6x, 16% 5x and 12% 3x.

Fourth Phase

This runs from 1814 to 1819. Sample size is 14 comprising chiefly 35.7% 12c, 14.3% 8c, 14.3% 15c and 14.3% 4x.

Fifth Phase

This runs from 1820 to 1829. Sample size is 161. comprising chiefly 22.4% 30c, 9.94% 12, 9.94% 12c, 7.45% 18c, 5.59% 24, 5.59% 9c.

Sixth Phase

This runs from 1830 to 1843. Sample size is 770. comprising 27.7% 30c, 25.6% 18c and 25.2% 6c. During this phase from c1840 onwards he makes increasing use of olfaction and LM potencies.

Other Data:

1. In a photograph of part of the contents of a Hahnemann medicine case from the Robert Bosch collection in Stuttgart, approximately dated c1840, the following remedies and potencies are clearly visible:

Ran b 24; Coccion 24; Aethusa cynap 12; Sabad 18; China 18; Rhus 24; Vinca 24; Natrum carb 24; Capsic 18; Selen 18; Opium 24; Spongia 12; Bryonia 12; Teucrium?

mar 18; Calc hydr? 24; Merc sol 24; Cantha 24; Staphy 24 and ? 18 and ? 24. If we process this we get as follows:

Potency	Number	per Cent
12	3	15
18	6	30
24	11	55
Total	21	100

2. Data from another, though undated, medicine case held in Stuttgart is as follows:

Coffea 6; Drosera 12; Aurum pur 30; Graph 30; Bryonia 12; Ignatia 12; Kali carb 30; Acid phos 9; Ipecac 6; Lachesis 30; Cina 6; Cantharides 12; Veratrum 6; Alumina 18; Rhododendron 6; Cuprum 18; Phos 30; Dulc 12; Hepar sulph 18; Calc carb 30; Platina 30; Chamomilla 6; Antim crud 18; Natrum mur 12; Carbo veg 18; Baryta carb 30; Arsenicum 18; Aconitum 6; Acid nitri 12; Nux vom 12; Staph 18; Cocculus 12; Belladonna 12; Colocynthis 12; Euphrasia 6; China 12; Arnica 6; Hyoscyamus 12; Pulsatilla 12. [This data kindly supplied by Martin Dinges of the Bosch Institute in Stuttgart in a private communication.]

If we process this we get :

Potency	Number	per Cent
6		24
9	1	2.5
12	14	35
18	7	17.5
30	8	22

These two sets of data are so clearly different that they must come from quite separate periods of Hahnemann's life. The first being most similar to Bradford's late Paris medicine chest (c1841), but the above one being much earlier, before his extensive use of potency 24, being more similar to his 1820-29 period, during which he was still making extensive use of potencies 6, 9 and 12.

We can therefore conclude that he changed his views on potency very frequently and mainly in the light of clinical experience rather than 'neat theories'. It is also clear that he was moving higher and higher and that in his later phase he settled both on Olfaction and the LM or Q potencies as being especially gentle and effective methods of drug administration. He regarded them as superior for practical reasons, not out of any quasi-mystical notions.

LM OR 'Q-POTENCIES'

Finally, in 1838 the LM potencies make their first appearance. It is also interesting to point out that Hahnemann never specifically mentioned 3x, one of the most popular English potencies of the last century, and still widely used on the Continent and in the Tissue Salts of Schuessler. Nor did he make great use of the now popular 6c before 1820, though he used it extensively in his closing years (1830-43).

We can deduce from all this, that to truly call oneself a Hahnemannian homoeopath one would likewise have to use potencies 12, 18, 24 and 30 for at least three quarters of one's overall prescribing.

It seems therefore a distortion of the facts, as far as we can ascertain them, to point to LM potencies or to higher centesimal potencies and claim them as being something Hahnemann was headed towards. We must surely try to base our understanding of his work upon what he actually did on a day to day basis, and not upon idle speculations about what he might have done. And as we can see, the above data clearly shows the medicine chests that he habitually carried with him in his last years in Paris.

General Korsakoff, the Russian, 1829, in Archiv of Hom Med addressed a letter to Hahnemann recommending tubes or phials for remedies, suggesting globules of lactose and moistened with 2-3 drops of liquid potency (Bradford, p191); Dudgeon says Korsakoff was the real originator of the high potencies (in his 'Letters on Hom' p351, publ in the Archiv fur die Hom Heilkunst, viii pt 2, p161), Bradford p191).

The final phase of his prescribing runs from 1830 to 1843, comprising 27.7% 30c, 25.6% 18c and 25.2% 6c. Also during this phase (from c1840 onwards) he makes increasing use of olfaction and the LM potencies.

We can therefore conclude that he changed his views on potency very frequently and mainly in the light of clinical experience rather than 'neat theories'. It is also clear that he was moving higher and higher and that in his later phase he settled both on Olfaction and the LM or Q potencies as being especially gentle and effective methods of drug administration. He regarded them as superior for practical reasons, not out of any quasi-mystical notions.

If we add up all of the potencies mentioned in Rima Handley's *A Homoeopathic Love Story*, (pp117-143) we get yet another snapshot of his use of potency in the 1835-43 period, as follows:

pot	No	%
3	2	3.4%
6	3	5.1%
9	1	1.7
12	4	6.8
18	6	10.2
24	9	15.3
30	16	27.1
100	1	1.7
200	12	20.3
M	2	3.4
LM's	3	5.1
sum	59	100

Another good source of data is that of Michalowski et al (1989) based upon Paris Casebook DF5 dated 1838-42. (Arnold Michalowski, Sabine Sander & Karl-Otto Sauerbeck, Therapiegeschichte Materialen zu Samuel Hahenamanns Pariser Praxis, (rough translation - therapeutic historical material from Samuel Hahnemann's Paris Practice) Med GG 8, 1989, pp171-196, Stuttgart)

The results for their data is as follows

sum	59	100
pot	No	%
3	1	0.424
6	2	0.85

pot		percent
9	1	0.424
12	7	2.97
18	22	9.32
24	59	25
30	104	44.1
LM's	40	16.95
sum	236	100

Finally, by combining and re-averaging all the above data we can obtain a final or global average for his last years in Paris. This includes the Stuttgart medicine cases 1 and 2, Bradford 1 and 2, Rima Handley, the 6th phase and the Michalowski data.

This is as follows:

pot	percent	range
3	0.581	0-3.8
6	9.13	0.85-25.2
9	1.36	0.42-3.02
12	13.4	2.97-35
18	17.98	9.32-30
24	22.83	15.3-55
30	27.6	22-44.1
100	2.26	0-1.7
200	3.06	0-20.3
M	0.53	0-3.4
LM's	3.33	0-16.95
sum	774 samples	

To assess how accurate this final % is we can compare it with the previous data. This is shown in the range column, which gives the max and min for that potency (excluding 0 for some) and thus indicates how widely from the mean the samples vary or are spread. The most compact samples (closest to the mean) are potencies 3, 9, 18, 24 and 30. This means they have a narrow range, cluster tightly about the mean and thus the average shown can be considered to be a very reliable indication of Hahnemann's actual prescribing habits for that potency. It means that most people agree on his actual use of that potency and that there is much less variation in his use of it. I think we can safely assert that an analysis of 774 cases is fairly good and statistically very significant.

Those other potencies with much wider ranges (6, 12, etc) were clearly subject to more variation by the man himself, i.e. he used them a lot at times and little at other times. It also means that those potencies with narrow ranges (mainly 3, 9, 18, 24 and 30) he was generally happy with and made frequent use of compared to those with wide ranges with which we can assume he had problems and his use of them therefore varied more over time.

Finally, we can safely say that Hahnemann at the end of his career mainly used potencies 12, 18, 24 and 30 and that this comprised some 81% of his total prescribing . If we then add potencies 6 and 9, we cover some 94% of his total prescribing. Clearly it is true that he was beginning to experimnt with higher potencies and was making increasing use of the LM's for reasosn already stated. Those homoeopaths who can with honesty say they use mainly potencies 12, 18, 24 and 30 can truly call themselves Hahnemannian. The rest cannot.

Most of this flies in the face of what most people think he did and of course, with his directions in the 5th edition of the Organon and also it conflicts with Kent's directions, amongst others. Much more detail will of course be found in Rima Handley's forthcoming book on the same subject.

■

A GUIDE TO HAHNEMANN'S TRANSLATIONS

'When he left Hermannstadt [now Sibiu in Romania], at the age of 22 years, he was master of Greek, Latin, English, Italian, Hebrew, Syriac, Arabic, Spanish, German, and some smattering of Chaldaic... here he was unwittingly preparing himself for his great future.' [Bradford, p.28]

As a twelve year old boy he mastered Latin and Greek...later he learned French, English and Italian and he availed himself during his sojourn in Hermannstadt of the opportunity to become acquainted with the languages of that mixture of peoples who had gathered together in this extreme southeasterly town of Europe. [Haehl, Vol 1, p.259]

'[Hahnemann]... must have read in Hebrew, Greek, Latin, Arabic, Italian, French, English and German.' [Bradford, P.94]

PREAMBLE

Samuel Hahnemann's extensive translations of medical and chemical treatises into German was a key aspect of the man and his work, and yet the subject is often referred to casually 'en passant' or skated over very briefly by his biographers. This survey brings together extracts from much of the published material on this subject and hopefully conveys the extent and importance of these translations and how they formed a critical phase in Hahnemann's development as a scientist and physician.

Dudgeon, 1853, states, that if it weren't for his poverty Hahnemann would not have done all these translations and were it not for the translations there would have been no provings and thus no homoeopathy. Certainly there would have been no proving of Cinchona without his magnificent translation of Cullen's 'Materia Medica'. But one could equally argue that he was only poor because he gave up medical practice, due entirely to his own stubbornness and pedantic demands. While he was impatient with an imperfect system (allopathy), it is also true that his own conscience would not allow him to deceive patients into believing that allopathic treatment would cure them when his own experience told him that it wouldn't.

> '...he was not more clumsy or stupid than other doctors; he simply lacked that power to shuffle off responsibility which enabled them to face every failure'. [Gumpert, p.43]

So we have a complex network of reasons lying behind Hahnemann's abandonment of allopathy.

> 'Hahnemann...sat at his desk writing until his fingers were sore. There was no more talk of medical

practice. The doctor was a fanatic devotee of the quill-pen, who now drowned his sorrows over his lost medical career in a sea of ink..' [Gumpert, p.61] Nor is it true that Hahemann gave up medicine because he 'was unable to earn a living' from it (Bradford, p.36).

'Had he wished he could have remained in Gommern [1781-84], for means for his ample living were assured. According to the statements made by his contemporaries and by himself, he had become disgusted with the errors and uncertainties of the prevalent methods of medical practice, and wished earnestly, to seek for some better method. He reduced himself and his family to want for conscience sake.' [Bradford, p.36]

He moved to Dresden in the autumn of 1784:

'He did not practise medicine, but devoted himself to his translations from the French, English and Italian. He also pursued with renewed zeal his favourite, chemistry.' [Bradford, p.37]

He translated 24 texts from other languages into German during the period from 1777 to 1806. Apart from 6 of them, all of these translations were done during the 1780's and 1790's, when he was conducting various chemical experiments and when he was first formulating, through research and experimentation, the outlines of his system of homoeopathic medicine, derived originally from his extensive critique of the medical system of his day - Old Physic. A critique which grew in its simmering impatience and intensity throughout the 1780's.

12 F

By around 1784, Hahnemann very reluctantly and very sorrowfully gave up the practice of medicine. At least this allowed him to channel his energy and time into translating chemical and medical treatises from English, French and Italian into German. This gave him a bit of an income, and also stimulated his further investigations of drugs poisonings and diseases, and gave him more time for historical research into actual medical cases in various languages.

> 'Thus he arrived at the decision to give up his practice "and to treat scarcely anyone else medically, so as not to injure him" and to occupy himself "merely with chemistry and writing"...'
> [Haehl, Vol 1, p.267]

> 'The more definitely Hahnemann passed into oblivion as a doctor, the greater grew his reputation as a writer on medical subjects. Orders for translations poured in on him from Leipzig.'
> [Gumpert, p.58]

Taken together, these changes which Hahnemann made in his life, provided him with the opportunity he needed to devote a lot of his time, to reading, writing and thinking. We also know that he conducted chemical experiments in the laboratory of his father-in-law, Herr Häesler, the apothecary in Dessau, and step-father of his first wife.

> 'But the sole consolation of Hahnemann's existence in Dessau was his daily visit to the apothecary, Häesler, in whose laboratory he could continue his study of chemistry.' [Gumpert, p.26]

> 'The time he spent in Dessau afforded him a welcome opportunity of pursuing his chemical

research in the laboratory of the Moor Apothecary Shop — work which was so significant for his pioneer activities in medicine.' [Haehl, Vol 1, p.265]

'Hahnemann devoted himself entirely to chemistry and writing, according to his own admission. He puts chemistry first. In this science he was self-taught. He had never received any definite course of instruction in the subject or possessed a laboratory except during his stay in Dessau (1781), where he had found a suitable place in the Moor Apothecary Shop for his experiments and probably also an occasional tutor in the person of the Apothecary Häeseler.' [Haehl, Vol 1, p.268]

Apart from the loss of his medical practice, which seems to have become an agony his conscience would not allow him to prolong, he now placed himself in a more favourable position for making some fundamental medical discoveries. He was partly in medicine and partly out of it, sort-of on the margins of it, a place he was to occupy for the rest of his life, though later on for very different reasons.

It is clear from the sheer mass and volume of these translations, that Hahnemann must have been one of the best read physicians of his day and certainly therefore, a person well-placed to observe and criticise some of the wilder absurdities of the medicine of his day, which had indisputably become a veritable mass of conflicting theories, not one of which had been tested by experiment, but merely composed as an exercise in rhetoric and then used to further the career of its inventor:

'At this period there was a complete anarchy in the domain of therapeutics. Theories Hippocratico-

vitalistic, Galenic, Mathematical, Chemical, Humoral, Electro-Galvanic, formed an inextricable tissue of variable opinions. Hahnemann had abstained from a search for therapeutical indications in this mass of hazardous theories. He had adopted a simple medication partly expectant, that corresponded more fully with his ideal of the art of healing.' [Rapou 'Histoire de la doctrine medicale Homeopathique, Paris, 1847, quoted in Bradford, p.34]

Hahnemann utterly despaired at the irrational nature of the medicine of his day, and its learned professors in the university medical schools, who he felt did more harm than good through their quarrelling:

'No learned brains could unravel the skein of hypotheses and theories which entangled the professors and set them all at odds...the words of an arrogant and incomprehensible professorial language were in themselves without results, but the applicaion of those same professors' erroneous deductions killed thousands of men and women. There were no experiments, there was no painstaking research; there were only odd and eccentric systems which were exalted into dogmas, without any possibility of testing senseless methods of treatment.' [Gumpert, p.15]

Hahnemann did not merely translate these texts, but he also annotated them with extensive commentaries and suggestions of his own, liberally disagreeing with the text wherever he felt inclined to do so. His first few translations he had selected himself, but many of the later ones were

A Guide to Hahnemann's Translations

commissioned by his fellow members of the Leipsic Economical Society - often rich industrialists.

It is also important for us to recall that Hahnemann also published an increasing number of papers of his own composition, during the same period of time, and of particular importance were the 'Essay On A New Principle' of 1796 and his 'Fragmenta de viribus' of 1806.

THE TRANSLATIONS

The original lists of Hahnemann's translations appear both in Dudgeon, 1851 (pp.xi-xiii), in Haehl (Vol 2, pp.511-12) and also in Bradford (pp.515-16).

> *'[Hahnemann] was not able to indulge in the social life of the University [of Leipzig] as all his spare time was spent earning his own living; he translated at least four books from English into German during his stay...' [Cook, p.32]*

1. **'Physiological Experiments and Observations with Copper'** of **John Stedman** (c1730-c1800), London 1769, trans. 1777 from the English; publ J G Muller, Leipsic, 134 pages.

2. Nugent's **'Experiment on Hydrophobia'**, London 1753, trans. 1777 from the English; publ J G Muller, Leipsic; 150 pages

Christopher Nugent, c1720-75, English physician, elected FRS in 1765, obtained his MD in France, practised medicine in Bath (**Rheumatic Hospital, Bath**), moved to London in 1764, wrote on Hydrophobia in 1753, an original member of the Literary Club, died 1775 [CDNB, p.2208].

3. **Falconer's 'Experiments With Mineral Waters and Warm Baths Used at Bath'**, 1775, 2 volumes, trans. 1777, from the English; published by Hilscher, Leipsic in two parts 355 pages and 439 pages.

William Falconer, 1744-1824, English physician, MD Edin 1766, then studied in Leyden MD 1767, physician to the Chester Infirmary 1767-70; elected FRS 1773; physician at Bath 1784- 1819; intimate of Dr Parr; published many medical essays [CDNB, p.965]. Dr Bartholomew Parr, 1750-1810, MD Edin 1773, physician at the Devon & Exeter Hospital 1775, published a very influential tome: the 'London Medical Dictionary' in 2 volumes in 1809, [CDNB, p.2305].

Courtesy David Falconer)   Courtesy David Falconer)

4. **Ball's 'Modern Practice of Physic' or 'Newer Art of Healing'** trans. 1777 and 1780 from the English; with annotations under the name of Spohr; publ Leipsic.

This is probably Peter Ball or Balle, d1675, c1620-75, physician, doctor of philosophy and Physic at Padua 1660; Hon FRCP 1664; an original FRS.

> *The translations... were taken also from the province of medicine (Stedtmann's Physiological Experiments'; Nugent's 'Hydrophobia'; Falkoner's 'Mineral Waters and Baths'; Boll's 'Newer Therapy'.)*
> [Haehl, Vol 1, p.265]

5. **de Machy's 'Procedes chimiques...' or 'Laboratory Chemist On The Preparation of Chemicals for Manufacture as for Art'**, 1769, reprinted 1780, Neufchatel, trans. 1784 from the French; publ by Joachim Crusius at Leipsic in 2 volumes 302 pages and 396 pages respectively; with supplements and copper plates; 2nd edition 1801.[Jacques Francois De Machy, 1728-1803, French chemist (in Hyamson)]

'[in 1784]... he translated Demarchy's 'The Art of Manufacturing Chemical Products' from the French. It was an elaborate work in two volumes, to which he made numerous additions of his own.' [Gumpert, p.34]

'[this book]... augured the development of the chemical industry which was to change the face of Europe in the century which followed. Hahnemann's own annotations in this book are evidence of his increasing competence in chemistry.' [Cook, 1981, p.45]

'Demachy was one of the first chemists of the day, and the French Academy had published his book in order that the people of France might learn the various processes of the manufacture of chemical productions... Demachy quotes a French analyst without giving his name, but Hahnemann gives not only the author's name, his book, and the particular passage in question. On every page his notes appear.' [Bradford, pp.30-31]

'His researches in chemistry drew Hahnemann's attention to the Frenchman, Demachy... a well-recognised man in chemistry who had been made a member of the Paris and Berlin academies on account of his writings and investigations... Hahnemann now translated the whole work, not merely mechanically, but inserting numerous footnotes, supplements, independent references, etc...' [Haehl, vol 1, p.28]

'It was on Gommern that Hahnemann commenced his translation of two volumes by the French chemist Demachy... a member of the Berlin Academy, as well as of his own French Academy in Paris. This book... concerned matters of universal importance to trade... so as to encourage the chemical industry to break down the monopolies of those firms which, especially in Holland, guarded the secrets with assiduity... Hahnemann took upon himself the responsibility of annotating the original work. Besides footnotes he added supplements giving independent references.' [Hobhouse, p.57]

6. **de Machy and Debuisson's 'Art of Distilling Liquor'**, [L'Art du destillateur liquoriste] Paris 1775, trans. 1785 from the French; in two parts vol 1, 332 pages and vol 2, 284 pages, publ Leipsic; trans and enriched with additions by the translator.

   '...all producers who need distilling installations should entirely discard the old Distillery apparatus, and use the French arrangement clearly described by Hahnemann.' [Westrumb in Crell's Chem Annals, 1792, I, p.490; quoted in Haehl, vol 2, pp.18-19]

7. **de Machy's 'Art of Making Vinegar'**, [L'Art du vinaigrier'] Neufchatel, 1780, trans. 1787 from the French; publ by J Crusius in Leipsic, 276 pages with additions by the translator and one supplement.

   'Hahnemann could invent a number of dazzling diversions in the twinkling of an eye. He translated Demarchy's 'The Art of Distilling Liquor' [in 1785] and 'The Art Of Manufacturing Vinegar' [in 1787] from the French. His name was becoming famous, and his assistance sought by rich and enterprising merchants...' [Gumpert, p.51]

   '...the writings of De Machy deserve more

appreciation; and it is of value that they should have been made known to the Germans by translations... Dr Hahnemann has put the author right on many points... and to correct many errors by annotations... the supplement of Dr Hahnemann on vinegar brewing... is as thorough as it is clear.' [The New Medical Literature, by Schlegel & Arnemann, 1788, pp 56-59; quoted in Haehl, vol 2, p.19]

'His translation of the works of Demachy, who was one of the most esteemed chemists of the time, led him to suggest means whereby chemical products might be produced wholesale for general use, and good liquor and vinegar obtained by manufacture.' [Haehl, Vol 1, p.268]

8. A la Haye of Brussells **'Falsification of Medicines'**, [Les falsifications des medicaments devoilees...'] 1784, trans. and publ 1787 in Dresden, from the French

One cannot avoid suspecting that this is a mistake on the part of Dudgeon and that it is in fact the very same work as we list next.

9. **'Signs of The Purity and Adulterations of Drugs'**, by **J B van den Sande**, chemist in Brussells, publ. 1787 by Walther of Dresden, 350 pages; trans. from the French.

'During his stay in Dresden, between 1785 and 1789, Hahnemann translated five major works: De Marchy's Art of Distilling Liquor and The Art of the Manufacture of Vinegar...B Van Sanden's Signs of the Purity and Adulteration of Drugs... De Marchy and Debuisson's The Manufacture of Liqueur, from the French, and, from the English, The History of the Lives of Abelard and Heloise.' [Cook, pp.50-51]

'*Professor Baldinger writes regarding this work in the Medicinal Journal, 1789: this work is very important and is indispensable for every practitioner... much that is good is taught in this important and indispensable book; I cannot sufficiently recommend it.*' [in Haehl, vol 2, p.22]

'*...van den Sande was an apothecary at Brussels, who had in 1784, published a book with the above title... it is in this publication that [Hahnemann] first gives his celebrated Wine Test... This test was greatly praised by the chemical and scientific journals of the day. Trommsdorff's Journal of Pharmacy stated that 'ignorance of Hahnemann's Wine Test was damning evidence of the incompetence of many apothecaries.' (Ameke, pp.21-29).*' [Bradford, p.39]

'*... The signs of purity and adulteration of drugs' by B van den Sande, apothecary in Brussels, and Hahnemann. The greater part of the essay was written by Hahnemann... he repeatedly complains of the unreliability of the pharmaceutical preparations... his 'Wine Test' is also mentioned for the first time.*' [Haehl, Vol 1, p.32]

10. '**Life of Abelard and Heloise**', by **Sir Joseph Barrington**, 1787, Birmingham and London, trans. 1789 from the English; 638 pages, publ. in Leipsic. The first translation of 'History of Abelard and Heloise' was made by Sir Joseph Barrington in 1787.

'*In 1789 he translated the History of the Lives of Abelard and Heloise from the English of Sir Joseph Barrington. This translation was mentioned by the critics as being correct and fluent and of value to romantic history.*' [Bradford, p.39]

> *'The translation of the 'Story of Abelard and Heloise' from the English (638 pages) proves that Hahnemann had studied foreign classic literature thoroughly and not just as a pastime. 'Algemeine Deutsch Bibliothek' of 1792 (Vol 106, p.243) says of the above story... 'Hahnemann translates faithfully and fluently, and we should be justified in recommending this work....' [Haehl, Vol 1, p.32]*

> *'If we bear in mind that during the years 1785-89 Hahnemann published more than 2200 printed pages, including translations, original works, and essays, and that he further worked strenuously...at his own medical profession, we must marvel at the unusual capacity for work, at the energy, the industry and zeal with which the man of thirty to thirty four years accomplished this task.' [Haehl, Vol 1, p.32-33]*

11. **'Inquiry into the Nature, Causes & Cure of Consumption of the Lungs'**, by **Michael Ryan** MD, FRAS Edin, London 1787, trans. from the English; publ. 1790 in Leipsic by Weygand, 164 pages

> *'In 1790 he published a translation from the English: 'Ryan on Diseases of the Lungs'.' [Bradford, p.43]*

Michael Ryan, c1720-1800, Irish physician, MD Edin, FRCS Ireland, practised in Kilkenny, then removed to Edinburgh, MRCS London; publ. medical works.

A person of the same name of Michael Ryan published: Prostitution in London, with a comparative view of that of Paris and New York, as illustrated of the capitals and large towns of all countries... & account of the nature and treatment of the various diseases, caused by abuses of the reproductive function. London: H. Bailliere, 1839. xx447pp. [From an internet book search] This could well be another Michael Ryan, 1800-41, who was MRCS and MRCP London and physician to the Metropolitan Free Hospital[CDNB, p.2618]

12. **Fabroni's 'Art of Making Wine in Accord with Sensible Principles...'**, Florence 1787, 2nd edition 1790, trans. 1790 from the Italian with additions; published by Barth in Leipsic, 278 pages; '...adding as was his custom, many notes.' [Bradford, p43] [Angelo Fabroni, 1732-1803, Italian biographer]

> *'In 1790 he published a translation... from the Italian: 'Fabroni On the Art of Making Wine on Rational Principles', adding, as was his custom, many notes. [Bradford, p.43]*

Fabroni also published:Angelo Fabroni, 'I Dialoghi Di Focione'. Venice: Giuseppe Orlandelli, 1789. This translation of Phocion, Athenian statesman and general who was a pupil of Plato and close friend of Xenocrates, is from the French of the abbé de Mably. It was first printed at Rome in 1763 and excited some controversy, thanks to which Fabroni (1732-1803) removed to Florence. Despite a later reconciliation with the Vatican, he chose to remain under the protection of the Grand Duke of Florence where he published several noted biographies before devoting himself entirely to religious pursuits. Melzi I, 290. Sm. 8vo, xxiii, 238pp. [From an Internet booksearch]

13. **'A Treatise of Materia Medica'** of **William Cullen**, trans. 1790, 2 vols from the English, 468 pages and 672 pages with annotations by the translator. publ by Schweickert in Leipsic [Professor William Cullen, Edinburgh, 1710-90, Scottish Professor of Physic]

'It is not probable that when he commenced upon 'Cullen' Hahnemann had any particular medical theories, but only a growing disgust for the medical fallacies of the day... it is not to be wondered at that he should translate the work at that time. He was translating for money, for the booksellers and publishers of Leipsic, and it is not likely that he selected the books which he was to translate.' [Bradford, pp.43-44]

> 'Cullen published the first edition of this book in London in 1773. Another edition was issued in 1789 in two volumes, and it was this edition that Hahnemann used in translation.' [Bradford, p.44]

> 'It may be mentioned that Hahnemann was not the first to translate Cullen's Materia Medica into German. In 1781 Dr G W C Consbruch made the translation: it was published in Leipzig by Weygand. A second edition was issued in 1790.' [Bradford, pp.49-50]

> 'His eight translations from English, French and Italian into German included a work of considerable significance, A Treatise on Materia Medica by Dr William Cullen...it is probable therefore, that it was on the initiative of the Leipzig publishers that Hahnemann was given the task of translating the work...' [Cook, p.58]

> 'Dr Hahnemann has completed these translations with great diligence notwithstanding the obscurity of the original...the annotations of the translator are for the most part very instructive, and his occasional corrections increase the value of this important work' [Med Chir Zeit, 1791, 1, pp.117 & 231; quoted in Haehl, Vol 2, p.25]

When we consider that every work he translated, he carefully annotated (often copiously) with comments, hints and suggestions of his own. These rather impudent notes in the margins were included to help the reader grasp a point or technique more clearly. Some of these annotations disagreed profoundly with the original work. How natural therefore, for Hahnemann, when reading about the specific symptoms of a specific drug, how perfectly natural for him to ingest a small non-lethal dose of the drug in question so as to check and see if it can produce the same symptom in himself? Arguably, it was his incurable urge to experiment and test things out for himself, combined with his insistence on disagreeing with people he knew were wrong, which led him to discover the proving technique.

In this manner he became his own medical laboratory for testing the drugs he read about, so as to confirm or deny the assertions of other medical writers. This remarkable and profoundly original method is certainly a measure of how methodical he was. And it also reveals the fundamental basis for the perfection of the technique into the more formal procedure of the proving as such.

In his Textbook of Materia Medica, first published in 1789, which Hahnemann translated into German in 1790, Professor William Cullen (1710-90) stated that the action of Cinchona relied upon its effects upon the stomach. This single statement greatly puzzled Hahnemann and presented him with a huge problem. He knew this was incorrect and said so in the annotations of his translation. He knew from his own use of it that Cinchona presents very few stomach symptoms.

But Cullen was Professor of Medicine at Edinburgh 1751-5, Professor of Chemistry 1756, Clinical Lecturer 1757,

Professor of the Theory of Physic 1766, President of the Edinburgh College of Physicians 1773-5 and, his crowning glory, he was elected Fellow of the Royal Society in 1777, which, then as now, is the highest scientific honour in Britain [Concise Dictionary of National Biography, Oxford Univ. Press, 1995, pp.706-7]. It is no exaggeration to say he was held in such high esteem in medicine that he was often called the 'Scottish Hippocrates' [Gumpert, p.65] and at that time he was regarded as the very highest authority on all medical matters. So that gives a measure of the man Hahnemann chose to disagree with!

Thus the Cinchona experiment derives precisely from Hahnemann's annotation of a medical work he was translating into German. And he primarily took the powdered bark himself to confirm or deny the stomach symptoms claim of Cullen. If Cullen had not been such an authority, to disagree with him would not have posed such a problem. But Hahnemann had to know for certain — and that was his nature.

> *'Cullen was wrong. It was not the attack on the mucus membrane of the stomach that cured fever...'* [Gumpert, p.66]

> *'The old teachers of materia medica have been copied up to the most recent times, together with their shallowness, their indecision, their fairy tales and their untruths by everybody (with few exceptions) and neither the old originators nor their weak followers deserve to be spared. We must tear ourselves violently away from these idealised authorities, if we desire to shake off the yoke of uncertainty and superstition in one of the most important branches of practical medicine. It is now*

high time.' [Hahnemann in Cullen, quoted by Haehl, Vol 1, p.273]

'Hahnemann having, by his simple and rational experiment with Cinchona bark in 1790, conclusively established the great therapeutic law, that to cure diseases medicines must be used which possess the power of exciting similar diseases, at once perceived that the whole edifice of the old Materia Medica must be rebuilt from the very foundation, as that Materia Medica furnished nothing positive regarding the [true] pathogenetic actions of drugs.' [Dudgeon, 1853, p.176]

14. **'Annals of Agriculture'** by **A Young**, FRS, trans. 1790 and 1791 from the English, publ in Leipsic by Crusius in 2 vols 290 and 313 pages respectively.

Arthur Young, 1741-1820, British agriculturist and author of 'Travels in France', editor. Annals of Agriculture and Other Useful Arts. Collected and published by Arthur Young. London: printed for the editor, and sold by H. Goldney, 1785. First edition. 8vo. iv, 527pp. + 3pp. index. Begun in 1784, forty-seven volumes appeared continuously till 1809.

15. **'Precautionary Measures For The Female Sex'** by **John Grigg** (c1750-c1810), accoucheur and surgeon to the Bath workhouse, London 1789, trans. 1791, from the English; publ in Leipsic by Weygand, 285 pages

'John Grigg's 'Rules of Conduct for the Female Sex...' was translated by Hahnemann from the English without additions or remarks. In addition to the 21 chapters which comprise 225 pages, an appendix is added 'on the treatment of children in the first

> *period of life' (59 pages). Here Hahnemann confines himself entirely to the translation of the original work without additions or annotations.' [Haehl, vol 2, p.27]*

Although Hahnemann was poor [Bradford, p.49 and p.75] he was honoured as a scientist. He was elected a member of the Leipzig Economical Society and as a Fellow of the Academy of Mayence [Bradford, p.49].

16. **Monro's 'A Medical and Pharmaceutical Chemistry and the Materia Medica'**, by Donald Monro, MD, physician to St George's Hospital, FRCP London and FRS London 1788, trans. 1791 from the English, publ by Beer in Leipsic in two volumes, 480 and 472 pages respectively, with annotations by the translator; 1794 2nd edition.

Donald Monro, 1727-1802, Scottish physician, [son of Alexander Monro, 1697-1767, Professor of Anatomy at Edinburgh] MD Edin 1753, army physician, LRCP 1756; physician at St George's Hospital, London 1758-86; FRS 1766, FRCP 1771, censor 1772, 1781, 1785, 1789; Croonian Lecturer 1774-5, Harveian Orator 1775, publ works on medicine and soldier's health [CDNB, p.2058]

> *'The translation of this work was very desirable... Dr Hahnemann has amplified, verified and corrected it. This gives the translation many advantages over the original work... through his careful corrections, Hahnemann has earned new honour from readers of this class of literature.' [Crell's Chem Annals, 1792, p.138; quoted in Haehl, vol 2, p.27]*

'Donald Monro, M.D, A Treatise on Medical and Pharmaceutical Chemistry, and the Materia Medica: To Which is Added an English Translation of the New Edition of the Pharmacopoeia of the Royal College of Physicians of London, 1788. Cadell, 1788 Monro, Donald, M.D. 3 vols., London: First Edition. A man of considerable skill in his profession, Monro was for many years a physician with the British armies in Germany and later with St. George's Hospital in London.' [from an Internet secondhand book search]

'The translator is Dr Hahnemann, a man who has rendered many services to science both by his own writings on chemistry, and by his excellent translations of important foreign works. His services have been already recognised, but deserve to be still more so.' [Crell in the Annalen, quoted in Bradford, p.48]

17. **Rigby's 'Chemical Observations on Sugar'**, 2 vols, London 1788, trans. 1791, from the English with annotations by the translator; publ in Dresden by C C Richter 82 pages.

Edward Rigby, 1747-1821, English physician and physiologist, publ work On Uterine Haemorrhage in 1776 trans into German and French, visited France 1789; practised in Norwich and became mayor of Norwich in 1805, [CDNB, p2536]

An Edward Rigby, also published: 'A System of Midwifery', A Whittaker, 1853 1st ed. 8vo. Text and ills. [From an internet booksearch] 18. de la Metherie's 'Essai analytique sur l'air pur et les differentes especes d'air' On

Pure Air and Different Kinds of Air', De la Metherie, doctor of medicine and member of the Dijon and Mayence Academy, Paris 1758, trans.1791 and 1792 from the French, in 2 vols 450 pages and 498 pages; publ by Crusius, Leipsic

19. **Rousseau's 'Principles on Education of Infants'**, trans. 1796 from the French; also called 'Handbook for Mothers'; published Fleischer, Leipsic; 2nd edition 1804. [Jean Jacques Rousseau, 1712-78]

    '...it is nothing more than a translation of [Rousseau's] work, with a few additions and one or two alterations by the translator.' [Dudgeon, 1851, p.xiii]

    'He translated from the French, Rousseau 'On the Education of Infants' under the title of 'Handbook for Mothers'...' [Bradford, p.57]

20. **Taplin's 'Equerry or Modern Veterinary Medicine'**, from the English, part 1 in 1797 Leipsic, 387 pages; part 2 in 1798, 304 pages.

This is quite clearly William Taplin, c1750-c1830, who also published as follows:

William Taplin, The Sportsman's Cabinet; or, a Correct Delineation of the Various Dogs used in the Sports of the Field, Including the Canine Race in General, London: J.Cundee, 1803-1804 First Edition. 2 vols., 4to.

William Taplin: The Gentleman's Stable Directory; Or, Modern System of Farriery. Comprehending the Present entire improved Mode of Practice: Likewise All the most valuable Prescriptions and approved Remedies, accurately proportioned and properly adapted to every known disease to which the Horse is incident. Interspersed with Occasion

Remarks upon the dangerous and almost obsolete Practice of Gibson, Bracken, Bartlet, Osmer, and Others. Also Directions for Feeding, Bleeding, Purging and getting into Condition for the Chase. To which are now added, useful instructions for buying and selling; With an Appendix, Containing experimental observations upon the Management of Draft Horses, their Blemishes and Defects. Inscribed to Sir John Lade, Bart. The Seventh Ed, London: Printed for G. Kearsley..., 1789, 1791. 2 volumes. 8vo, pp. [iii] - xxiii [xxiv blank], 434; viii, 419 [420 adverts], with engraved portrait of author as frontispiece to volume 1.

Bound with: William Taplin: Practical Observations upon Thorn Wounds, Punctured Tendons, and Ligamentary Lameness in Horses, with Experimental Instructions for their Treatment and Cure. Illustrated by a recital of cases, interspersed with a variety of useful remarks. To which is added a successful method of treating The Canine Species, in that destructive disease called The Distemper. The whole forming a supplement to The Gentleman's Stable Directory. London: printed for G. Kearsley..., 1790. 8vo, pp. 86. Three parts in two volumes. The last short item is bound at the end of volume 1.

Taplin first published The Gentleman's Stable Directory in 1778. While the first volume claims to be a 7th edition, Taplin claims in the second volume that the work has gone through "ten large editions." [from an internet booksearch]

21. **'New Edinburgh Dispensatory'** trans 1797-8 from the English with annotations by the translator; publ in Leipsic by G Fleischer Jnr, part 1 1797, with 3 copper plates 583 pages; part 2 1798, 628 pages with annotations

'In addition, Hahnemann completed several translations, including Rousseau's Handbook for Mothers, from the French, and the New Edinburgh Dispensatory, from the English....again the reviewers of Hahnemann's writings were complimentary, and their comments suggested that he had by this time established a reputation for his work. For example, 'a work of this kind by a man who had made a name for himself in Germany as a chemist and as a practitioner, deserves special recommendation.'. In Tromsdorff's Journal of Pharmacy a critic wrote of his translation of the New Edinburgh Dispensatory, 'The work is welcome, especially as the translation is an improvement on the English original on account of the notes by the learned Dr Hahnemann." [Cook, pp.76-77]

'Although there is no lack of treatises of this kind in Germany, yet the present work is welcome, especially as the translation is an improvement on the English original on account of the notes by the learned Dr Hahnemann.' [Tromsdorff's Journal of Pharmacy, 1799, quoted by Haehl, vol 2, p.49) 'He translated...from the English, the 'New Edinburgh Dispensatory' in two volumes..' [Bradford, p.57]

'The usefulness of this work has been recognised and it is enhanced by the translator's notes' [Hufeland's Journal, 1798, V, p.469; quoted in Haehl, Vol 2, p.49]

Two examples of the numerous editions and authors of this work are as follows:

1. Lewis, Dr. The Edinburgh New Dispensatory: Containing, 1. The Elements of Pharmaceutial Chemistry. II the Materia Medica; Or, An Account of the Different Substances Employed in Medicine. III. The Pharmaceutical Preparations and Medicinal

Compositions of the Latest Editions of the London and Edinburgh Pharmacopoeias. Philadelphia: Thomas Dobson, 1796. 4th edition. 6 copper plates (2 folding), xvii, 612pp, 2pp of ads in back, 8vo. In his work as a translator he could not restrain himself from giving outspoken expression of his divergent views. In 1798, for example, in translating the Edinburgh Dispensatorium', he availed himself of a footnote to mock at the multi-compounded prescriptions...' [Hahel, Vol 1, p.307]

2. Andrew Duncan, the Edinburgh New Dispensary: Containing 1. The elements of pharmaceutical chemistry. II. The Materia Medica, or the natural, pharmaceutical, and medical history of the substances employed in medicine. III. The pharmaceutical preparations and compositions... Edinburgh, 1810, 5th edition, revised & enlarged xxii, 822pp, 6 copper plates 8vo. [from an internet booksearch]

'The first hints of dilutions are to be found in the translation of the second part of the ŒEdinburgh Dispensatorium' (1798). Silver nitrate was recommended by Boerhaave in doses of 2 grains, worked up into pills with breadcrumbs and sugar; Hahnemann considered that too strong, and suggested a very diluted preparation.' [Haehl, Vol 1, p.312]

'The translation of the Dispensatory called forth from the chemists of Germany unstinted praise. As was his custom, he enriched it with copious notes.' [Bradford, p.57]

22. **'Thesaurus medicaminum — A New Collection of Medical Prescriptions'** trans. 1800, from the English;

composed by a member of the London College of Physicians; 412 pages with a preface and annotated notes by the translator; publ. by G Fleischer Jnr at Leipsic.

'In 1800 Hahnemann translated from the English the 'Thesaurus Medicaminum', which was a collection of medical prescriptions... which was published anonymously... he continues to argue against compound prescriptions and in favour of single remedies... he denounces the body of the work... he ridicules placing drugs antagonistic to each other in the same prescription and advises a return to the simpler methods of Hippocrates.' [Bradford, pp.71-72]

'...denouncing more and more energetically the absurdities and errors of ordinary medical practice. One of the most remarkable articles in this style is his preface to a translation of a collection of medical prescriptions, published in 1800, which preface is the best antidote to the contents of the work itself...the English original of this work, which contained nought but a collection of the abominable and nonsensical compounds which he had been inveighing against for the last 5 years...' ...as for the contents of this book, they are the grossest imposition ever palmed upon man, a confused jumble of unknown drugs — mostly poisons — mixed together in what are called prescriptions...none of which possesses the qualities attributed to it... it contains a multitude of anarchical elements that totally disqualify it for any orderly action whatever... the best counsel I can give you, dear reader, is to place the main body of this book into the fire...' [Dudgeon, 1853, pp.xxvii-xxviii]

'In 1799 he suddenly announced without particular explanation very small and so-called infinitesimal doses... in the 'Treasury of Medicine' or the ŒCollection of Selected Prescriptions' (1800) there is an increasing number of remarks concerning very much smaller doses...' [Haehl, Vol 1, p.312]

'In the Preface and footnotes to his translation of the Thesaurus medicaminum' — Treasury of Medicines or Collection of Selected Prescriptions' (1800) — Hahnemann was, if possible, more outspoken in his contempt for every mixture of medicines.' [Haehl, Vol 1, p.308]

'Three years later (1800) Hahnemann translated a 'Treasure of Medicine or Collection of Chosen Prescriptions' (Thesaurus Medicaminum) from the English....he wrote a preface to the book, in which he promptly dismissed as worthless the long recipes translated, with their medicinal hashes, and ridiculed them...' [Haehl, Vol 1, p.69]

23. **Home's 'Practical Observations On the Cure of Strictures of the Urethra by Caustics'**, publ. in 1800 Leipsic by G Fleischer Jnr; trans. from the English with annotations by the translator, 147 pages

This is Dr E Home, English surgeon, also known as Sir Everard Home (1756-1832) first Baronet and pupil of the great English physician John Hunter (1728-93), elected FRS 1785, lecturer in anatomy 1792 and surgeon at St George's hospital London 1793-1827; Master (1813) and first President (1821) of the Royal College of Surgeons; Hunterian

Orator 1814 and 1822, baronet 1812, surgeon to the Chelsea Hosp 1821-32; published Lectures on Comparative Anatomy 1814 and other medical works, [CDNB, p.1466].

> *Sir Everad Home. Lectures on Comparative Anatomy in which are examined the preparations in the Hunterian collection. Illustrated by engravings. London Printed by W. Bulmer and Co. for G. and W. Nicol 1814 First edition. Home, Sir Everard. Lectures on Comparative Anatomy. London: 1814-1828. First edition. Six quarto volumes. With 371 engraved and lithographed plates. [from an internet websearch]*

> 'In the year 1800 Hahnemann translated...a little English book by Dr E Home. As with almost all his translations, here he also adds his personal views and experiences in the form of annotations and footnotes. Home was a disciple of the genius Hunter, a specialist on diseases of the genital organs...and it was no small merit to [Hahnemann] to have acquainted the medical profession, through his superior translation of Home's work...' [Haehl, Vol 2, pp.49-50]

24. **von Haller's 'Materia Medica'** trans. 1806 from the Latin, according to Bradford (p.80) but from the French, according to Haehl (vol. 1, p.73), publ. by Steinacker in Leipsic. As in most matters, we can generally assume Haehl as being more often correct than Bradford.[Albrecht von Haller, 1708-77, Swiss anatomist, physiologist, writer and botanist]

> 'In 1801 he published in Hufeland's Journal some observations on 'Brown's Elements of Medicine' in which he again pleads against the use of so many

drugs in one prescription, and earnestly recommends simpler methods of treatment. With the exception of von Haller's 'Materia Medica' translated in 1806, this was to be the last of Hahnemann's translations.' [Bradford, p.72]

'...the next year, 1806, Hahnemann translated the Materia Medica of A von Haller, from the Latin. This was the last book he translated.' [Bradford, p.80]

'In the year 1806 he completed his last translation: Albrecht von Haller's 'Materia Medica of German Plants, Together with their Economic and Technical Use.'...in which 462 plants are described...Hahnemann's work is a translation from the French... Haller [was] a physician of Lausanne...' [Haehl, Vol 1, p.73]

The totals are 17 books from the English, 6 from the French, 1 from the Italian, and 1 from the Latin, and totalling over 9400 pages of text, a pretty staggering achievement for any accomplished linguist. Besides all these longer books, and during the same years, Hahnemann also translated numerous short papers on medicine and chemistry, from a similar range of languages, which were published in various scientific and medical journals of the day [Bradford, p.32].

DISCUSSION

It seems clear from this survey, that it was very largely through his translation work, that Hahnemann finally attained his later and more mature views on medicine. Through continually struggling, in great detail, with what he so often found to be the absurd and disagreeable views of others (ie. allopaths) - and which he criticised vehemently and extensively in his many footnotes - thus he arrived at his more final views about an ideal form of medicine. Many of us tend not to know what we really want, but through mixing with something we dislike we soon begin to formulate some ideas about a better alternative. I think this theme forms a sound basis for much of Hahnemann's early work. The theme recurs wherever we look.

From an initially unsure and sceptical position (a position so ambivalent that he desisted from medical practice entirely), he gradually developed, with increasing confidence and certainty, his own views and ideas about the single drug, the law of similars, reduced doses and the proving — which are the central pillars of homoeopathy. These ideas must have been formulated in Hahnemann's mind as 'shadows' of the main pillars of allopathy, which he had identified as complex drugs, contraries, strong doses and signatures.

Hahnemann abandoned medical practice for fear of its harmful effects and through a profound dissatisfaction with its dismal clinical results. He thus became paralysed into medical inactivity through a profound uncertainty about the usefulness of its main techniques and with what he was going to do with the rest of his life. His apparently stop-gap solution to this problem was both intelligent and deeply pragmatic: keep translating to earn a living and given time some truth might just emerge out of a terrible darkness.

> 'The future looked very dark to the honest seeker after truth. He had lost his faith in medicine. Of this time he writes: 'Where shall I look for aid, sure aid? Sighed the disconsolate father on hearing the moaning of his dear, inexpressibly dear sick children. The darkness of night and the darkness of

a desert all around me; no prospect of relief for my oppressed paternal heart.' [Hahnemann in Hufeland, Lesser Writings, p.513, quoted in Bradford, p.51]

Thus, far from being a side-issue in his development, the translations seem to sit much closer to centre-stage than we realise. Indeed, they seem to form the absolute bedrock of his own medical and scientific development, and by looking at them, we gain a valuable insight into how he fashioned the central ideas and techniques of his homoeopathic system from some of the wildest absurdities of eighteenth century allopathy.

Two useful analogies spring to mind. Firstly, acting as a rich and fertile soil, the translations actively informed and inspired his thinking and enriched all his other writings, experiments and discoveries. Second, more like a river, the work of his translations flowed on into all other areas of his life, depositing, wherever it went, a fine sediment of new ideas. Thus, through his coming to know intimately what he increasingly felt was 'wrong' in the medicine of his day, and by daily mixing his mind with it, he gradually perceived and formulated, that which he felt was 'right', and apparently with increasing clarity and confidence. Thus, based upon his reading and translating, he was then able to identify more clearly the fundamental errors of allopathy (ie. why it did not work). This undoubtedly informed his experimentation — the Cinchona experiment, probably being the best example.

As we survey the impressive mass of these translations (9400 pages in 29 years is 324 pages per year, or roughly 1 page per day, every day!), several other points should also become clear. From a starting position of quite passively translating allopathic medical texts into German in order to make a livelihood, Hahnemann began to adopt a more fiercely critical stance, finally becoming openly hostile to allopathy and confidently ridiculing the contents of some of the texts, such as two of his last translations: the 'New Edinburgh Dispensatory' and the 'Thesaurus medicaminum', the contents of which he lampooned as absurd to the point of madness. It seems he just could not resist the temptation to pass comments about what he was translating, even though he was being paid to do it.

My assumption is that Hahnemann gave up translating simply because he had had such a bellyful of the material he was translating that he just could not bear to do any more — so profoundly did he come to disagree with and detest their subject matter. And above all else, he had outgrown them, and was becoming totally preoccupied with his new creation - homoeopathy.

In effect, therefore, he used his translations as a platform from which first to probe the depths of allopathy, and then later, to launch into massive and sustained attacks against it. That was by no means his starting position, but it was certainly how things ended up. No wonder, then, that he never flinched in his furious arguments with allopaths after 1806: he had probably seen and rehearsed all their arguments during his translations and had already demolished their positions point by point. He had in fact attained a state of renewed medical certainty, which others interpreted as stubborn arrogance. He can only have attained this through his translations, backed up by his experiments.

'He now saw full well that he must not look to his medical brethren for assistance in his great aim, but he did not despair; on the contrary, this very

> opposition of his colleagues made him more resolute in his determination to carry out his plans alone, or with what casual assistance he could procure from non- professional friends.' [Dudgeon, 1853, p.181]

Thus his translations gave him an unparalleled insider's knowledge of the 'enemy camp' and uniquely prepared him for every future battle. Like a brilliant military commander, he knew intimately all their weapons and how they would be used. As a result, they stood before him entirely disarmed. The only weapon they had left was contempt, which they rained down upon him without mercy.

> 'There is a principle which is a bar against all information, which is proof against all arguments, and which cannot fail to keep a man in everlasting ignorance — that principle is contempt prior to investigation.' [Herbert Spencer, quoted in Barker, p.1]

Then there is the Hahnemann as the 'secret agent' theory:

> 'Hahnemann... practised his profession only to obtain definite proofs against it... he was in the fortunate position [in Dresden, in 1785] of being able to examine a very large number of patients and to treat them according to his own discretion, while large experimental stations were at his disposal.' [Gumpert, pp.49-50]

I suppose allopaths must have felt betrayed by 'the learned Dr Hahnemann', a qualified doctor and respected scientist who was once their dear friend. A person, in fact, who had worked alongside them just like one of them, but who, it turns out, was more like a spy operating in the enemy camp, working not for them but against them; studying and practising allopathy, as Gumpert says, purely 'to obtain definite proofs against it'. He was covertly working to obtain the downfall of allopathy. Once he had calculated its main errors, once he had identified its major flaws and absurdities and once he had formulated a more rational alternative to it, he would turn against it, betray it and strive to see it destroyed. This is a slightly overdramatic and possibly entertaining version of events, but it is a distortion to portray Hahnemann as deliberating the downfall of allopathy in this calculating way. Maybe towards the end of his Leipzig battles he was operating as a major enemy towards allopathy. He was an enemy of untruth, and felt very passionately that he had found a new truth in medical science. But his essential gameplan all along, had merely been to find out why allopathy did not work and to correct it, such that it worked reliably and predictably. Surely a just, noble and worthy objective by anyone's standard?

> *'Hahnemann's assaults on the ancient medicine had rendered him thoroughly distasteful to his colleagues; he was now no more to be trusted, and was henceforth regarded as an outcast and a Pariah, whose companionship was shunned for evermore.'*
> [Dudgeon, 1853, p.181

In a profound sense, therefore, only through his sustained and intimate mixing with what he regarded as a form of 'medical darkness' - or untruth, which he detested - was he able to grope towards a form of light or truth in which he quite clearly delighted. In Hahnemann's mind homoeopathy therefore came to seem like the perfect 'light' of allopathy's dark shadow, the other side of the same coin, the opposite pole and yet also (in the modern psychological sense) its complement. The yin and the yang, perhaps. There seems no doubt that he forged the one through wrestling with the ideas of the other, but in an entirely opposite fashion, the 'dark twin' and the light. In this sense, we might say that the light was borne out of the darkness in an almost poetic, Blakeian or spiritual manner, even though, Heaven forbid, Hahnemann himself would never have permitted the use of such language. First and last he was, of course, a practical man of science.

It seems fairly clear that by 1806 Hahnemann had emerged from that 'darkness', and returned from that lonely 'desert', having answered this same question entirely to his own satisfaction, and found in the homoeopathic system of his own making, the 'sure aid' and the 'relief' his heart had yearned for. And at a deeper level, creating homoeopathy would seem to have closed another circle of his life, one which had started thirty years before, in the wild mountains of Trannsylvania, while working as a young man, at the start of his career, for his beloved Patron:

> *'[In 1777] he carefully catalogued Baron von Bruckenthal's immense library of books and rare manuscripts. It was during the quiet, scholarly days, in the secluded library at Hermannstadt [Sibiu], that he acquired that extensive and diverse knowledge of ancient literature, and of occult sciences, of which he afterwards proved himself the master, and with which he astonished the scientific world. [Bradford, p.28]*

Bradford might be distorting the facts a little here, because it is more accurate to say that Hahnemann shocked and horrified the scientific community rather than astonished them with his great knowledge.

Hahnemann had selflessly donated his great talents for the benefit of medicine and science and thus for all humanity, and conferred upon his followers a revolution in medicine. A revolution derived entirely from experimentation and clear thinking. Through identifying what he saw as the fundamental errors in allopathy, he had formulated a working system with sound underlying principles. Thus, looking back, he might have permitted himself the modest indulgence of realising that he had succeeded in doing precisely what he had set out to do. Not many of us can say that. As his Paris gravestone so aptly says: 'Non inutilis vixi' - 'I have not lived in vain'.

■

HAHNEMANN - THE REAL PIONEER OF PSYCHIATRY

The Ballad of the Army Waggons.
A poem by Tu Fu, 2nd March 1982 - Peter Morrell

"Hahnemann was less keen to explore the psychological or psychic causes of sickness and he seemed to play down the significance of such factors. Moreover, in homoeopathy, that still remains a more or less blank sheet even to this day."

Reflection upon this point has prompted me to consider this matter further.

This short survey attempts to explore Hahnemann's treatment of mentally ill patients, his aphorisms in the Organon on the same subject and finally the uncomfortable position 'mental illness' occupies within the conceptual fabric of homoeopathy as a whole.

As Dudgeon tells us, Hahnemann *"settled for a time in 1792,"* in Georgenthal, and it was while residing there that he *"accepted an offer of the reigning Duke of Saxe-Gotha to take charge of an asylum for the insane,"*. In a letter of May 1792, Hahnemann states that the Duke would soon be *"handing over to me his hunting castle in Georgenthal,",*], and it was here that Hahnemann was able to *"pursue his painfully interesting investigations,"*, eventually establishing a dramatic cure of a patient, Herr Klockenbring. The account of this cure was published in 1796 [see Lesser Writings, 243-49] and this proves Hahnemann was *"one of the earliest, if not the very first,"* to advocate a *"treatment of the insane by mildness rather than coercion,"*. In fact, it was on 2nd

September in the year 1793, that *"Pinel made his first experiment of unchaining maniacs in the Bicêtre,"*, which was some fifteen months **after** Hahnemann had commenced treating Klockenbring.

This single incident undoubtedly provided Hahnemann with some pioneering ideas about the nature of mental disease and how sufferers ought to be treated. Whether it gave him any conception of mental illness, as a separate category of sickness seems unlikely, because such an idea clearly flies in the face of the holistic views inherent to homoeopathy itself. These events also lie close to the years when Hahnemann was conducting his first provings and just before he published what might be termed his 'first sketch' of materia medica in the *Fragmenta de viribus medicamentorum positivis*, published in 1805. Therefore, this incident actually occurred at a very busy and important time when Hahnemann was consumed with his formulation of the homoeopathic system for the first time.

There seems little doubt that Hahnemann *"possessed an extraordinary understanding for the nervous and mental activities of his patients...and [possibly] considered psycho-therapy in certain cases to be more important, more applicable than the use of homoeopathic medicines."*. He also seems to have been *"far in advance of his time in this province."*. Everyone seems to be agreed that he exhibited a *"fine understanding...for the unfortunate victims of mental derangement,"*

**Johann Christian Reil
(1759-1813)**

and he acquired a reputation for the same, attracting many patients with mental problems. This was in the 1790s before homoeopathy was yet established and during which time he was not a regular medical practitioner. His cure of Klockenbring *"caused a sensation,"* at the time and certainly reveals him as the originator of *"entirely new methods in the treatment of mental patients, independently of his famous contemporaries Pinel and Reil."*. *"'We lock up these unhappy beings like criminals in cells,' exclaims Reil in 1803."*

The anatomist and psychiatrist Reil (*1759-1813*), was *"a friend of Goethe and publisher of various medical journals, who was the first to use the term "psychiatry;" warned against the indiscriminate administration of drugs and, instead, emphasized the use of psychogogics, occupation, playing music, and acting in his therapeutic program, "Rhapsodies" on the application of emotional cures on rain of the mind." The treatment of melancholy included pleasing physical stimuli such as heat, studying esthetic paintings, strolling, and swinging."*

Phillippe Pinel [1745-1826], a French physician, M.D. Univ. of Toulouse, 1773. After moving to Paris in 1778, he was appointed (1793) Director of the Bicêtre Hospital and shortly thereafter of the Salpêtrière. His Traité médico-philosophique sur l'aliénation mentale (2d ed. 1809), based on observations in both these hospitals, advocated humane treatment of mentally ill persons, then called the insane, and a more empirical study of mental disease. He further contributed to the development of psychiatry through his establishment of the practice of keeping well-documented psychiatric case histories for research."

TREATMENT OF KLOCKENBRING

The chief resource that is alluded to by others in support of Hahnemann's superior and prophetic views on mental illness is his treatment of Klockenbring in Georgenthal in 1792. This event was certainly critical in formatively creating his own views on this subject.

At the time in question, Hahnemann declared that he had *"been for several years much occupied with diseases of the most tedious and desperate character in general..."*, including several cases of hypochondria and insanity. Hahnemann then wrote of establishing *"a model asylum for the treatment, by gentle methods, of the insane of the higher classes of society."* Publicity for the new asylum was given in a local journal, The Anzeiger, in March 1792 yet *"in spite of the clear intention to restrict its use...to persons of...good social standing...the document breaks out compassionately into a plea for a rational treatment of the countless victims of insanity who were kept in confinement in the asylums."*

Hahnemann's entry into the psychiatric field *"was four years before William Tuke, the English Quaker had finally established the Retreat in York...and a year before Pinel reformed the Bicêtre Asylum in Paris."*

William Tuke, *"was head of the Quaker family that founded the York Retreat in 1792...located in a rural setting,* provided humane institutional care of people with mental illness. Its reduced use of restraints and confinement, and therapeutic use of occupational tasks, especially farming chores, were duplicated in scores of later institutions." Tuke [1732–1822], was an English merchant and philanthropist, who succeeded at an early age to the family business at York in wholesale tea and coffee. Apart from founding the York Retreat, he also spawned a whole family of individuals, all with pioneering links to humane treatment of the poor, the destitute and the mentally ill. The York Retreat was "an influential early institution for the intelligent and humane care of the insane."

William Tuke
(1732-1822)

At the time of Hahnemann's incursion into this field, the insane were *"treated like wild animals...chained in dungeon-like cells."* The usual treatment at the time was *"by violence...whipping and dungeons."* Haehl states that Hahnemann *"acquired a knowledge of psychiatry...greater than Pinel...[upholding] the cause of humane treatment,"* [Hobhouse, 93], Hahnemann additionally laying out *"the foundations of a new medicinal treatment of mental illness,"* [ibid. 93]. Hahnemann also appreciated the importance of the 'law of similars' when he referred to a cure *"by Hippocrates of his friend's mania by the use of Hellebore...[which can] produce the symptoms of mania."* Apparently, this observation provided one confirmation for his idea of the central importance of similars in medicine.

During the two years following his translation of Cullen's Materia Medica, and the epochal Cinchona bark proving in 1790 that derived from it, Hahnemann *"continued to experiment upon himself and on his family and certain of his friends with different substances,"* but he had not yet *"tested the truth of this new principle on the sick. The insanity of Klockenbring gave him the opportunity."* However, for the first few weeks *"Hahnemann simply observed Klockenbring without giving him any medical treatment."*

Klockenbring had been *"Hanoverian Minister of Police and Secretary to the Chancellery...[and] in his fast life, he developed great eccentricity,"* but he became the subject of a satire claiming he was a close associate of drunken brothel keepers and that he had *"the most dangerous venereal disease and moral vices ranging from drunkenness to fraud."* As a public figure and family man who could not stand such accusations, he *"became violently insane."*

"In June 1792 he was brought to Georgenthal," being *"so violent that he was escorted by two well-built men to keep him under control."* His face was *"covered with large spots, was dirty, and imbecile in expression. Day and night he raved. He was afflicted with strange hallucinations...would recite Greek...actual words of Hebrew text...he destroyed his clothing and bedding, took his piano to pieces...and exhibited the most perfect forms of excitable mania."* Yet, Hahnemann had succeeded in curing him by *"March 1793."* As Cook suggests, it seems likely that his ravings were indeed *"those of the tertiary stages of syphilis."* as his cruel satirist had suggested in the first place.

IN THE ORGANON, HAHNEMANN ON SO-CALLED 'MENTAL DISEASES'

Several things are apparent to anyone who reads about *"mental and emotional maladies,"* [Aph.229] and *"mental and emotional disease,"* in the Organon. For example, Hahnemann is consistently very careful indeed not to fall into the allopathic trap of classing them as a separate category of sickness. He very specifically qualifies his reference to them as diseases, preferring to allude to them as mental symptoms of the whole person. For example, he states that *"what are termed mental diseases...do not, however, constitute a class of disease,"* [Aph. 210], and employing various phrases, he refers to them as an *"altered state of the disposition and mind,"* [Aph. 212], *"the so-called mental and emotional diseases,"* [Aph. 215], *"the state of the mind and disposition,"* [Aph. 213], *"the symptom of the mental disturbance,"* [Aph. 216], etc.

Hahnemann refers to *"derangement of the mind and disposition,"* [Aph. 215], to *"insanity or mania (caused by fright, vexation, the abuse of spirituous liquors..."* [Aph. 221]; *"attack of the insanity,"* [Aph. 223]; *"a real moral or mental malady,"* [Aph. 224]; *"furious mania...doleful, querulous lamentation...senseless chattering...disgusting and abominable conduct..."* [Aph. 228]; *"destruction and injury of surrounding objects,"* [Aph. 228]; *"the violent insane maniac and melancholic,"* [Aph. 229]; *"an acute mental or emotional disease,"* [Aph. 222]; *"periodic or continued mental derangement,"* [Aph. 223]; *"mental or emotional disease of long standing,"* [Aph. 222]; *"there are incredibly numerous varieties of them,"* [Aph. 230]. Taken together, these observations clearly demonstrate the amount of careful attention he had personally directed towards such cases.

From the depth and detail of his knowledge of emotional disorders, Hahnemann then reveals a clear familiarity with patients who are *"obstinate, violent, hasty...intolerant and capricious, or impatient...lascivious and shameless,"* [Aph. 210]; cases of *"insanity...melancholia...mania,"* [Aph. 216]; disease states resulting from *"faults of education, bad practices, corrupt morals, neglect of the mind, superstition or ignorance,"* [Aph. 224]; *"the melancholic...the spiteful maniac...the chattering fool,"* [Aph. 224]. All such references suggest Hahnemann's minute observation of many cases and the thoughtful and compassionate attitude that such experiences must have inspired in him towards *"such unfortunate beings,"* [Aph. 222] who possess a *"clouded spirit,"* [Aph. 229], for he sees in each of them *"the soul that pines or frets in the chains of the diseased body,"* [Aph. 229].

He himself is clearly one he calls *"the accurately observing physician,"* [Aph. 211], that such disorders *"can only be detected by the observation of a physician gifted with perseverance and penetration,"* [Aph. 216]. Being very empathic towards such patients in whom *"the emotional and mental state, constituting the principal symptom of such a patient,"* [Aph. 230], he also makes vague attempts at explanation of mental illness based upon his own extensive observations. He proposes that they *"originate and are kept up by emotional causes, such as continued anxiety, worry, vexation, wrongs and the frequent occurrence of great fear and fright,"* [Aph. 225]; *"emotional diseases...first engendered and subsequently kept up by the mind itself,"* [Aph. 226]; and that they require a *"carefully regulated mode of life,"* [Aph. 228].

Hahnemann also condemns outright the fact that the mentally deranged patient of his day all too *"often witnesses* the occurrence of ingratitude, cruelty, refined malice and propensities most disgraceful and degrading to humanity, which were precisely the qualities possessed by the patient before he grew ill," [Aph. 210] and which are very clearly uncurative and injurious that only aggravate the condition of the patient. He insists that the physician should adopt an "*appropriate psychical behavior towards the patient,*" [Aph. 228], employ "*an auxiliary mental regimen,*", "*without reproaching the patient for his acts*" [Aph. 228]. This should not include "*corporeal punishments and tortures*" [Aph. 228] or "*the employment of coercion,*" [Aph. 228]. He is astonished and appalled at "*the hard-heartedness and indiscretion of the medical men,*" [Aph. 228] for "*torturing these most pitiable of all human beings with the most violent blows and other painful torments,*" [Aph. 228], which he condemns as a "*revolting procedure,*" [Aph. 228].

Such physicians he says "*debase themselves...[by]...their uselessness,* [Aph. 228]. He denounces "*harshness towards the pitiable, innocent sufferers,*" [Aph. 228] and proclaims that "*they are equally pernicious modes of treating mental and emotional maladies,*" [Aph. 229]. And he advises physicians in general that "*I can confidently assert, from great experience, that the vast superiority of the homoeopathic system over all other conceivable methods of the treatment is nowhere displayed in a more triumphant light than in mental and emotional diseases of long standing,*" [Aph. 230], acknowledging the general point that "*the disposition of the patient often chiefly determines the selection of the homoeopathic remedy,*" [Aph. 211], as examples of the key feature of mentals in remedy selection, he then furnishes us with some examples - "*Aconite will seldom or never effect a rapid or permanent cure in a patient of a quiet, calm, equable disposition; and just as little will Nux vomica be serviceable where the disposition is mild and phlegmatic, Pulsatilla where it is happy, gay and obstinate, or Ignatia where it is imperturbable and disposed neither to be frightened nor vexed,"* [Aph. 214].

Always emphasising that *"a homoeopathic medicinal pathogenetic force - that is to say, a remedy which in its list of symptoms displays, with the greatest possible similarity, not only the corporeal morbid symptoms present in the case of disease before us, but also especially this mental and emotional state,"* [Aph. 217], for *"a disease of the mind and disposition,"* [Aph. 218], or *"disorder of the mind,"* [Aph. 220], Hahnemann then identifies remedies like *"Aconite, Belladonna, Stramonium, Hyoscyamus, Mercury,"* [Aph. 221], as being especially useful for such patients, but though *"a lucid interval and a transient alleviation of the psychical disease"* [Aph. 219] may be obtained, that they can only be *"cured by antipsorics,"* [Aph. 223], that *"mental and emotional diseases...can only be cured by homoeopathic antipsoric medicine,"* [Aph. 228], that one must select *"the antipsoric remedies selected for each particular case of mental or emotional disease,"* [Aph. 230], and administer *"a radical, antipsoric treatment,"* [Aph. 227] as being *"the only efficacious mode of curing such disease,"* [Aph. 228].

This short account provides an accurate survey of what Hahnemann says in the Organon regarding emotional disorders.

DISCUSSION

Although Hahnemann, in the Organon, and most homoeopaths since, do consider the mental symptoms - the *"always predominating state of the mind and disposition"*

[Aph. 217] - as being very important and significant in defining the disease or selecting a remedy, yet nowhere in homoeopathy is there any coherent theory of mind or mental illness in the same sense that is found in allopathy. Indeed, mind is merely regarded as another part of the whole person: *"the almost spiritual, mental and emotional organs, which the anatomist has never yet and never will reach with his scalpel"* [Aph. 216]. In other words, all homoeopaths since Hahnemann have predominantly ignored mind as a *separate field* of disease causation, except insofar as it is merely a field wherein symptoms make themselves manifest either as a product of the drug or of a disease and always when viewed holistically - in the round.

Hahnemann does however acknowledge that such mental disorders do give an impression, an apparition of being a separate class of disease: *"as though it were a local disease in the invisible subtle organ of the mind or disposition,"* [Aph. 215], but because homoeopathy fails to take cognisance of mental illness as a separate entity, apart from any other holistic disease entity, then it seems to ignore all theories of mental disease in exactly the same way that it ignores all allopathically construed theories of physical disease, as being largely irrelevant to its 'modus operandi' or worldview. It adopts this position because all disease is construed as a *"dynamic aberration of our spiritlike life,"* [Close, 67]; *"a perverted vital action,"* [Close, 70]; *"disease is the suffering of the dynamis,"* [Close, 72]; *"disease is primarily a morbid disturbance or disorderly action of the vital force,"* [Close, 74]. Close is most emphatic in insisting that disease is *"not a thing, but only the condition of a thing,"* [Close, 70]. Because homoeopathic drugs correct the vital force, so, after which, by domino effect [so to say], the entire organism automatically becomes corrected - including mind. We might therefore ask where is the concept of mental illness in homoeopathy? There is NO such concept - there is no concept of mental illness per se in homoeopathy.

Clearly, the Organon's conception of 'mental illness' does not dovetail too easily with the conventional definition of mental illness or, the way it is applied by modern practitioners. In this sense, homoeopathy clearly has no separate category of 'mental illness'. Even though, the symptom of the one-sided illness may involve mental illness [in the conventional sense] an obsession, illusion, delusion, hallucination, fear [phobia?], suicidal impulses, depression, etc., to homoeopathy it is only an illness of a deeply deranged vital force, deranged at the most fundamental level, never of the mind itself in isolation from the whole person.

The essence of this view is peppered throughout the Organon and in Kent and Close and Boger - it states simply that mind and body comprise one holistic unit [conventionally regarded as two arenas] in which symptoms make themselves manifest. It depicts a *"functional unity of the psychic state...and somatic state,"* [Verspoor, 103]. Boenninghausen also repeats this dual unity of Aphorisms 224-226 [Verspoor, 118]. However, Hahnemann is clear that the ultimate source of all symptoms is derangements in the "life force." A view incidentally he shared with Paracelsus, Stahl, and van Helmont. Remedies remove these derangements and so the flow of symptoms - to whichever arena - is slowed and then ceases. These views are stated repeatedly by Close and Kent, for example, and obtain ample repetition by all 'the greats'.

Jean-Baptiste Van Helmont (1577-1644)

Hahnemann leaves no doubt that the fundamentally holistic nature of homoeopathic philosophy, rails repeatedly against materialistic and allopathic constructs, which seek to slice the person up into organs or systems and he condemns any 'treatment of parts' that always flows from such a reductionist perspective. Kent likewise condemns this approach in his own emotional manner. The only option therefore is to regard all 'disease' so-called as an expression of an internal disorder resident in the life force, which remedies reach and eliminate, and then the flow of symptoms ceases. Clearly, the remedies must be chosen based on their totality and similarity to the entire person, rather than upon the disease as an entity — which was originally an idea of Paracelsus interpreted differently in the material school leading to allopathy from the view in vitalist schools including van Helmont [Paracelsus' chief interpreter] and Stahl. This stream leads directly to Hahnemann - even though he never states that overtly.

'Disease as entity' was a spiritual concept of invasion of the life force - this concept was created by Paracelsus, but poorly described by him, receiving much clearer expression by van Helmont. This point was also amplified extensively by Kent in his idea that the cause of disease invades the vital force first, as a spiritual entity, and then outflows its bad effects into the entire organism 'from within outwards'. This view comes close to that of some modern homoeopaths who believe in *"the all-encompassing state of mind,"* [Verspoor, 125].

Whether this is truly *"Hahnemann's conception of the 'highest disease'...those that are 'spun and maintained by the soul' but ultimately rooted in the arch beliefs of the human spirit [Aph. 224],"* [Verspoor, 130], is very hard to say. It almost suggests *"the idea of disease as a delusion,"* [Verspoor, 268], which again sounds like Hahnemann as a disease *"first spun and maintained by the soul,"* [Verspoor, 299]. However, it is hard to see to what extent such modern ideas about the significance of mind or mental symptoms in homoeopathy truly derive from the words of Hahnemann. One suspects that his own words have been hammered on an anvil of modern psychology into very distorted word shapes, belonging to a lexicon of concepts that would have been entirely alien to Hahnemann himself. This clearly remains a matter of opinion and debate.

❖ ❖ ❖

FATE VERSUS WISH

*Written by Dr. P. Krishnan, Tutor in Pharmacy,
Govt. Homoeopathic Medical College, Calicut, Kerala, South India.*

Madame Melanie d' Hervilly, the second wife of Dr. Samuel Hahnemann was a native of France. Her diplomatic activities in the last episodes of Hahnemann's life at Paris contributed them fame, monitory benefit, freedom and everything. Even then the life and personality of Madame Melanie has been often misrepresented whenever people say anything about the life of Dr. Hahnemann.

Writers and Biographers were ignorant about the life and situation of a widow in 18th century and the worthy task of keeping all the literary remains of Dr. Hahnemann till it was published.

The tragical events in the life of Madame Melanie d' Hervilly should be studied and she should be remembered as a person who had done a lot for the survival and propagation of Homoeopathic Medical Science. The life of

Dr. Hahnemann and the history of Homoeopathy would be complete only if the life of Madame Melanie is properly considered.

From childhood itself Melanie had a burning desire for acquiring knowledge. She was talented in music, painting, science, etc. But these extraordinary faculties were considered as certain negative qualities and so was neglected by her mother. This created some domestic troubles. Knowing all these facts, Melanie was adopted by Gullion le Thiere's family. This was a matter of much relief to Melanie.

Melanie learned the basics of painting from Gullion le Thiere, who himself was a painter. It might be for facilitating a better life and fame later that she became the life partner of Dr. Hahnemann.

Melanie was only 43 when Dr. Hahnemann died in 1843. The journey to Paris which opened an opportunity for all kind of progress in the life of Dr. Hahnemann during his last decade, provided much financial security for her also. It was to keep up this financial status, Melanie created hatred among Dr. Hahnemann's family members.

Even at the time of Dr. Hahnemann's passing away, Malanie was worried about the crooked ways of maintaining the patients visited him. That was why she informed nobody about the death, instead she pretended as if he was alive and thus continued the practice. It was because of this she was compelled to keep the body embalmed and preserved it for about nine days and then buried it without informing anybody.

But the Homoeopathic Doctors in France protested and became violent at this and they turned against Melanie because of her wretched attempt to keep the existence of Dr. Hahnemann in chaos and to go on with the practice. Doctors even filed a writ petition in the court against her practice who had neither studied in any Medical College nor had any Medical Degree, but had only a Diploma granted by Pennsylvania Homoeopathic Academy. All this happened in 1846.

Objecting the statements and complaints of the Doctors, Madame Melanie submitted a counter petition. One could find so many sentences in it which were abusive to Doctors. She even highlighted the point that surgery was developed through well experienced barbers. Another point of her argument was that doctors who practice medicine merely based on the descriptions given in the leaflets published by Pharmaceuticals were quite stupid. Moreover, she expressed her doubt whether those doctors had any such medically oriented experiences like herself, who provided immense help in the observations and research projects of Dr. Hahnemann.

But the verdict of the Court was against Melanie because it observed that she had no basic qualifications to practice Medicine. Moreover she had to pay 100 Francs as fine.

Even if her attempts failed, Melanie was not ready to succumb to defeat. After Hahnemann's death, even though many eminent personalities including Dr. Boenninghausen came forward to procure and publish the articles and books containing the latest medically related observations and inferences of Dr. Hahnemann, Melanie kept them away with an attitude of revenge.

Again Melanie came forward with certain new calculations. She decided to adopt a girl namely Sophie and planned to give her in marriage to any of the Homoeopathic Doctor and expected that they might live with her so that she could also continued the practice in another form.

Dr. Suss Hahnemann, Dr. Constantine Hering and Dr. Dayce were ready to publish the articles of Dr. Hahnemann. But their attempts were discouraged by the lame arguments of Melanie. She was of the opinion that the real works of Hahnemann might loss their individuality and gravity by the attempts of corrections, additions or omissions, which the publishers might do and thereby degrade Hahnemann's name and fame. Moreover, she told that she might think about the publication only after subsiding the rage of Apothecaries towards Hahnemann. But these lame excuses came from her with an intention to sell the books to those who promise highest rate.

Notwithstanding the attitude of an enemy she kept up towards Dr. Boenninghausen related with the price of books, Melanie expected Dr. Karl Boenninghausen, the son of Dr. Boenninghausen, to be the husband of her foster daughter Sophie. Both the families agreed on this and the marriage took place on 12th December 1855. The couple lived with Melanie and the medical practice was on. Melanie used to visit the clinic to help Dr. Karl who was unfamiliar with French.

It was told by the Biographers that in those days Melanie provided immense help and support to Amalie and Suss Hahnemann, children of her husband as they were badly in need of financial help.

In 1865 Luds of Kothen illegally published the 6th edition of *Organon of Medicine*. After making certain corrections, this was republished by Suss Hahnemann. Melanie was very much annoyed.

Even though a team of doctors of Philadelphia Homoeo Medical College of America headed by Dr. Dunham came to buy the books, they had to withdraw themselves from the attempt because Melanie demanded 50,000 Dollars and share of the profit from its publication. Although they agreed with her demands later, the second attempt also failed because of the death of Dr. Dunham amidst the settlement.

In 1870 when war broke out between France and Germany, and in search of safety, Sophie and Dr. Karl went to their native place West Phalia in Germany. Though Melanie whose age and physique was not favourable then for such a journey, also accompanied them. But, as the war ended soon, she returned to Paris again.

When the war broke out again in the next year Melanie lost her residence and all possessions. Since the valuable books of Hahnemann were taken to Germany by Sophie till that time, they survived.

Thereafter, the life of Melanie was miserable. Living in a hut, she drew paintings and earned her livelihood by selling them. Neither the foster daughter Sophie nor the son in law, who were still in financially sound position bothered about her who was quite alone.

This might be the reason why in 1872, the French Government permitted Melanie to practice Homoeopathy. But by that time, as a matter of negative fate, she got seriously ill and lost the integrity for consultation.

Thus, on 27th May 1878, following a pulmonary disease Melanie passed away; her last days being witnessed by a few. The mortal remains were buried in the common tomb of Le Thiere family at Montmartre cemetery, near that of her husband.

After the death of Melanie the right of publication of Hahnemann's books were entrusted with Sophie. As per the constant request from American Doctors, even though she agreed to reduce the amount from 50,000 dollars to 25,000 Dollars, this discussion also however failed.

Later in 1880 Dr. H.N. Guernsey of Philadelphia College visited Sophie and promised to pay 10,000 dollars (only 10,000 dollars!!). But as she stick to her demand that she should get a share of the profit also, it resulted in the failure of another talk.

After 17 years, though Sophie granted oral permission to Dr. Richard Hael for publishing the books, due to the unexpected death of Sophie, the attempt reached nowhere. Since Sophie had no children, Dr. Karl Boenninghausen became the next heir of the entire collection of books.

Again, after 7 years, in 1906, though Dr. Richard Hael and Dr. William Boericke went to Germany and met Dr. Karl Boenninghausen, no proper solution could be formulated. Sorry to say that Dr. Karl Boenninghausen also died soon.

Later in 1920 it was only for 10,000 dollars Dr. Richard Hael bought the books from the then heir of Dr. Hahnemann's possessions! Thus all the remaining works of Dr. Samuel Hahnemann could be published in 1921, i.e., about 78 years after his death.

∎

DETAILS OF HAHNEMANN'S FAMILY MEMBERS

First wife: Johanna Leopoldine Henriette Kuchler.
Second wife: Madame Melanie de Hervilly.
Hahnemann had 11 children with Johanna.

1. **Henriette**

    Eldest Daughter.

    Born in 1783 at Gommern.

    Her husband - Christian Friedrich Forster was a Minister. Had two male and two female children. Died at Dresdorf.

2. **Friedrich.**

    Eldest son.

    He had rickets.

    Intelligent as well as eccentric.

    Married and had 3 male and 2 female children. From 1828 onwards, he was missing due to psychic problems.

3. **Wilhelmine**

    Second daughter.

    Married to Music Director Richter and died in 1818.

4. Amalie

Third daughter.

Hahnemann's most lovable daughter.

It was her duty to keep patient records properly and to reply the letters of her father. Her first marriage was with Dr. Suss, who died while she was pregnant. It was this child who was later known as Dr. Leopold Suss Hahnemann.

Later Amalie was married to Mr. Liebe, but got divorced.

Died on 7th December, 1857.

5. Karolene

Fourth daughter.

Unmarried.

Died in 1830.

6. Ernst

Second son.

Died in an accident at Molschleben.

7. Friedrike

Fifth daughter. She was deaf. Firstly married to Mr. Andra.

After the death Mr. Andra, she was married to Mr. Dellbrucks. After the death of Mr. Dellbrucks she was found murdered in the backyard of the house.

8. The stillborn child.

9. Elionore

Sixth daughter.

Married twice.

Elionore published a book in 1834 called "Homoeopathic

Adviser for the Home". Dr. Hahnemann strongly criticised the book.

Found murdered in a pond.

10. Charlottle

Seventh daughter.

Unmarried.

Died in 1863.

11. Luise

Eightth daughter.

Her husband was Dr. Mosdorf, Assistant of Dr. Hahnemann. Divorced. Died in 1878.

❖ ❖ ❖

THE HAHNEMANN FAMILY

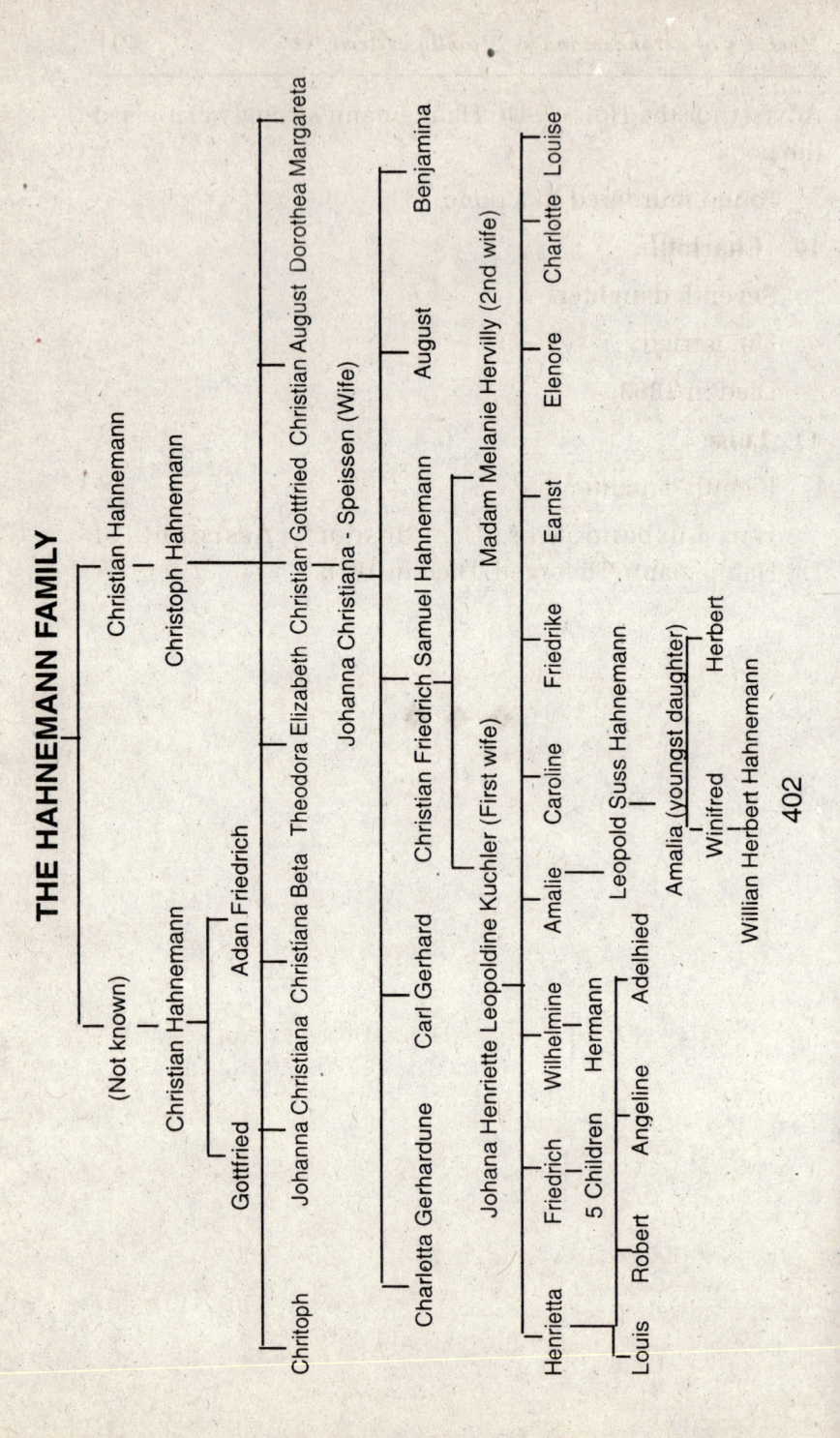

```
                                    Christian Hahnemann
                                           |
                                    Christoph Hahnemann
                                           |
        ┌──────────────────────────────────┼──────────────────────────────────┐
   (Not known)                                                          
        |                                                               
   Christian Hahnemann                                                  
        |                                                               
   ┌────┴────┐                                                          
Gottfried  Adan Friedrich                                               
                                                                        
Chritoph                                                                
   |                                                                    
   ┌──────────┬──────────────┬──────────────┬──────────────┬──────────────┐
Johanna    Christiana      Theodora      Christian      Christian      Dorothea
Christiana  Beta          Elizabeth     Gottfried       August        Margareta
                                                                        
                    Johanna Christiana - Speissen (Wife)
                                    |
                    Christian Friedrich Samuel Hahnemann
                                    |
              ┌─────────────────────┴─────────────────────┐
        (First wife)                              Madam Melanie Hervilly (2nd wife)
   Johanna Henriette Leopoldine Kuchler                   |
                    |                                  August — Benjamina
   ┌────────┬──────────┬─────────┬─────────┐
Charlotta  Carl      Amalie   Caroline  Friedrike   Earnst   Elenore   Charlotte — Louise
Gerhardune Gerhard                                  
                    |
              Leopold Suss Hahnemann
                    |
        Amalia (youngst daughter)
                    |
           ┌────────┴────────┐
        Winifred          Herbert
                             |
                    Willian Herbert Hahnemann

Henrietta — Friedrich — Wilhelmine — Hermann
                |
            5 Children
Louis — Robert — Angeline — Adelhied
```

402

BIBLIOGRAPHY

A C Siddall, *History of Homeopathic Medicine at Oberlin, Ohio, 1833-1933*, Ohio State Med. Jnl, 74, pt. 2, 1978, 121-124

A Michalowski, S Sander & K-O Sauerbeck, 1989, *Therapiegeschichtliche Materialen Zu Samuel Hahnemanns Pariser Praxis*, Stuttgart: Med. GG 8, 171-196

Andrew R Aisenberg, Book Review: *Constructing Paris Medicine*, by C Hannaway and A La Berge, [Eds.], Rodopi, Amsterdam, 1998, in Social History of Medicine, 14.1, April 2001, 145-6

Arthur K Rogers, *Students History of Philosophy*, New York: MacMillan, 1935

B Jain, *A Brief Life of Hahnemann*, India: B Jain, 1977

Barbara Griggs, *Green Pharmacy: a History of Herbal Medicine*, London: Jill Norman & Hobhouse, 1981

Bertrand Russell, *A History of Western Philosophy*, London: Unwin, 1943

C Boenninghaussen, *Obituary*, BJH, 1864, Vol. 22, 351

C Boenninghaussen, *The Lesser Writings*, Trans. Bradford, 1844, Jain India Edition 1994

C S Cameron, *Homeopathy in Retrospect*, Trans. Stud. Coll. Phys. Philadelphia, 27, 1959, 28-33

CDNB - *Concise Dictionary of National Biography*, Oxford, 1997, 3 vols.

Charles Webster, *From Paracelsus To Newton, Magic And The Making Of Modern Science*, USA: Barnes And Noble, 1982

E C Whitmont, *Psyche and Substance*, USA: N Atlantic Books, 1980

E K Ledermann, *Body, Mind And Spirit*, BHJ 50:4, 1961, 273-81

E K Ledermann, *Good Health Through Natural Therapy*, UK: Prism Books, 1976

E K Ledermann, *Homeopathy and Natural Therapeutics*, BHJ 35:1, 1945, 30-46

E K Ledermann, *Implications of Hahnemannian Homeopathy*, BHJ 46:4, 1957, 166-70

E K Ledermann, *Philosophy and Medicine*, 2nd Edition, London: Gower, 1986

E K Ledermann, *The Philosophical and Scientific Basis for Allopathic and Homeopathic Medicine*, BHJ 34:2, 1944, 76-94

E K Ledermann, *The Vital Force in Homeopathy and General Medical Practice*, BHJ, 58:4, 1968, 148-160

Elizabeth Danciger, *The Emergence of Homeopathy: Alchemy into Medicine*, London: Century-Hutchinson, 1987

F Treuherz, *The Origin of Kent's Homeopathy*, JAIH, 77:4, 1984, 130-149

H Bloch, *Thomas Sydenham, MD (1624-1689): the Father of*

Clinical Observation, Journal of Family Practice, 1994 Jan; 38 (1): 80-1

H Pietschmann, *Medicine: A Discipline Between Art And Science*, BHJ 72:3 [July 1983], pp.155-61

Harris L Coulter, *Divided Legacy - a History of the Schism in Medical Thought*, 3 Vols., Washington: Wehawken Books, 1973

I Kant, *Critique of Pure Reason*, 1781

I Swedenborg, *The Principia*

IGM, *Hahnemann Casebook DF12*, (1840-42), Stuttgart, microfiche, 1997

IGM, *Krankenjournale DF5* by Samuel Hahnemann (1838-9), Stuttgart, Book form, 1995

Isaiah Berlin, *Against the Current - Essays in the History of Ideas*, London: Pimlico, 1979

Isaiah Berlin, *Against the Current: Essays in the History of Ideas*, London: Pimlico, 1997

Isaiah Berlin, *The Sense of Reality: Studies in Ideas and their History*, London: Pimlico, 1996

J B Blake, *Homeopathy in American History*, Trans. Stud. Coll. Phys., Philadelphia, Series 5, vol. 3, 1981, 83-92

J D Bernal, *Science In History*, 4 Vols., London: Penguin, 1969

J E G Brieger, *Methodological Obstacles in Homeopathic Research*, BHJ, 50, 1961, 239-45

J H Clarke, *Hahnemann and Paracelsus*, London: Homeopathic Publishing Co, 1924

J Jacobi, [Ed] *Paracelsus, A Selection of His Writings*, Princeton: Princeton Univ Press, 1979

James T Kent, *Lectures on Homeopathic Philosophy*, USA: North Atlantic Books, 1900

Jean Pharamond Rhumelius, *Medicina Spagyrica Tripartita*, 1648

John H Clarke, *Obituaries And Appreciations of Clarke*, BHJ, April 1932

John H Warner, *The Therapeutic Perspective - Medical Practice, Knowledge And Identity In America 1820-1885*, Cambridge: Harvard Univ. Press, 1986

John Milton, *Paradise Lost*, 1667

John Pert, *Telephone Conversation With P Morrell on History of Scottish Homeopathy*, Feb. 1991

Julian Winston, *The Faces of Homeopathy - A History of the First 200 Years*, New Zealand: Great Auk Publishing, 1999

K D Keele, *The Sydenham-Boyle theory of morbific particles*, Medical History, 1974 Jul; 18 (3): 240-8

Keith Thomas, *Religion And The Decline of Magic*, New York: Scribner's, 1971

Kenneth Dewhurst, Dr Thomas Sydenham, *His life and Original Writings*, Los Angeles: Univ. California Press, 1966

L W Hull, *History And Philosophy of Science*, London: Longmans, 1959

Margaret L Tyler, 1942, *Homeopathic Drug Pictures*, UK: Health Science Press, 1942

Margery Grace Blackie, *The Patient Not The Cure, the Challenge of Homeopathy*, London: MacDonald & Janes, 1976

Martin Dinges, [Ed], *Weltgeschichte Der Homoöpathie: Lander, Schulen, Heilkundige*, Muchen: C H Beck, 1996

Martin Gumpert, *Hahnemann - The Adventurous Career of a Medical Rebel*, L B Fischer Publ. Corp., New York, 1945, [Translated From The German By Claud W Sykes]

Martin Kaufman, *Homeopathy in America*, Baltimore: Johns Hopkins Univ. Press, 1971

Meilhammer, B, D H Paper, G Franz & Robert Juette, 1994, *Globuli aus Hahnemann Hausapotheke*, Deutsches Apotheker Zeitung, 134-17, 28-4-94, 17-21, Stuttgart

Michael Neagu, *Homeopathy In Rumania*, Paper to Stuttgart Conference, April 1995

Michael Neagu, *Homoopathie Ein Rumanien*, In Dinges, 1996

N Gevitz, *Sectarian Medicine*, Jnl Amer. Med. Assoc., 257, 1987, 1636-40

Nicholas Culpeper, *An English Herbal, Spittalfields*, London 1643

Nicholas Culpeper, *The Complete Herbal*, Spittalfields, 1652

Nicholas Goodrick-Clarke, [Ed] *Paracelsus Essential Readings*, London: Crucible, 1990

Paracelsus in Das Buch Paragranum

Paracelsus, Alchemical Medicine, Wisconsin, 1987

Paracelsus, *Concerning the Spirits of the Planets*, Wisconsin

Paracelsus, *Selected Writings*, [Edited By J.Jacobi], London: RKP, 1951

Paracelsus, Sieben Defensiones

Penelope Gouk, Book Review: *Religio Medici: Medicine and*

Religion in 17th century England, by O. P. Grell and Andrew Cunningham, Scolar Press, Aldershot, UK, 1997, reviewed in Social History of Medicine, 11.2, August 1998, 317-318

Peter Ackroyd, Blake, London: Sinclair-Stevenson, 1995

Peter Morrell, *Coming Out of the Darkness like a Meteor: Dr Hahnemann Builds His Materia Medica*, NEJH Summer 2001, The Homeopath, October 2001

Peter Morrell, *On Hahnemann's Workloads and Consultation Times in his Paris Practice*, JAIH, July 1998

Peter Morrell, *Samuel And Melanie In Paris*, The Homeopath 62, 1996

Peter Morrell, *Some Reflections on the Origins of Hahnemann's Ideas*, Heilkunst, Canada, July 2000

Peter Morrell, *The Character of Hahnemann and the Nature of Homeopathy*, The Homeopath 68, Oct. 1997

Peter Morrell, T*he Proving, Potentisation and the Law Of Similars, Some Historical Perspectives*, Resonance, Vol. 20:3, USA, May-June 1998

Phillip A Nicholls, 1988, *Homeopathy and the Medical Profession*, London: Croom Helm, 1988

Phillip A Nicholls, *The Scientific Investigation of Homoeopathy*, Richard Hughes Memorial Lecture, Faculty of Homoeopathy, London, 2 May 1991

Pierre Schmidt, *The Life of James Tyler Kent*, Geneva, c.1950

R P Patel, *Observations and Experiences With 50 Millesimal Potencies*, Student Homeopath 37, Nov. 1995, pp.19-21

Rapou, *Histoire de la doctrine medical Homoepathique*, Paris, 1847

Richard H Shryock, *The Development of Modern Medicine, an Interpretation of the Social and Scientific Factors Involved*, Philadelphia: Univ. Penns Press, 1936

Richard Palk, *The Grave of Hahnemann*, In ONEM, and Society of Homeopaths Newsletter 39, Sept. 1993.

Richard Tarnas, *The Passion of the Western Mind*, London: Pimlico, 1996

Rima Handley, *A Homeopathic Love Story*, USA: North Atlantic Books, 1990

Rima Handley, *Classical Hahnemannian Homeopathy or What Hahnemann Really Did - Preliminary Observations*, The Homeopath 7:3, Spring 1988 pp.106-114

Rima Handley, *In Search of the Later Hahnemann*, UK: Beaconsfield, 1997

Robert E Dudgeon, *Lectures on The Theory And Practice of Homeopathy*, 1853, India: B Jain, 1978 edition

Rosa Waugh Hobhouse, *Life of Samuel Hahnemann*, India: World Homeopathic Links, 1933

Roy Porter, *The Greatest Benefit To Mankind, a Medical History of Humanity*, New York: W Norton & Co, 1998

S C F Hahnemann, *The Chronic Diseases, their Peculiar Nature and their Homeopathic Cure*, 1828, Jain Edition, India

S C F Hahnemann, *The Organon of The Healing Art*, Sixth Edition, Tr. Kunzli, Naude & Pendleton, 1810, London: Gollancz, 1983 edition

S F Mason, *A History of The Sciences*, London: Heinemann, 1953

S Hahnemann, *On the Effects of Coffee From Original Observations*, Leipzig, 1803

Samuel Hahnemann, *Aesculapius In the Balance*, 1805, in Hahnemann's Lesser Writings, 1895, edited by Dudgeon, 423-6

Samuel Hahnemann, *Essay on a New Principle for Ascertaining the Curative Powers of Drugs*, 1796

Samuel Hahnemann, *On The Helleborism of the Ancients*, 1812, in Hahnemann's Lesser Writings, 592

Samuel Hahnemann, *On the Value of the Speculative Systems of Medicine*, 1808, in Hahnemann's Lesser Writings, 489-90

Samuel Hahnemann, *Organon of Medicine*, Dudgeon/Boericke Translation, Combined 5th/6th Edition, 1921, Jain Reprint

Samuel Hahnemann, *The Lesser Writings*, Edited By Dudgeon, Jain Edition, 1895

Serena Lambrughi, *A Question Of LM Prescribing*, Student Homeopath 36, Oct. 1995, 23-26

Sir John Forbes, *Homeopathy, Allopathy and Young Physic*, New York: Radde, 1846

Stuart Close, *The Genius of Homeopathy: Lectures and Essays on Homeopathic Philosophy*, New York, 1924

Stuart Close, *The Genius of Homœopathy, Lectures & Essays on Homoeopathic Philosophy*, Delhi: Jain reprint, 1924

Thomas L Bradford, *Life and Letters of Hahnemann*, Jain, 1895 1986 Edition

Trevor M Cook, *Samuel Hahnemann, the Founder of Homoeopathy*, Wellingborough: Thorsons, 1981

U C Adler, 1994, *Nachweis von 681 Q-Potenzen in der franzosischen Krankenjournalen Samuel Hahnemanns*, Stuttgart: Med GG 13, 135-166, 1994

Wilhelm Pelikan, *The Secrets of Metals,* Anthroposophical Press, New York, 1988

William G Rothstein, *American Physicians in the Nineteenth Century From Sects To Science,* Baltimore: Johns Hopkins Univ Press, 1972

William Gutman, *Homoeopathy: the Fundamentals of its Philosophy and the Essence of its Remedies,* Bombay, India: Hom. Medical Publishers, 1978

William Shakespeare, *Romeo and Juliet*

❖ ❖ ❖